HARVARD HISTORICAL MONOGRAPHS
XXIV

PUBLISHED UNDER THE DIRECTION OF THE DEPARTMENT
OF HISTORY FROM THE INCOME OF

THE ROBERT LOUIS STROOCK FUND

The Incidence of the Emigration During the French Revolution

BY

DONALD GREER

GLOUCESTER, MASS.

PETER SMITH

1966

TO MY WIFE AND MY SON
MARY AND DAVID GREER

ACKNOWLEDGMENT

THOUGH this study engages my responsibility alone, it owes much to the generous collaboration of others. Primarily, a Grant-In-Aid from the Social Science Research Council made possible the research work in France. For this aid and for the courtesy of the Council in permitting me to use it at my convenience, I wish to express my appreciation. My sincere thanks are offered to many of the departmental archivists of France for a great deal of help in locating and occasionally in transcribing materials in their archives, and I am deeply indebted to M. Georges Bourgin of the Archives nationales, who arranged to have an almost incredible quantity of material sent from various Archives départementales to the Archives nationales for my use.

Of the counsel and criticism necessary to works of scholarship my friends have given freely. Professor Crane Brinton of Harvard University encouraged me to undertake this project and to persist in it. Mr. Frederick G. Fassett, Jr., of the Carnegie Institution of Washington, and Dr. Lester C. Houck, formerly of the American Academy in Rome, applied their skills as editor and classicist, respectively, to reading the manuscript, and rendered invaluable suggestions. Miss Rene Sanford of Washington, D. C., read the proofs, and to her discernment is due the elimination of numerous errors and the clarification of many a passage. And Mary Marshall Greer, who made the cartogram illustrating the geographic incidence of the emigration, was constantly helpful in all the steps of my work.

Donald Greer

West Gloucester, Massachusetts
October 21, 1950

CONTENTS

ABBREVIATIONS

AD—Archives départementales. *Example:* AD Gironde, Q 1477, *for* Archives départementales de la Gironde, Série Q, no. 1477.

AN—Archives nationales.

BN—Bibliothèque nationale.

CHAPTER I

INTRODUCTION

1. Objectives

DURING the last decade of the eighteenth century, France, convulsed by a great revolution, cast out victims of change, refugees from readjustment, fugitives from violence, disorder, and economic stress. These were the *émigrés* of the French Revolution. A few of them spent a quarter of a century in exile; some of them died abroad; most of them returned to France before the end of the Revolution. But absent or present, in war or peace, during the Revolution, the Empire, and the Restoration—for over forty years—the émigrés, or at least a portion of them, played an important, sometimes sinister, and often decisive part in the crucial events of the life of France.

Worms and Coblenz, the flight of the King, the Brunswick manifesto, the civil wars of 1793, the White Terror, the plots and intrigues of the Directory—mere mention of these evokes the presence, the action, or the influence of the émigrés. Nor does the record end with the Revolution. Even after the amnesties accorded by Bonaparte, the irreconcilables remained abroad or slipped into France only to conspire. When Bonaparte disappeared to Elba, they escorted Louis XVIII back to Paris; and by their immediate clamor for all that the fleur-de-lys once had signified they winged the eagle for his flight from Elba to the capital and thus precipitated the interlude of the Hundred Days. Unbenefited by experience, they continued to agitate during the Restoration until, at last, by forcing the passage of the law indemnifying them for property confiscated during the Revolution, they contributed heavily to the ultimate disaster of the Bourbon monarchy.

The very patency of these facts has forced the light on certain aspects of the emigration, leaving others completely shadowed. The external history of the movement—the peregrinations of the royal family, the vicissitudes of the army of Condé, the picturesque details of émigré life in Brussels or London or Hamburg—has been written and rewritten;[1] the nexus between the flight from France and the counterrevolution has been meticulously examined;[2] the intellectual history of the emigration has furnished the substance for a brilliant exposition;[3] valid, though not comprehensive, conclusions have been reached concerning the property readjustments consequent upon the great expatriation, and the famous billion franc indemnity of 1825 has been studied in one of the most exhaustive research works of our time.[4] All this constitutes an imposing body of information—and we have alluded only to salient topics. Yet, paradoxically, it is incomplete, for the basic facts remain veiled.

The volume, the incidence, the periods, and the motivation of the emigration have not been revealed. How many persons emigrated from France between 1789 and 1799? What regions were most, or least, affected? To what social classes did the émigrés belong? Were most of them privileged (nobles and clergy) or unprivileged (bourgeois, artisans, and peasants)? Why did they emigrate? Were they impelled by fear? By fashion? By treason? Or by other motives? When did they go? Under the Monarchy?

[1] Ernest Daudet, *Histoire de l'émigration pendant la Révolution française* (2 vols.; Paris, 1904–1905); Henri Forneron, *Histoire générale des émigrés* . . . (3 vols.; Paris, 1884–1890).

[2] Emmanuel Vingtrinier, *La contre-révolution, première période, 1789–1791* (2 vols.; Paris, 1924–1925); Louis Madelin, *La contre-révolution sous la Révolution, 1789–1815* (Paris, 1935); Émile Gabory, *L'Angleterre et la Vendée* (2 vols.; Paris, 1930–1931); André Lebon, *L'Angleterre et l'émigration française de 1794 à 1801* (Paris, 1882). For other relevant works see R. Baret, "Bibliographie critique sur les relations du gouvernement britannique avec les émigrés et les royalistes de l'Ouest," *La Province du Maine* (1935), XV, 177–186.

[3] Fernand Baldensperger, *Le mouvement des idées dans l'émigration française, 1789–1815* (2 vols.; Paris, 1924).

[4] André Gain, *La Restauration et les biens des émigrés* . . . (2 vols.; Nancy, 1928).

Under the Republic? When, if at all, did they return? And to each of these queries there are many corollaries.

Except for a few departments and districts treated in scholarly local monographs, the answers thus far given to these questions have been vague, suppositive, or erroneous. Estimates of the total number of émigrés have varied between one hundred thousand and two hundred thousand. André Gain *inferred* the geographic incidence of the emigration from the distribution of the indemnities;[5] and though we shall have to resort to his hypothesis in a few instances where the sources fail us, it remains a vague gauge. The persistent *assumption* that most of the émigrés were nobles or clergymen has distracted attention from the mass migrations such as that which occurred in Alsace late in 1793 when thousands of peasants and village artisans crossed the Rhine to Germany.[6] The phrase "the émigrés of fear" has become a sort of cliché blanketing the motivation of the emigration; but, even if it proves to be true that "fear" was the primary impulse, there are nuances of fear, ranging from apprehension to panic and frenzy. A first, a second, sometimes a third wave of flight have been distinguished, but they have not been clearly differentiated as to volume and social composition. It is agreed that most of the émigrés returned to their native soil, but the periods of this reflux have been only vaguely indicated.

Of course, it is easier to ask than to answer such questions, and some of them may be beyond any definitive answer. The documents pertaining to the emigration have suffered heavily from the toll of time and destruction.[7] Even when passably intact, as indeed they are in the greater part of the local archives of France, the records vary immensely in informative quality, and at best they leave much to be desired.

[5] *Ibid.*, II, 178, and tables, pp. 183, 188, 202, 452–454.

[6] Cf. Marc Bouloiseau, *Liste des émigrés, déportés et condamnés pour cause révolutionnaire dans le district de Rouen* (Paris, 1937), 8–9.

[7] A striking example of the condition of some of these documents is the comprehensive list for the Bouches-du-Rhône (AD Bouches-du-Rhône, Q 37–38). Apparently having been exposed at some time to moisture it is in part stained and faded to the point of illegibility and in part so fragile that its pages crumble at the touch of the hand.

Yet, on the whole the difficulties are not insurmountable, and this study is an attempt to illuminate the internal history of the emigration. The period covered extends from July, 1789, when the Comte d'Artois and his friends crossed the frontier into the Austrian Netherlands, to December, 1799, when Bonaparte closed the lists of émigrés. The territory comprised is the France of the Revolution and the greater part of the nineteenth century, thus including Alsace and Lorraine, Nice, Savoy, and Avignon and the Comtat Venaissin (the Vaucluse).[8] The principal immediate objectives are the discovery of the volume, the geographic, social, and temporal incidences—in other words, the fundamental patterns— of the emigration during the French Revolution.

The means, the only feasible means, are those of statistics: counting, sorting, tabulating. For us the émigrés represent constituent units of French society during the revolutionary ordeal. Their significance is numerical and categorical, not individual or personal. Except when their names are evoked as labels for examples or unique cases we shall allow them to remain anonymous. The unit that represents the Duc de la Rochefoucauld-Liancourt, the Cardinal de Rohan, or the Princesse de Conti is neither more nor less important than that which figures Jean Bertin, a Breton beggar;[9] Georges Hastmann, an Alsatian chimney sweep;[10] or Julie Hannequin, a Provençal prostitute.[11] Numbers for symbols, rather than names with all their connotations, will enable us to approach our problem directly; and, if the result has the colorlessness of a silhouette, it may also have a silhouette's clarity.

At the outset, then, our methodology is avowed. Statistics, as we shall use them, constitute a language of reference to specific and

[8] The Haut-Rhin, the Bas-Rhin, part of the Meurthe, and most of the Moselle, annexed by Germany in 1871, recovered by France in 1919; the Alpes-Maritimes and Mont-Blanc (Savoie and Haute-Savoie), annexed by France in 1792, recovered by Piedmont in 1814 and 1815, and reannexed by France in 1860; and the Vaucluse, annexed in 1791 and retained by France.

[9] "Liste générale des émigrés du département de la Mayenne," 18 fructidor an IV. AD Mayenne, Q 103.

[10] "Liste supplétive des émigrés du district de Wissembourg," 7 brumaire an IV. AD Bas-Rhin, Q unclassified.

[11] Louis Honoré, "L'émigration dans le Var, 1789–1825," *Bulletin de la Société d'études scientifiques et archéologiques de Draguignan* (1923), XXXIV, 645.

tangible things in the strictly material world. Their immediate meaning may be no more than that which meets the eye. Yet even this primary function will serve to reconstruct the vital patterns of the emigration and thus to lay the foundations of our study. Then we can proceed by means of analyses, correlations, and inferences to interpretations. An examination of the geographic incidence in the light of local circumstances, inherent or occasional, may partially explain the emigration; and an analysis of the regional variations of the social incidence may further our understanding. The relation of the flux and the reflux of the movement to the events of the Revolution will no doubt throw light on the motivations. And what is known concerning the émigrés abroad may confirm what we shall learn about them as they emigrated. These and other exercises will be undertaken in the belief that inside the dry bones of statistics lies a marrow of significance.

2. Sources

THE basic sources for our study are the lists of émigrés and deportees prepared in compliance with the legislation of the period. Beginning in the spring of 1792, each commune, or municipality, established a list of local émigrés; the communal lists were combined in district lists, the district lists in departmental lists, and the departmental lists in a national list. Supplements, local and national, were issued from time to time until 1799, or, in a few cases, until 1801. According to the prescription of the law of March 28, 1793, the full names of the emigrants were to be followed by their rank, their profession, their last residence in France, and a brief description of their property. Until the autumn of 1793, separate panels of banished clergy were maintained, and in some departments this practice was continued throughout the period; but the law of September 17, 1793, assimilated the deportees to the émigrés, and therefore records published subsequent to that date should include them.[12]

The number and the chronology of the lists issued in different departments depended in part on the importance of the local emi-

[12] For an excellent brief discussion of the legislation concerning this matter see Marc Bouloiseau, 20–24.

gration, in part on the zeal of the local authorities. Where the
emigration was light or where the officials were apathetic, the first
lists appeared late and the last supplements appeared early. In the
Basses-Alpes, for instance, the first of the four lists issued was
dated March 10, 1793, the last July 23, 1794.[13] On the other hand,
in the Meuse, where the emigration was heavy and the authorities
were zealous, ten lists were published between October 16, 1792,
and March 17, 1798.[14] These are typical cases; but in some departments—the Ain, for one—lists were issued as early as March, 1792,
or—as in the Tarn—as late as March, 1800.[15] As for the national
list, the first sections appeared in 1793, the last in 1801.

Compiled in manuscript, the lists then were printed. Occasionally they were cried in the streets of cities, and one may well
imagine that they sold like hot cakes. Each departmental archive
should contain at least one manuscript and one printed copy of the
local lists, but it is not surprising that, after a century and a half,
a number of them have disappeared. Moreover, in some departments the *série Q*, the usual repository of these documents, has not
been classified; in others it has been classified but not catalogued;
and in either case access to the records may be difficult, though not
necessarily impossible. In some places the manuscripts have survived though the printed lists have vanished; and in others the
individual dossiers of the emigrants and the deportees, easily
located because of their bulk, are available as a means of reconstruction. In a few departments all resources fail. Fortunately,
however, it was the practice of local administrations to circulate
copies of their lists for the information of other departments, and
consequently certain departmental archives contain collections of
lists.[16] Easily the most important of these, undiscovered until the

[13] AD Basses-Alpes, Q unclassified.

[14] Jean Dubois, *Liste des émigrés, des prêtres déportés et des condamnés pour cause
révolutionnaire du département de la Meuse* (Bar-le-Duc, 1911), *passim.*

[15] Eugène Dubois, *Histoire de la Révolution dans l'Ain* (3 vols.; Bourg, 1931–1933),
II, 435–437, "Supplément à la quatrième liste [des émigrés du Tarn]," 13 ventôse an
VIII. AD Tarn, Q 451.

[16] Especially valuable is the collection in the Archives départementales of the Pyrénées-Orientales, at Perpignan. Among other important lists it contains the following
which can not be found in the archives of the departments of their origin: "Liste . . .

summer of 1939, is that in the departmental archives of the
Gironde, at Bordeaux. In addition to numerous lists of which
copies exist elsewhere, it contains twenty-five lists not to be found
in the archives of the localities of their origin.[17]

Now, theoretically, the cumulative "Liste générale par ordre
alphabétique des émigrés de toute la République" (and its supplements), of which numerous copies are extant,[18] should furnish a
unique resumé of most of the information necessary for our work.
In reality it is virtually useless. It is a veritable repertoire of errors,
for a century and a half the object of ridicule, stricture, and oppro-
brium. It mirrors all the mistakes, innocuous, tragic, and grotesque,
committed in the confection of the local panels. Names are duplicated over and over again, misspelled, distorted beyond all hope of
identification; many persons who never emigrated are included,
and others, especially clergy, who did leave France are omitted;
not more than one profession in ten, not more than one residence
in three is given. Unreliability on the one hand, paucity of information on the other, make the "Liste générale des émigrés de
toute la République" one of the curios of the Revolution, and
void its value as a source of information.

There remain the local lists—departmental, district, and communal. Their quality is extremely uneven: few of them are perfect;
and many of them, especially the earlier ones, are quite as faulty as
the "Liste générale," of which, indeed, they were the source. But
whereas the errors of the former are practically incorrigible, those
of the latter are susceptible to partial correction. Aside from the
mutilation of proper names, which does not seriously interfere

---

des émigrés du département de Paris," Paris, an II (two copies); "Liste générale des
émigrés du département de Vaucluse," 4 prairial an II; "Premier supplément à la liste
générale des émigrés des Hautes-Pyrénées," 13 vendémiaire an III; etc.

[17] For a repertoire of these lists and an appraisal of their value see Donald Greer,
"A guide to source material on the émigrés of the French Revolution," *Journal of
Modern History* (1943), XV, 39–46. The writer also left a manuscript repertory with
the administration of the Archives nationales in Paris, in 1939.

[18] In the Bibliothèque nationale, the Archives nationales, and in many of the Archives
départementales. Lucien Dorbon, 156 Boulevard Saint-Germain, offered sections of the
Liste générale for sale in the summer of 1939. See his *Catalogue de livres, pamphlets . . .
et ouvrages curieux sur les évenéments . . . de la Révolution française* (Paris, 1939).

with our purpose, their flaws may be grouped in four categories: the inclusion of non-émigrés; the omission of authentic émigrés; multiple inscriptions of the same names; omission of the professions or description of them in loose, indefinite terms.

Nearly every scholar who has dealt with the emigration has signaled the innocent people inscribed on the fatal lists. Indeed, some writers would have us believe that the majority of the "émigrés" never saw foreign soil. M. Montarlot asserts that 358, or nearly 60 per cent, of the inscriptions in the Saône-et-Loire were erroneous;[19] M. Gaugain dismisses the principal list for the Mayenne as "a masterpiece of high fantasy";[20] and M. Jacob scoffs at the idea that 245 persons, most of them peasants, artisans, or tradesmen, emigrated from the single *canton* of Villenauxe in the Aube.[21] Extreme opinions of this sort, however, must be taken with strict reservations, for they are based either on *a priori* incredulity (as in the cases of MM. Gaugain and Jacob), or on a *parti pris* for the very dubious documents attesting non-emigration—certificates of residence, etc.—accepted by complaisant Thermidorian or Directorial officials (the case of M. Montarlot).

Still it is incontestable that the non-émigré group was both large and heterogeneous. It included shades of the dead as well as representatives of the living: the executed and the proscribed; ministers and diplomats in the service of the State; soldiers and sailors actually in the armed forces; deserters and prisoners of war; foreigners and phantasms; *chouans* and refractory clergy hidden in France; and, above all, persons merely absent from their habitual domiciles.

A sizable catalogue could be filled with specific examples; a few must suffice. Among the most notorious, of course, was the case of Monge, inscribed on the list of the Ardennes while he was serving as Minister of Marine in 1792; but more iniquitous (because it was

---

[19] Paul Montarlot, "Les émigrés de Saône-et-Loire," *Mémoires de la Société éduenne* (1913), XLI, 122.

[20] Ferdinand Gaugain, *Histoire de la Révolution dans la Mayenne* (Laval, s.d. [1917]), 315.

[21] M. Jacob, "Villenauxe et l'émigration," *La Révolution dans l'Aube, année* 1909, pp. 65–66.

deliberate) was the inscription of Admiral Truguet while he was ambassador at Madrid in 1798.[22] General Brunet, executed in Paris in 1794, was resurrected as an émigré in the Basses-Alpes;[23] Kervélégan, proscribed Girondin deputy, was pronounced an émigré in the Morbihan;[24] and Jean Cottereau, whose presence in France under the sobriquet "Jean Chouan" was hardly a secret, appeared as an émigré in the records of the Mayenne.[25] The Baron de Schauenbourg, an officer on active service, was inscribed in the Haut-Rhin;[26] and Finance du Fey, a soldier captured by the Austrians at Marchiennes (Nord) on October 3, 1793, was listed in the Saône-et-Loire.[27] The Directory of the same department eventually decided that the émigré Étienne Capclin had never existed;[28] four of the "émigrés" of the district of Rouen had been dead for years;[29] and, according to the *Répertoire général des émigrés de l'Aude* itself, two of the Bertrand brothers had been absent for thirty years, the third for forty years.[30] The Austrian generals Beaulieu and Wurmser were figured as émigrés, the former in the Dyle,[31] and the latter in both of the Rhenish departments.[32] The list of the Haut-Rhin was graced with the names of several German princes, among them the Duc des Deux-Ponts, future Maximilian I of Bavaria.[33] But the real crown remains to be placed on our brief

[22] Paul Barras, *Memoirs* (Eng. tr.; 4 vols.; New York, 1896), III, 308–312.

[23] "Troisième liste supplétive des émigrés [des Basses-Alpes]," 5 thermidor an II. AD Basses-Alpes, Q unclassified.

[24] "Liste supplétive des émigrés . . . du Morbihan," 7 prairial an II. AD Gironde, Q 1477.

[25] Liste générale . . . des émigrés . . . de la Mayenne," 18 floréal an II. AD Mayenne, Q 103. Cf. Ferdinand Gaugain, 315.

[26] Félix Schaedelin, *L'émigration révolutionnaire du Haut-Rhin* (Colmar, 1937), 84.

[27] Paul Montarlot, *loc. cit.* (1920–1923), XLIV, 67–68.

[28] *Ibid.* (1919), XLIII, 20–21.

[29] Marc Bouloiseau, 11.

[30] AD Aude, Q 139.

[31] "Troisième liste supplémentaire des émigrés [de la Dyle]," s.d. AD Gironde, Q 1475.

[32] "État général des émigrés du district de Strasbourg," 15 janvier 1793; duplicated in the lists for the districts of Wissembourg and Haguenau. AD Bas-Rhin, Q unclassified; Félix Schaedelin, 84.

[33] Félix Schaedelin, 84–85.

repertoire of examples: the department of the Côte-d'Or listed as an émigré "Louis Capet, last of the tyrants"![34]

Errors so grotesque are all but incredible, and inevitably they have been ascribed to the deliberate intention of vicious or ignorant revolutionary officials.[35] Indeed, no one is likely to maintain that all the Jacobin authorities were innocent of the insolence or the ineptitude of office or to deny that some of them "manufactured" émigrés. The truth is, however, that the majority of the errors sprang neither from intention nor ineptitude, but from the literal application of the laws or from circumstances quite beyond official control. Specifically, as Marc Bouloiseau has insisted,[36] the cause of a very large number of them was the law of April 8, 1792, which, in effect, defined as émigrés all persons absent from the department in which they possessed property.[37] Such persons could, it is true, obviate inscription by sending certificates of residence from the department of their domicile to the department or departments where they possessed real property. Some of them, usually nobles or bourgeois living in cities where the law was conspicuously placarded, complied; but, because of carelessness or ignorance, most of the "absent" neglected the formality which would have saved them.[38]

The consequences were bizarre. The first three lists of the district of Rouen carried the names of 160 "absent" domiciled in other departments; a handful of them had, in fact, emigrated, but 146, or more than 50 per cent of the total inscriptions, were at home.[39] Identically "painful surprises," as Marc Bouloiseau calls them,

[34] "Département de la Côte-d'Or. Liste des noms et des biens des émigrés. Quatorzième liste," 29 perminal an II. AD Côte-d'Or, Q 514.

[35] The classic indictment is that by Marcel Marion, "Quelques exemples de l'application des lois sur l'émigration . . .," Revue historique (1911), CVII, 272–284; CVIII, 28–48.

[36] Marc Bouloiseau, Liste des émigrés . . . dans le district de Rouen, 11; and, by the same author, Le séquestre et la vente des biens des émigrés dans le district de Rouen, 1792–an X (Paris, 1937), 30ff.

[37] For the text of the law see Marcel Ragon, La législation sur les émigrés, 1789–1825 (Paris, 1904), 201–208.

[38] Marc Bouloiseau, Le séquestre et la vente des biens des émigrés, 32.

[39] Ibid., 31; and, by the same author, Liste des émigrés . . . dans le district de Rouen, 11.

afflicted absentees everywhere in France. Now, too, the incredible inscriptions of the dead and the vanished, the notoriously present and the legitimately absent, become explicable, especially when one allows for bureaucratic literalism. The four dead men of the district of Rouen and the long-departed Bertrand brothers of the Aude appeared in the old registers as property owners. Of course Louis XVI held real property in the Côte-d'Or;[40] certainly Monge was absent from his home in the Ardennes, and surely it would have been unwise for Cottereau, *dit* Chouan, to live at his home in the Mayenne. As for the soldiers and the prisoners of war, by one of the strangest oversights in the history of legislation the law of April 8, 1792, did not specifically exclude them. No doubt the clause excepting from inscription "ceux qui ont une mission du gouvernement" was intended to cover them, but its vague comprehensiveness presumed on the part of petty officials more talent in deductive reasoning than many of them possessed.

The literal application of this same act also enveloped foreigners who owned real property in France; and if the law of March 28, 1793, narrowed the definition to those absent from their French residences, it also broadened it to include those who enjoyed French citizenship, irrespective of property tenure.[41] Moreover, this legislation was applied in annexed territory—in Belgium, for instance. In quarters where Jacobinism was anything but a hot flame prior to the administrative purges of the summer of 1793, the authorities, strangely unable to discern the absence of compatriots, scrupulously listed all the foreigners. At Gex, in the Ain, for example, the district, pressed by the department to keep a closer watch on the emigration, inflated its meager panels with the names of all the Swiss (and Genevan) subjects who owned summer residences in the circumscription.[42] Even Paris supplemented its ample quota with a number of foreigners, among them such no-

---

[40] The property of the *condamnés* also passed to the nation, but the list containing the name of Louis Capet is distinctly a list of émigrés.

[41] Marcel Ragon, 224–225. (Section III, Article 6 of the law of March 28–April 5, 1793.)

[42] Eugène Dubois, III, 126.

tables as Frederick Grimm, author of the *Correspondence*, and the English banker Boyd, whose case became notorious.[43]

On the other hand, circumstances rather than legislation explain the inscription of numerous clergymen who did not leave France. The law of August 26, 1792, prescribed exile, failing which, deportation for nonjurors, and most of them obeyed. Some of them, however, took passports merely as a blind, remaining hidden within the country, while others simply disappeared, *sans formalité*.[44] In either case, they usually were listed as émigrés or deportees. How, for instance, were the authorities of the Maine-et-Loire to know what had become of the hundred or more priests released from the prisons of Angers by the Vendeans in June, 1793?[45] Probably every department had its contingent of deportables who remained at home. As random examples, there were twenty-three in the Loiret-Cher,[46] seventy-seven in the Landes,[47] about three hundred in the mountains of Auvergne (Haute-Loire),[48] and they were very numerous in the entire region of the Vendean war. To these nonémigrés must be added some of the old or infirm *réfractaires*, interned instead of exiled, but nevertheless often listed as deportees.[49]

Thus, law and circumstance incubated a large company of fictive emigrants, but it must immediately be emphasized that probably as many, or more, authentic émigrés escaped official cognizance. Some of the officials of the early Republic deliberately ignored the

---

[43] "Liste . . . des émigrés . . . de Paris," Paris, an II. BN, Lb⁴¹ 3338; also AD Pyrénées-Orientales, Q 730.

[44] Élie Rossignol, *Les prêtres du Tarn persécutés pendant la Révolution* (Albi, 1895), 19–20; J. Gallerand, *Les cultes sous la Terreur en Loir-et-Cher* (Blois, 1928), 13; E. Sevestre, *Les problèmes religieux de la Révolution et de l'Empire en Normandie* (2 vols.; Paris, 1924), II, 795.

[45] Most of them followed the Vendean army when it evacuated Angers. See Émile Queruau-Lamerie, *Le clergé du département du Maine-et-Loire pendant la Révolution* (Angers, 1899), *passim*.

[46] J. Gallerand, 11–15.

[47] Abbé Légé, *Les diocèses d'Aire et de Dax pendant la Révolution française* (Aire, 1875), 181–188.

[48] Ernest Gonnet, *Essai sur l'histoire du diocèse du Puy-en-Velay, 1789–1802* (Paris, 1907), 210.

[49] A common occurrence. Some of the lists indicate the "reclus"; others include them without indicating them. In the Haute-Garonne nearly 500 were listed without indication of their status.

emigration. In the spring of 1793, Barras and Fréron, deputies on mission, could see in the streets of Embrun (Hautes-Alpes) returned émigrés, who, apparently, were invisible to the local authorities, their acquaintances.[50] The municipal councilors of Londe (Seine-Inférieure), all either relatives or tenants of the Marquis Le Cordier de Bigars, persistently refused to list him as an émigré, though his absence was a matter of local notoriety.[51] And as late as Messidor of the Year II, the Protestant communes of Riquewihr and Beblenheim (Haut-Rhin) submitted completely negative reports, though it was well known that the emigration had been heavy in both villages.[52] Even where vigilance was not lacking, the Jacobins were neither omniscient nor omnipresent, and in every department (especially in the cities) at least a few departures must have been unnoticed and unrecorded.

But above all, thousands of real émigrés were lost in the anonymity of crowds, in the confusion of panic, or in the smoke of civil war. Where the emigration was heavy, it was difficult for the authorities to maintain anything like a complete census. In the Moselle, for example, André Gain has estimated that there were nearly a thousand omissions.[53] Where panic made the flight torrential, it was impossible to record it. In the Var, for instance, Louis Honoré was able to discover the trace of 5,331 émigrés, but he believes that the real total exceeded 10,000;[54] and, though the official documents of the Bas-Rhin reveal 20,510 fugitives, contemporaries talked of forty or fifty thousand from the two districts of Haguenau and Wissembourg alone.[55] Finally, where civil war accompanied by punitive devastation led not only to mass

[50] F. A. Aulard, *Recueil des actes du Comité de Salut public* . . . (27 vols.; Paris, 1889–1933), IV, 92–95 (Barras and Fréron to the Convention, May 10, 1793).

[51] Marc Bouloiseau, *Le séquestre et la vente des biens des émigrés*, 24. The case was notorious, and the Department finally declared Cordier de Bigars an émigré despite the refusal of the *commune* to denounce him.

[52] Félix Schaedelin, 26–27. M. Schaedelin ascribes these deliberate omissions to the "confessional solidarity" of the Protestants.

[53] André Gain, *Liste des émigrés, déportés et condamnés pour cause révolutionnaire du département de la Moselle* (2 vols.; Metz, 1925–1932), II, 737.

[54] Louis Honoré, *loc. cit.*, pp. 12–13.

[55] R. Reuss, *La grande fuite de décembre 1793 et la situation politique et religieuse du Bas-Rhin de 1794 à 1799* (Strasbourg, 1922), pp. vi, 15–18.

migrations, but also to complete disruption of local administrations, the recorded emigration is a mere token of the reality.[56]

Errors of commission and omission thus may balance one another, but duplications of names complicate the numerical problem. They occurred everywhere; few records are entirely free from them. They amount to 187 in the lists of the Var;[57] they represent 20 per cent of the inscriptions in the Eure;[58] and they are so numerous in the Côtes-du-Nord that they deterred Léon Dubreuil from tabulating the émigrés of the department.[59] Yet these intra-departmental duplications present the least difficulty, since, on the whole, they are corrigible. It is when the same name is duplicated in the lists of different departments that the difficulty may be insuperable. In this connection the law of April 8, 1792, which identified absentee property owners and émigrés, was again at fault, and again some curious consequences ensued. The Bourbons, the Condés, the Rohans, the La Rochefoucaulds, the Montmorencys—all the great proprietors of France—were inscribed in a dozen or more departments. When the subjects were so notable it is a simple matter to eliminate the duplications from list to list, but many absentee landlords lacked any signal lustre, and in these cases there is no practicable means of eradicating the inter-departmental duplications.

Still more serious impediments to the achievement of our purpose are sundry descriptive vagaries, especially the omission of professions. Vocation is to be our principal social denominator, and when the sources omit or garble it, we are obliged either to abandon social classification or to resort to other and often less positive indices. In some lists, such as those of the Seine-et-Oise, the columns reserved for professions are virgin. In others we are offered

[56] "Les listes officielles ne comprennent pour le département de la Vendée qu'une quantité négligeable de noms d'émigrés," remarks C. de Saint-Marc, "Les émigrés du Poitou et des anciens grands gouvernements d'Angoumois, Aunis et Saintonge, 1792–1793," *Mémoires de la Société historique et scientifique des Deux-Sèvres, année* 1905, p. 173.

[57] Louis Honoré, *loc. cit.*, p. 13.

[58] AD Eure, Q 11–12. Eliminated in tabulating lists.

[59] Léon Dubreuil, *La vente des biens nationaux dans le département des Côtes-du-Nord, 1790–1830* (Paris, 1912), 175.

quaint comments, as amusing as they are baffling. The limp of "Gaillard le boiteux" (Vaucluse), the big thigh of "Arnaud, dit la grosse cuisse" (Bouches-du-Rhône), the light pocketbook of "Julien, dit paye-leger" (Vaucluse), and the red hair of "Praol, dit poil rouge" (Bouches-du-Rhône) shed little light on their social status.[60] And it aids us not at all to know that Mme. Delanney of Lille was the "widow of Gilbert," that Messien of Bergues (Nord) was a "married man,"[61] or that Joseph Tuiller of Verme (Mont-Terrible) was an "imbecile."[62] Plural inscriptions introduce another element of imprecision: Jean Martin "et toute sa famille" (men, women, or children?) emigrated from the Var;[63] the Cortet "heirs" (how many?) from the Saône-et-Loire;[64] and from the Nord went "Dubusseret, his son, his daughter-in-law, and nine servants plus two children and a grandson of M. Podéna"![65] Even the property designations, useful as guides and less frequently omitted than vocations, often fail us. La Bascle d'Argentueil owned "un mauvais chateau" at Loches (Indre-et-Loire),[66] and all we know of Jean Ballyat is that he was the proprietor of a "trunk full of clothing" at Landau (Bas-Rhin).[67]

In the light of all these defects, one may ask, "Of what value are the lists of émigrés?" None, in a few cases. But most of them are or can be made serviceable. In the first place, the most baroque of the errors are almost self-corrective. In the second place, our critique, though it applies to the lists of all dates, bears particularly on the earlier ones. Their mistakes and deficiencies were patent, and both law and practice were amended to mitigate them.

[60] "Liste générale des émigrés . . . de Vaucluse," 4 prairial an II. AD Gironde, Q 1478; "Relevé général des émigrés . . . des Bouches-du-Rhône," 15 nivôse an II. AD Gironde, Q 1475.

[61] "Liste générale des émigrés . . . du Nord," 20 août 1793. AD Nord, L 1080; "District de Bergues. Liste supplétive des émigrés," ms., s.d. AD Nord, L 1095.

[62] "Liste générale des émigrés . . . du Mont-Terrible," 21 ventôse an II. AD Gironde, Q 1477.

[63] Louis Honoré, loc. cit., p. 66.

[64] Paul Montarlot, loc. cit. (1919), XLIII, 94.

[65] "Liste générale des émigrés . . . du Nord," 20 août 1793. AD Nord, L 1080.

[66] "État général des émigrés . . . de l'Aube," s.d. [1793]. BN, Lb[41] 3034.

[67] "État général des émigrés du district de Haguenau," 7 février 1793. AD Bas-Rhin, Q unclassified.

The confusion of absentees and émigrés being the most prolific error-breeder, the decree of March 28, 1793, clearly defined émigrés as persons who actually had left France. True, absentee proprietors still were required to prove residence within the country, and it was not until November 15, 1794, that the law forbade the inscription of émigrés in districts other than those of their domiciles. Eventually, however, these and other amendments had effect, and from the middle of 1793 onward most of the departments issued revised or recapitulative lists of much better quality than those of the early vintage.[68]

In the third place, all but a few of the lists are susceptible to correction and completion by means of other source material. The unofficial registers, often compiled by administrative agents for their own use, the lists of the relatives of émigres, prepared in accord with the law of September 12, 1792, the lists of canceled émigrés, and the lists of the beneficiaries of the amnesties of 1795, 1800, and 1802, besides being necessary for some aspects of our study, are sometimes more accurate and more informative than the panels of émigrés themselves. Still more important are the dossiers of the individual émigrés and deportees, which contain a variety of papers—denunciations, correspondence, petitions, to say nothing of material pertaining to émigré property. When these files are complete, they constitute a rich resource. Used in conjunction with the catalogues of relatives, of canceled, and of amnestied émigrés, they may serve to confirm, to supplement, or to reconstruct the picture of the emigration.

Local scholars have followed essentially this procedure in critically editing the lists for a few departments,[69] and we have applied it when necessary and possible in our research. A great many of the

[68] The Marne, for instance, in 1794 issued separate lists of resident and nonresident "prévenus d'émigration." AD Gironde, Q 1477.

[69] In addition to the works of Louis Honoré, André Gain, Jean Dubois, Félix Schaedelin, Marc Bouloiseau, and Paul Montarlot, already cited, the following are the best of these edited lists: Victor Forot, *Les émigrés corrèziens avec la nomenclature et la valeur de leurs biens séquestrés* (Paris, 1922); L. Gauthier, *Les émigrés de la Haute-Saône* (Gray, 1913), based on petitions for cancellation in the Archives nationales, and therefore incomplete; and François Descostes, *Les émigrés en Savoie, à Aoste et dans le pays de Vaud, 1790–1800* (Chambéry, 1903).

errors have thus been eradicated. Obviously, however, it would require more than one lifetime to subject every case to microscopic analysis. Nor is it likely that the final results would vary substantially from those represented in our tables. Not critical technique but miraculous divination would be needed to restore, after a hundred and fifty years, utter veracity of detail in a matter which baffled contemporaries themselves. Probably, as Mathiez believed, the errors favored the émigrés, especially those of the lower classes. But even if it be true, for example, that there were 1,500 rather than 1,186 émigrés from the Gironde and that the artisan exodus was a few percentage points higher than our tables indicate, the Gironde remains a department of moderately heavy and predominantly upper-class emigration. The utmost precision would serve us little better in our attempt to discover the incidences of the emigration.

Our statistics, then, cannot pretend to absolute exactitude. They include an irregular margin of error. In a few places it may infringe as much as fifty per cent (e.g., the Var), in others it narrows to insignificance (e.g., the Basses-Alpes), and it probably averages not more than ten per cent. We shall signal in passing the great indentations, which, for the rest, can be partially compensated by indicating probabilities equivalent to certitudes. But the greatest error of all would be to assume that approximate statistics have no value. On the contrary, they are almost, if not quite, as conclusive for our purpose as would be the most perfect precision. We are seeking to reconstruct the pattern of the emigration from France during ten years of revolution, and to that end broad, bright threads are primarily necessary. The categories of our tables are these threads, and their colors are indelible within their error-faded edges.

CHAPTER II

THE EMIGRATION

1. Volume and Perspective

MORE than a century and a half after the fall of the Bastille no definitive conclusion had been reached concerning the volume of the emigration from revolutionary France. In October, 1800, on the eve of Bonaparte's first amnesty, the *Liste générale* and its supplements gave the names of 145,000 uncanceled émigrés. The official figures, however, were suspect; and, though Taine accepted 150,000 as a fair appraisal of the total number of exiles, other scholars believed that he erred by 50,000 one way or the other.[1] These, as well as other estimates, had one thing in common: they were based on the national lists. True, no serious scholar urged the reliability of these sources, but it was sometimes forgotten that they comprised the "émigrés" from conquered territory which remained French for only a few years. In some annexed districts, especially in Belgium and Porrentruy, the emigration was numerically important.[2] Hence, all estimates derived from the *Liste générale* were weighted not only with the notorious unreliability of the

---

[1] Hippolyte Taine, *The French Revolution* (Eng. tr.; 3 vols.; New York, 1910), III, 291–292; André Gain, *Liste des émigrés . . . de la Moselle*, I, 4; and, by the same author, *La Restauration et les biens des émigrés*, II, 177–178.

[2] From Porrentruy alone there were 1,186 émigrés ("Liste générale des émigrés du département du Mont-Terrible," 21 ventôse an II. AD Gironde, Q 1477). The majority of the Belgian clergy were *réfractaires*, and the lay emigration seems to have been heavy ("Première [deuxième] liste supplémentaire des émigrés du département des Forets," s.d., and "Troisième liste supplémentaire des prévenus d'émigration du département de la Dyle," 9 germinal an VI. AD Gironde, Q 1475). As for Luxembourg, the "Liste des personnes prévenues d'émigration du département des Deux-Nèthes . . .," 19 fructidor an IV (AD Gironde, Q 1475) gives 87 names.

source, but also with the inclusion of foreigners who should not have been classed as French émigrés.

In quest of a more secure basis, we have resorted to the local sources. These, when pared in so far as possible of their errors, give a total of 109,720 émigrés from seventy-two departments, that is to say 80 per cent of those included in Table I. In seven of the other fifteen the source materials either have disappeared or are inadequate; in three others they apparently exist but were inaccessible to the author; and in the remaining five they are fragmentary but very useful.[3] Most of these deficiencies probably are irremediable. We must, then, seek some other means of estimating the emigration from these departments.

André Gain postulated that there were five émigrés for every indemnity granted in 1825,[4] and this ratio applied to the indemnities of the seventy-two departments which we have studied in the sources gives results approximating those we have derived. In some cases there is a close approach to an equation; in others the difference between the hypothesis and the reality is wide, but in general the variation averages less than ten per cent.[5] The indemnity hypothesis, then, is acceptable as a means of determining

---

[3] The situation in the fifteen departments in question was as follows: In the Ain the documents pertaining to the émigrés were inaccessible; in the Eure-et-Loir, the Loiret, the Loire-Inférieure, and the Charente-Inférieure materials were nonexistent or totally inadequate; there was in the Côtes-du-Nord and the Pas-de-Calais considerable fragmentary material which, if intensively processed, might serve for a partial reconstruction of the original lists; the apparently complete lists in the Lot-et-Garonne, the Vienne, and the Haute-Vienne were not available; and incomplete materials for Calvados, the Jura, the Loire, the Puy-de-Dôme, and the Sarthe were used in preparing this study.

[4] André Gain, *La Restauration et les biens des émigrés*, II, 178ff. See especially the tables and cartograms showing the incidence of the indemnity.

[5] Examples of near equations: Finistère, 408 indemnities, 2040 hypothetical émigrés, 2086 actual émigrés; Aude, 144 indemnities, 720 hypothetical émigrés, 759 actual émigrés; Lozère, 67 indemnities, 335 hypothetical émigrés, 338 actual émigrés. For the Manche, with 401 indemnities, the 2,005 hypothetical émigrés exactly equal the 2,005 tabulated émigrés. Examples of wide differences: Moselle, 1652 more actual than hypothetical émigrés; Bouches-du-Rhône, a surplus of 4,200 actual émigrés (an extreme case); Nord, a deficiency of 2,225 actual émigrés. Examples of average differences: Ardennes, hypothetical émigrés, 1,305; actual émigrés, 1,201; Doubs, hypothetical émigrés, 1735; actual émigrés, 1930.

the approximate volume of the emigration where the sources fail us. The figures for eleven of the departments carried in our tables of the geographic incidence are based entirely on this hypothesis, and in four other cases incomplete or fragmentary source material supported the results derived from the formula.[6] The number of émigrés thus added to our tabulation from the documents is 19,379, or 15 per cent of the total, which becomes 129,099. Granting the inevitable margin of doubt, it still is certain that this end result is the most accurate now attainable.

There were, it is true, other emigrants—the unlisted fugitives. As we have seen, they were numerous in the regions of invasion and civil war, but there is no way of ascertaining even their approximate number. Perhaps it has been somewhat exaggerated, for in the very districts where cataclysmic events scattered populations like autumn leaves in a gale many of the fugitives went to other parts of France.[7] In any case, the shroud of confusion is impenetrable, and one competent opinion is as good as another. Probably the unofficial émigrés numbered somewhere between 20,000 and 30,000. Perhaps, then, Taine was right after all, for our computation gives a total of about 150,000 exiles.[8]

Presently, however, we are concerned only with the 129,099 official émigrés. In view of all the circumstances, the number was not large. It represented only one half of one per cent of the population of France, or only about five persons in every thousand. The past had known and the future was to know greater exoduses than this one. In the smaller France of 1685 the revocation of the Edict of Nantes precipitated the flight of 200,000 Protestants,

[6] See the Bibliography for the departments for which our statistics are derived wholly or in part from Gain's hypothesis.

[7] Indeed, there was forced evacuation from certain districts in the West. Early in ventôse an II, Hentz and Francastel, representatives on mission, ordered the deportation of the inhabitants of the Vendée to other departments; and on the sixteenth of the month (March 6, 1794) they informed the Committee of Public Safety that ten thousand persons had been evacuated (Léon Dubreuil, *Histoire des insurrections de l'Ouest* [2 vols.; Paris, 1929–1930], II, 2).

[8] André Gain (*La Restauration et les biens des émigrés*, II, 177–178) estimated a total of two hundred thousand "including the fugitives from the Bas-Rhin, the Var, and the Vendée."

and it is estimated that a million left the country in the forty years following the revocation.[9] As for the revolutionary Europe of the twentieth century, its hordes of displaced persons are as yet uncounted, but the total would run into the millions. Yet perspective can be deceptive, and if the French emigration, like the French Revolution itself, seems to pale in the glare of the conflagrations of our time it nonetheless was one of the facets of a period of dynamic change.

2. *Modalities under the Monarchy*

THIS flight from France is best envisaged not as a series of waves but as a stream rising as a rivulet in midsummer, 1789, gathering volume as the Monarchy weakened and toppled, swelling to a torrent in the climactic violence of 1793, and subsiding to a trickle after Thermidor. But description of each phase of this changing stream has remained more or less in the province of impressionism. Of course, the character of the early emigration is well known. It was a mode induced by the example of the Comte d'Artois, who fled from Versailles early on the morning of July 17, 1789. Within a fortnight or so most of the courtiers had followed. Among those leading the procession were the Princes of Condé and Conti; other early deserters from France were the Lorrains, the Polignacs, the Rohans, de Broglie's seven daughters and their husbands, and, especially, the Queen's favorites—for instance, the Princesse de Lamballe, who later fatefully decided to return.[10] Some of these pristine émigrés departed in grand style: the Duc de la Trémoëlle, his wife, and their four children appeared at Nice in August, 1789, with three carriages, a berline, a diligence "sur resorts," and a cabriolet, which the duke later sold for two thousand livres;[11] and the Marquis de Mirpoix, one of the richest seigneurs of

[9] Ernest Lavisse, ed., *Histoire de France depuis les origines jusqu'à la Révolution* (9 vols. in 18; Paris, 1900-1911), vol. VII, pt. 2 ("Louis XIV, de 1643 à 1685 [2e partie]," by Ernest Lavisse), p. 80.

[10] Henri Carré, *La noblesse de France et l'opinion publique au XVIIIe siècle* (Paris, 1920), 365-368.

[11] Georges Doublet, "L'émigration française à Nice de 1789 à 1792," *Nice historique* (1928), XXXI, 128-129.

Languedoc, arrived in Rome a little later with half a million livres.[12] Others, however, left everything behind them, for very few of the early émigrés dreamed of a prolonged absence. The Comte d'Artois himself expressed their attitude when he remarked to the Comte d'Esterhazy, commandant at Valenciennes: "We shall return in three months."[13] Three decades would have been a better forecast, but the outraged seigneurs of 1789 contemplated only a temporary withdrawal from a scene unworthy of their presence.

Already, however, other motives than emulation dictated escape. No doubt the effects of the "great fear" of the summer and early autumn of 1789 have been magnified, and the conception of "spontaneous anarchy," Taine's magnificent distortion, lives on. Nevertheless, a few conflagrations made a great glare in the skies, a few murders assumed the appearance of massacres; and soon the émigrés of disdain were joined by the first "émigrés of fear," fugitives from the burning chateaux. From the country as a whole they were not numerous; many departments were scarcely affected —for example, only three persons emigrated from the Var in 1789.[14] But from certain provinces, such as Burgundy, Franche-Compté, Dauphiné, and Languedoc, where the *jacquerie* was especially virulent and persistent, the exodus was heavier. Indeed, by the end of September emigrants from these regions were conspicuous in Turin, Chambéry, and the small Savoyard towns near the French border.[15]

But the march on Versailles, in October, is the first clearly discernible milepost in the history of the emigration. Coming after the tension of the summer, the October Days accentuated upper-class fears of mob violence and at the same time blighted aristocratic hopes for a coup d'état. The consequences were immediate. A number of grand seigneurs who, like the Duc de Choiseul and the Baron de Breteuil, had resisted the early current now de-

---

[12] Emmanuel Vingtrinier, *La contre-révolution, première période, 1789–1791*, I, 70.
[13] Henri Carré, 365.
[14] Louis Honoré, "L'émigration dans le Var, 1789–1825," *Bulletin de la Société d'études . . . de Draguignan* (1923), XXXIV, 16.
[15] Emmanuel Vingtrinier, I, 69–70.

parted.[16] The officers of the royal army, only the most compromised of whom had deserted after the fall of the Bastille, now began to emigrate in droves.[17] And hesitant prelates, such as Louis André de Grimaldi, Bishop of Noyon, who arrived in Nice in November, abandoned their sees.[18] Now, too, the flight involved bourgeois as well as seigneurs and ecclesiastics. Mounier's emigration created a sensation, and he was only one of numerous deputies who deserted their posts in the Assembly. As early as October 9, the president of that body announced that he had received three hundred requests for passports in two days! The moderates were alarmed and the radicals were enraged, but the Assembly, already stricken with a strange lethargy in regard to the emigration, took no legislative action.[19]

The current of the emigration, in synchrony with the pace of the Revolution, quickened during 1790. The abolition of hereditary nobility set the provincial nobles, hitherto passive, against the Revolution; the suppression of the *parlements* disaffected the *noblesse de robe* and a good many bourgeois as well; the Civil Constitution of the Clergy alienated virtually all of the upper clergy and a great many of the lower; and the rising tide of insubordination in the army accelerated the defection of the officers. Early in May, Lieutenant-Colonel de Hell, from his vantage point in Alsace, noted the daily passage of noble carriages on the route to Switzerland.[20] Every day new faces appeared in the émigré colonies around France—at Nice, Turin, Lausanne, Mannheim, Coblenz, Brussels; every day another episcopal see was vacant; and every day some regiments lacked some of their officers. Most of these emigrants were still of the privileged classes—"the most important families of the purely feudal nobility," remarked Felix Schaedelin in commenting on the early emigration from the Haut-Rhin.[21] But as the year drew to a close the movement broadened

---

[16] *Ibid.*, I, 83–84.
[17] L. Hartmann, *Les officiers de l'armée royale et la Révolution* (Paris, 1910), 118–122.
[18] Georges Doublet, *loc. cit.*, p. 59.
[19] Marcel Ragon, *La législation sur les émigrés, 1789–1825*, 11.
[20] Félix Schaedelin, *L'émigration révolutionnaire du Haut-Rhin*, 14.
[21] *Ibid.*

and deepened. "Until now there were hardly any émigrés from the Mayenne," the Department informed the Assembly, "[but] during the last eight days a large number leave Laval every night, and they announce loudly that they are going to join the malcontents."[22]

That last phrase is significant. By the end of 1790 there were already two Frances: that of the Revolution, within the frontiers, and that of the counterrevolution, at Brussels and Coblenz and Turin—and still the National Assembly had contented itself with inviting state functionaries and pensioners absent from the kingdom to return.[23] At the end of February, 1791, after the departure of the King's aunts had caused a furor in the radical press, Barnave proposed and the Committee on Legislation submitted a bill on emigration; but Chapelier, its reporter, said that it was unconstitutional, and Mirabeau assured its defeat when he swore that were it passed he would not obey it.[24] In effect, then, *pax vobiscum* was the word of the Assembly to the departing émigrés.

Their intentions were anything but peaceful, but the early movement was at least spontaneous. Pressure and propaganda, however, played a part in the growing exodus of 1791. Nobles already abroad urged their friends still at home to join them, and émigré agents within the country activated the movement. When persuasion failed, various forms of pressure were applied. Officers were threatened with the revocation of their commissions; caricatures of stay-at-home nobles were circulated, or to these gentry were sent little packages containing scissors, needles, and thread![25] Some parents virtually forced their sons to emigrate. Young Norvins, for instance, was summoned before a sort of court composed of his father, his mother, and the Count and Countess of Brienne and informed that he must go to Metz, where émigré agents would see him over the frontier.[26] Moreover, recruiting for

[22] Ferdinand Gaugain, *Histoire de la Révolution dans la Mayenne*, 314.

[23] Marcel Ragon, 12.

[24] *Ibid.*, 13–14. Mirabeau's words were: "Si vous faites une loi contre les émigrants. je jure de n'y obéir pas."

[25] Henri Carré, 478.

[26] *Ibid.*, 481.

the émigré army forming on the Rhine was openly conducted. The *Gazette de Paris* carried a notice offering a bounty of fifty livres for volunteers, announcing the rates of pay, and giving directions for reaching the concentration points.[27]

Indeed, 1791 was essentially the year of the military emigration. The Comte d'Artois established his headquarters at Coblenz in June, and the King was to join the émigré army gathering there. But Louis XVI was stopped at Varennes-en-Argonne, and the plot fell to the ground. Until then the higher officers, especially Bouillé, who commanded in the East, had detained their subordinates,[28] but the failure of the King's flight precipitated a general exodus. The hope of counterrevolution within the country no longer restrained the officers, and, since their attitude was notorious, insubordination on the part of their troops rising to mutiny rendered their professional rôles untenable. Some of them were stripped of their insignia and driven from the garrisons, and these expulsions often led to the desertion of other officers.[29] Those who remained with their units were subjected to intense propaganda from the émigré leaders. In July, all officers who passed as stanch royalists received letters ordering them, in the name of the "Regent of the Kingdom," to join in the "holy enterprise" of crushing the revolution. Those who failed to report to a designated place abroad on July 30 were to be dismissed from the army, dishonored, and ostracized.[30] And sometimes more effective than the general summons were the personal appeals addressed by the princes to their friends. "It is not certain," wrote the Comte de Puymaigre, "that my father would have emigrated, but after a letter from the Prince de Condé, to whom he owed his military career, he no longer hesitated. . ."[31] The desertions assumed mass proportions. "Aucun officier ne pouvait y tenir," confessed a Limousin lieu-

[27] Ernest Daudet, *Histoire de l'émigration pendant la Révolution française*, I, 103; L. Hartmann, 384.

[28] L. Hartmann, 206.

[29] *Ibid.*, 259. For example, the *chasseurs* of the regiment of Champagne expelled their colonel, and six other officers followed him.

[30] *Ibid.*, 314–316.

[31] *Ibid.*, 316.

tenant.[32] Within six weeks after the dramatic scene at Varennes some regiments were entirely without officers; others were reduced to two or three; and few indeed were the formations without conspicuous vacancies. By the end of the year some six thousand officers, about three-fourths of the corps of the royal army, were on foreign soil.[33]

The amazing fact is that the French Government did very little to prevent the evasion of so many of its nationals, both civilian and military. During the greater part of the period which Crane Brinton has defined as that of the first revolution (1789–1792), Frenchmen were free to go and come as they pleased. Until the King's flight, in fact, the frontiers were open and travel was unrestricted. Then, on June 21, 1791, the frontiers were closed. Six weeks elapsed, however, before a law on emigration was passed on August 6, and it was a prelude *dolce* to the later harsh legislation. It forbade French citizens to leave the country, and it enjoined those who had left after July 1, 1789, to return within one month. Those who complied were to suffer no penalties; those who disobeyed were to be fined by the triplication of their taxes concurrent with their absence. But the enforcement clauses of the law were inapplicable, and among the groups excepted from all its provisions were those "absent because of illness "[34]

Benign rather than punitive, the law of August 6, 1791, was in force only a little more than a month. The Constitution, accepted by the King on September 14, implicitly abrogated it, and the same day the National Assembly explicitly annulled it. Again the frontiers were open, and, since passport requirements were abolished, foreign travel was unrestricted. The consequences were ominous. The émigrés of yesterday met the émigrés of tomorrow on

---

[32] Thomas de Closmadeuc, *Quiberon, 1795* (Paris, 1898), 260.

[33] "État des officiers de tous grades déserteurs ou émigrés classés par régiments," Paris, 1793. BN, LF[196] 5. Cf. L. Hartmann, 258–261. For the Norman officers, 362 in all, at Coblenz in November, 1791, see P. Le Verdier, *Les émigrés normands à Coblentz d'après le registre de leurs délibérations* (Caen, 1931), *passim*.

[34] For the text see Marcel Ragon, 196–198. For a critique of the law see Marc Bouloiseau, *Le séquestre et la vente des biens des émigrés dans le district de Rouen*, 5–7. For example, twelve of the most notorious émigrés of Rouen turned up with doctors' certificates attesting their maladies.

the roads to the frontiers, and the latter outnumbered the former. Those who had hoped that the amnesty would inaugurate a phase of reconciliation were disillusioned and alarmed. Even Louis XVI was now apprehensive. On October 14 he declared that he owned as "his friends, his only friends" those who united with him to maintain the laws, and he summoned the émigrés to return to France, "the post of honor." Few of them responded; for most of the émigrés of this period "the post of honor" was Condé's army on the Rhine, and October was a month of heavy military emigration.[35]

The quick, signal failure of the policy of conciliation caused the Legislative Assembly to adopt far more severe measures against the émigrés. The bill of November 9, 1791, though somewhat equivocal, in effect required them to return to France before January 1, 1792, under penalty of death for disobedience.[36] This project, it is true, was stillborn, for the King withheld his sanction. Soon, however, the tide of events became irresistible. No one could ignore the war clouds on the horizon of 1792, and the air was full of the belligerent cries of the émigrés on the Rhine. On the first day of February the Legislative Assembly reëstablished passport requirements for travel; on the twelfth it decreed the principle of sequestration of émigré property; and on April 8, 1792, with war impending, it adopted the first great law on emigration.[37]

This act, primarily an implementation of sequestration, was aimed at property rather than persons, and its negligent definition of émigrés was to create irreparable confusion. Excepting persons whose departure antedated July 1, 1789, and certain other groups, all absentees from the departments of their property were to be considered as émigrés unless they proved the contrary, and local lists, pyramiding from the communes to the departments, were to be prepared. Emigrants who had returned to France since

---

[35] L. Hartmann, 346ff. Even Marie Antionette wrote her brother, Leopold II; "L'existance d'une armée d'émigrants sur la frontière suffit pour entretenir le feu et fournir un aliment aux accusations contre nous" (Ernest Daudet, I, 113-114).

[36] Marcel Ragon, 34, and 198–201 (text).

[37] Ibid., 38, and 201–208 (text of the law of April 8, 1792).

February 9, 1792, and those who returned within one month after the promulgation of the law were doubly taxed for the current year and deprived of their rights of active citizenship for two years; those who returned later were to be canceled from the rolls of active citizens for ten years.

If the purpose of this leniency was to arrest the emigration, it failed, for in 1792 the advent of war and the second revolution brought one phase of the movement to a climax. During the first three months of the year, the military emigration continued unabated, and the declaration of war, in April, was the signal for another surge of mass desertion.[38] The implacable fanaticisms engendered as the Monarchy moved to its fall, the tension that burst in the September massacres had results too obvious to require comment. The consequences of the foreign invasions and the French conquests of Savoy and Nice we shall treat later. Here it will suffice to note that the Austro-Prussian invasion of 1792, coming at a time when France was suspended, as it were, between the Monarchy and the Republic, was chiefly responsible for the heavy emigration from the Meuse and neighboring departments; and that the French conquests of Savoy and Nice caused the flight of several thousand inhabitants who later were listed as émigrés.

Seventeen hundred and ninety-two, however, was most distinctly the year of the clerical exodus. The law of November 27, 1790, had required priests, as state functionaries, to take an oath of loyalty to the Civil Constitution of the Clergy or to resign.[39] Many rejected the oath, and on May 27, 1792, the Legislative Assembly decreed that any nonjuror would be deported if twenty active citizens of his commune demanded it. The stage was now set for wholesale proscription. On August 26, 1792, the Assembly ordered the nonjurors, or *réfractaires*, as they were called, to leave France within fifteen days, after which period they would be physically deported. The old (those over sixty) and the infirm were

---

[38] L. Hartmann, 453–464.

[39] On January 4, 1791, the assembly further decreed that the oath must be taken, if at all, without reservations or restrictive preambles.

given the option of internment; but, on the other hand, ecclesiastics not subject to the oath, and hence not *réfractaires* (monks, for instance), were to be deported if they were denounced by six citizens of their municipalities. Since approximately 50 per cent of the secular clergy refused to swear the oath, the decree of August 26 banished about thirty thousand.[40] As we have seen, some of them evaded the law; others had emigrated earlier or were deported later; but the majority passed into exile during the autumn and winter of 1792.[41] And since, as we shall see, the character of the laws and the state of the records combine to render virtually impossible a clear differentiation of the categories of proscribed clergy—voluntary deportees, physical deportees, emigrants—we must use the word émigrés loosely, comprehending all the exiles, lay and clerical.

The passing of the Monarchy not only synchronized with a crescendo of emigration, but in certain departments it also marked the virtual end of the movement. In the Indre, with a total of 277 émigrés, only 16 departed after 1792; in the Creuse, with 280 émigrés, the subsequent departures numbered only 31; and in the Hautes-Alpes, out of 105 émigrés only 10 emigrated later.[42] Anticipating the statistical evidence, in France as a whole the preponderance of the noble and clerical emigration occurred prior to 1793. Many of the clergy, of course, were forced to go, but until September at least the exodus of the nobility was not generally a compulsory flight. It began as a mode; it continued as a protest; and it gathered volume as a counterrevolution. Presently a cordon of émigré colonies half-encircled France, from Turin to Brussels. The armed emigration gathered at Coblenz and Worms, the fashionable elements gravitated to Brussels and London, the shoddy to Lausanne and Fribourg.[43] With intrigue and with arms the émigrés attacked France, and to justify their treason they elaborated a new theory of patriotism: the *patrie* was no longer geo-

---

[40] For a discussion of the number of nonjurors see below, p. 83.
[41] See below, p. 81.
[42] See Table II.
[43] Ernest Daudet, I, 127.

graphic and demographic France; it was the association of the elite who had withdrawn from a demoralized society.[44] Blind, arrogant, and insouciant, the aristocratic émigrés of the period of the Monarchy abandoned France in the hope of reconquering France.

With these expatriated enemies of the Revolution, three corps of whom invaded the country with the Prussian army, there was no longer any ground for compromise. The blows directed against them now fell in quick succession. On September 6, 1792, the property of the émigrés was confiscated; on October 25 they were banished "à perpétuité" under penalty of death if they returned; and on November 15 those who already had returned were accorded fifteen days in which to re-emigrate.

These laws were succinct, but it remained for the act of March 28–April 5, 1793, to constitute a comprehensive code on emigration. Defined as émigrés and banished forever were those French nationals who had departed after July 1, 1789, and had not returned before May 9, 1792; those who could not prove continuous residence in France after the latter date; and those who had passed, or in the future passed, from intact French territory to territory occupied by the enemy. The Knights of Malta resident in the island were included, and even foreigners who had domiciles in France or who had "exercised the rights of citizens" fell under the ban if absent during the stated period. There were, of course, exceptions —government agents, their families, and their servants; merchants, tradesmen, and artisans whose normal occupations took them beyond the frontiers; and persons abroad for study. These exceptions, however, were so barricaded with restrictions that few people were protected by them. As for children, those less than ten years old were exonerated, but when they reached the age of ten they would be required to return to France within three months or to accept classification as émigrés. Lists of émigrés were to be prepared, printed, and posted, first in the communes, then in the districts, then in the departments, and finally in Paris, for France as a whole.

[44] Fernand Baldensperger, *Le mouvement des idées dans l'émigration française, 1789–1815*, I, 305–306. "Ou sont les fleurs de lys là est la patrie," was the shibboleth.

Persons inscribed by error could secure cancellation of their names by producing certificates of residence witnessed by eight persons (neither relatives, nor tenants, nor creditors, nor debtors, nor agents) of the communes in which they had resided, attesting their presence during the period of alleged absence. These certificates, if presented to departmental directories within one month after the publication of the lists containing the names of the accused in question, entitled them to temporary immunity and provisional recovery of their property, but definitive cancellation was a function of the Council of Ministers. Returned émigrés captured under arms were to be executed immediately; others who reentered France were, upon verification of their identity, subject to mandatory death sentence by the criminal courts.[45]

Nor were the clergy forgotten. On August 14, 1792, an oath of "liberty and equality" had been prescribed for all state pensioners, a group which included many of the regular clergy as well as other clerics. This oath was distinct from that of the Civil Constitution of the Clergy, and the Pope did not pronounce against it, as he had against the new constitution for the French church. Nevertheless, a number of the clergy refused it, and on March 23, 1793, the Convention required their deportation. A month later the same assembly imposed capital punishment for banished clergy who returned to France; on September 17 it placed them in the same category with émigrés; and, finally, on March 20, 1794, it assimilated all refractory ecclesiastics to emigrants. The nonjurors, like the lay émigrés, were now excised from the body of the nation.

3. The Temporal Incidence

So much for the open book of the emigration, the pages that everyone could read. But other pages remain uncut. Indeed, though we have carried the thread of legislation to 1794, the story of the emigration for the period of the Monarchy, which we have just sketched, is incomplete and superficial. It lacks amplitude. In the following chapters we shall call upon statistics to tell us

[45] Marcel Ragon, 223–244 (text).

what lay behind it, to supply substance. More than that, however, for the emigration did not end when the shrouds were drawn over the Monarchy. The great plebeian emigration, so little known— the frantic flight of thousands and thousands—was yet to come. The mortal struggle between the Republic and its enemies wracked French society to its base, and where the conflict raged in its acute forms the securities of life vanished and the fugitives from turmoil numbered in the thousands. But these are generalities, and the epic of the emigration will remain incomplete until its pertinent details are woven into links of cause and effect.

This is our purpose, and though we must relegate the detailed demonstrations to subsequent chapters, the temporal incidence of the movement will serve as a point of departure. A statistical curve of the emigration, rising from a base line in 1789, would mount steadily through 1790 and 1791, steepen in 1792, shoot to a peak in 1793, fall away early the next year, and drop almost vertically in August, 1794. Unfortunately the data for plotting such a curve do not exist. The first lists of émigrés did not appear until 1792, when they already comprised three years of arrears, and most of the later lists included at least some of the earlier émigrés who, for one reason or another, had escaped inscription. To mention one example among many, as late as 1798 the department of the Bas-Rhin still was listing the émigrés of 1793.[46] Nor do the apparent dates of emigration given in some of the sources (especially in the dossiers) solve the problem, for usually these dates are those of official cognizance, whereas the time lapse between departures and their discovery by the officials varied from hours to years. And, of course, the same imprecision applies to dates of property sequestrations. But if a graphic expression of the temporal incidence is precluded, it remains possible to determine for a large portion of France the approximate number of departures before and after January 1, 1793—in other words, roughly under the Monarchy and under the Republic. Obviously the lists confected prior to 1793 represent anterior emigration only, and from the lists made sub-

---

[46] For example, the extensive "Liste supplétive des émigrés . . . du Bas-Rhin," 2 prairial an VI (May 21, 1798). AD Bas-Rhin, Q unclassified.

sequently we have selected the cleanest records of the later emigration.

Our analysis (see Table II) thus comprises 36 departments and 68,154 emigrants, 53 per cent of the grand total (129,099). The sampling is broad. All the aspects of the varied physiognomy of France, all the types of local circumstantial environment, all the major themes of motivation are represented. The recapitulative figures, then, cannot be far wrong. Thirty-two per cent (21,336) of these émigrés left France before January 1, 1793; 68 per cent (46,570) escaped later. The ratio of one émigré under the Monarchy to more than two under the Republic may be too high for the country as a whole, but there is no denying that the emigration in the later period was much heavier than in the earlier.[47] Nor can it be mere coincidence that 31 per cent of the socially classified emigrants were of the privileged orders, 63 per cent of the Third Estate. On the contrary, the least that one is entitled to infer is that the upper classes participated principally in the lesser emigration during the Monarchy, while the greater flight under the Republic involved the masses.

A closer examination of our data will reinforce these conclusions. To facilitate analysis, we have established two categories: one includes the twenty-four departments where the preponderance of the emigration occurred prior to 1793; the other the twelve departments whence the majority of the emigrants departed later. The first group embraces 17,663 émigrés, 26 per cent of the tabular total. Of these about three-fourths (72 per cent) emigrated during the early period (1789–1792), *and* two-thirds (66 per cent) were priests or nobles; about one-fourth (27 per cent) fled in the later period (1793–1799), *and* about one-fifth (21 per cent) were com-

---

[47] See Table II, part 2, for preponderance probabilities. Assuming that three-fourths of the émigrés of category 1 departed prior to January 1, 1793 (as was the case in category 1 of part 1 of the table); that three-fourths of those of category 2 departed after January 1, 1793 (as was the case in category 2 of part 1 if we exclude the excessive weight of the Bas-Rhin); and that the division was about equal in category 3, we find that about fifty-two thousand persons, 40 per cent of the total, emigrated in the years 1789–1792, about seventy-seven thousand, 60 per cent of the total, in the years 1793–1799.

moners. Though the second group comprises only twelve departments, it renders 50,491 émigrés, 74 per cent of those represented
in the table. Approximately one-sixth (17 per cent) of them became
exiles during the years of the Monarchy, *and* one-fifth (20 per cent)
of them were *privilégiés*; nearly five-sixths (83 per cent) of them
went from France in the torrid republican years, *and* more than
three-fourths (76 per cent) of them belonged to the Third Estate.
It would be impossible to ignore these recurrent correlations,
irrational to deny their significance: they establish beyond reason-
able doubt the clerico-aristocratic quality of the monarchical emigration, the plebeian character of the republican exodus.

But why did the society of the emigration change? The explanation is implicit. In most of the twenty-four departments of predominately early and essentially privileged-class emigration, comparative calm prevailed throughout the Revolution. To some of
them, in fact, the shocks of the period came as expiring tremors.
In the high Alps and the high Pyrenees, the Revolution was
scarcely more formidable than thunder rolling over the mountain
tops;[48] in the Landes hardly more fearsome than wind in the local
pine forests; in the Creuse little more disturbing than a distant
fire in the *maquis*. And if the actualities of the Revolution were
quite unmistakable in the departments surrounding Paris, such
as the Oise, the Seine-et-Oise, the Seine-et-Marne, they themselves
were not arenas of combat. Here, as in the remote mountains or
in the deep interior, life could go on more or less normally; apart
from the clergy banished in 1792, most of those who emigrated
chose to emigrate; most of those who chose to emigrate were

---

[48] F. A. Aulard, *Recueil des actes du Comité de Salut public* . . . , IV, 92–95 (Barras
and Fréron to the Convention, May 10, 1793). The story of glacial indifference to the
Revolution in the Hautes-Alpes, as told by Barras and Fréron, is striking, even if we
discount a generous dose of artificial coloring. None of the revolutionary measures,
such as the disarmament of the suspects, had been applied. Indeed, the authorities
affirmed that there were no suspects in the department. Nonjurors were officially
ignored, and the assignats had not penetrated some districts. There were only three
or four Jacobin clubs in the department, and these served principally as reading rooms
for a few bourgeois who gathered on mail post days to read the *Journal de Perlet*!
"Patriotism" in the Hautes-Alpes, the representatives concluded, "has remained, so
to speak, under the snow, like the summits of the mountains."

nobles; most nobles who chose to emigrate departed in the dusk of the Monarchy. They did not, of course, go alone. They took servants with them; some bourgeois accompanied them; and Third Estate emigration was relatively heavy in a few departments where invasion (e.g., the Meuse), insurrection (e.g., the Lozère), or terrorism (e.g., the Gard) furnished broader and stronger incentives than political option. Yet the essential fact remains: where visible compulsions were few, cassocks and coats of arms symbolized the emigration.

Clerical and noble émigrés were still more numerous in the departments of our second category, but here they were heavily outnumbered by commoners. For here the impact of events broke all social frontiers. These twelve departments furnish examples of the violent convulsions that produced the great emigration—invasion, counterattack, and panic; insurgence, repression, and terrorism; bloodshed, devastation, and reprisal. We must not encroach on our later discussion of particular circumstances, nor is it necessary to do so at this point. No social group was immune to panic such as that which seized the populace of Toulon in December, 1793, when the republicans stormed the rebel city; impervious to horror such as that inspired in the Mayenne by the atrocities of the Vendean war; invincible to chaos such as that created in the Pyrénées-Orientales by the passage and repassage of undisciplined armies. And our present, illuminating the past, makes it easy for us to visualize the refugee-crowded roads, the semi-deserted cities, the abandoned homes. The tragedies of the Republic took their toll not only in human lives but also in human securities. When these were taken away, there remained the alternative of flight— flight for the thousands of common people who formed the mass of the emigrants from the Republic.

The change in the social complexion of the emigration thus reveals a curious paradox, for in 1793, the year of the birth of modern democracy, the emigration became democratic. Beginning as a clear stream of the elite, it had become a little clouded with popular elements in 1792, and a year later it had swelled into a turgid torrent of the populace. Then the flood had reached its crest; and, as the sound and fury of the Revolution died away, the emigration ebbed. Already, in fact, it had ceased in some departments. October in the Cantal,[49] November in the Lot,[50] December in the Seine-et-Oise[51] saw the publication of the last lists. In other departments there were only a few émigrés after the close of the year. In May, 1794, the Creuse and the Indre-et-Loire[52] compiled their last rolls, and even from the Var, a center of late terrorism, very few persons emigrated after the fall of Toulon.[53] From the still insurgent West the emigration probably continued to be heavy: the longest of the several lists issued in the Mayenne appeared on September 4, 1796,[54] and in the Morbihan the repression that followed the Quiberon expedition in 1795 threw up a final wave of emigration.[55] Elsewhere than in the West, however, all signs indicate a rapidly shrinking movement.

The Ninth of Thermidor ended the first phase of the modern battle for democracy, and as most of France sank into an exhausted, habitable lethargy the emigration expired of inanition. The reaction drove out a few ex-terrorists; there were a few fugitives after the abortive insurrections of Germinal, Prairial, and Vendémiaire, a few refugees or deportees during the political broils of the Directory. Some of these late exiles bore famous names—Barère, Carnot, Pichegru. But numerically the post-Thermidorian emigration was slight, except, perhaps, in the area of western insurgence.

[49] "Liste générale des émigrés . . . du Cantal," 5 octobre 1793. AD Gironde, Q 1475.

[50] "Département du Lot. Liste supplétive des émigrés . . . ," ms., 29 brumaire an II (November 19, 1793). AD Lot, Q 1. True, there is another supplement dated 27 vendémiare an VII. But it contains only two names.

[51] "Dixième liste des émigrés . . . de Seine-et-Oise," s.d. [December, 1793]. AD Seine-et-Oise, Q 373.

[52] "Liste supplétive des émigrés [de la Creuse]," 2 prairial an II (May 21, 1794). AD Gironde, Q 1475; "Liste supplétive des émigrés de l'Indre-et-Loire," 23 floréal an II (May 12, 1794). AD Indre-et-Loire, Q unclassified.

[53] Louis Honoré, *loc. cit.*, p. 60. M. Honoré asserts that there was only *one* case of emigration after the fall of Toulon.

[54] "Liste supplétive des émigrés . . . de la Mayenne," 18 fructidor an IV (September 4, 1796). AD Mayenne, Q 106.

[55] "Liste des individus du district de Vannes absens (*sic*) de leurs communes depuis le premier floréal dernier pour se réunir aux chouans et pour cette raison regardés comme émigrés . . . ," 7 nivôse an IV (December 28, 1795). AD Morbihan, Q 570.

In the Haute-Saône only twelve cases were recorded after 1794;[56] in the Gers,[57] the Cher,[58] and the Seine-et-Marne[59] four; in the Ardèche none.[60] And in many other departments the records end in the year of Robespierre's fall. July was the month of the last list in the Basses-Alpes,[61] August in the Saône-et-Loire,[62] September in Finistère,[63] October in the Hautes-Pyrénées,[64] November in the Côte-d'Or,[65] December in the Gironde.[66] Furthermore, the late lists were, for the most part, meager, some of them a single name, and retrospective. The emigration ran its main course from the fall of the Bastille to the fall of Robespierre; then it diminished to nothing because the struggle that had fed it had ended.

[56] "Quatrième supplément à la liste des émigrés de la Haute-Saône," 18 messidor an VI (July 6, 1798). Last previous list, 15 brumaire an III (November 5, 1794). AD Gironde, Q 1476.

[57] "Troisième supplément à la liste des émigrés . . . du Gers," 14 nivôse an VI (January 3, 1798), and "Quatrième supplément . . .," 19 brumaire an VII (November 9, 1798). Last previous list preserved, 25 floréal an II (May 14, 1794). AD Gers, Q 336.

[58] "Seconde liste supplétive des émigrés . . . du Cher," 1 floréal an VII (April 20, 1799). Last previous list, 12 vendémiaire an III (October 3, 1794). AD Cher, Q 399.

[59] "Quatrième liste supplétive des émigrés . . . de Seine-et-Marne," 23 floréal an V (May 12, 1797). Last previous list, 11 frimaire an III (December 1, 1794). AD Seine-et-Marne, 1Q 2310.

[60] Répertoire des émigrés . . . de l'Ardèche (typed manuscript), Privas, 1939. AN, Bureaux, no. 2753; also AD Ardèche, unclassified.

[61] "Troisième liste supplétive des émigrés . . . des Basses-Alpes," 5 thermidor an II (July 23, 1794). AD Basses-Alpes, Q unclassified.

[62] "Cinquième liste supplétive des émigrés . . . de la Saône-et-Loire," 4 fructidor an II (August 21, 1794). AD Gironde, Q 1477.

[63] "Liste générale des émigrés . . . de Finistère," 28 fructidor an II (September 14, 1794). AD Finistère, Q unclassified.

[64] "Premier supplément à la liste . . . des émigrés des Hautes-Pyrénées," 13 vendémiaire an III (October 4, 1794). AD Pyrénées-Orientales, Q 730.

[65] "Département de la Côte-d'Or. Vingtième liste . . . des émigrés," 17 brumaire an III (November 7, 1794). AD Côte-d'Or, Q 514, 515.

[66] "Supplément au relevé général des émigrés [de la Gironde]," 14 frimaire an III (December 4, 1794). AD Gironde, Q 1479.

CHAPTER III

THE GEOGRAPHIC INCIDENCE

1. General Views

THE cartogram opposite gives us a graphic glimpse of the geographic incidence of the emigration. Along the frontier from Flanders to the Alps, along the Mediterranean from Italy to the Rhône, through Roussillon to Spain, along the sea from the Gironde to Brittany, and along the Channel from Brittany to Flanders the emigration was heavy; in the regions bordering the inside of this broken band the emigration was moderate or uneven; and at the core of France it was light. The heavy periphery was thin in the East, thick in the West, and its principal interruptions were in the Alps, along the Mediterranean, and in the Pyrenees.

If we ignore for the moment the exceptions, the question of population, and other human circumstances, it is obvious that geography partially explains the varying incidence of the emigration. From Le Puy to the frontier was a long, expensive, and often hazardous journey; from Strasbourg one crossed the Rhine to Germany. Clearly the facility of flight stimulated emigration, and, in general, its incidence lightened as the distance from the frontiers lengthened. The Cher, with 239 émigrés, the Indre with 277, the Allier with 340 lie in the heart of France. The Nord (2,635 émigrés), the Alpes-Maritimes (3,000), and the Pyrénées-Orientales (3,845) are departments of double frontiers, both maritime and land. We should look in vain for a department of heavy emigration deep in the interior, or, apart from those on high mountain ranges, for one of very light emigration on the frontier. Other factors, of course, must enter into the explanation of the

variations of the geographic incidence; indeed, much remains to
be said concerning the examples just cited. Yet when all qualifications have been made, the influence of geography imposes itself
as a constant.

When, however, we translate our data from cartographic representation into the language of numbers (see Table III) the vast
inequalities of incidence compel attention. From the Hautes-Alpes
there were 105 émigrés, from the Bas-Rhin *two hundred times as
many* (20,510). In three departments there were less than 200
émigrés, in four between 200 and 300, and in seventeen less than
500. Compare these small numbers with those of the categories of
mass emigration: seven departments from each of which there
were more than 3,000 émigrés, ten departments with from 2,000
to 3,000 each. And between the upper and the lower groups were
twenty-six departments with from 500 to 1,000 émigrés each,
and twenty-seven with from 1,000 to 2,000. Moreover, the categorical totals and percentages further accentuate these differences.
The 44,900 émigrés of the seven departments of the heaviest
emigration constitute 33¾ per cent of the total number, while the
5,302 émigrés of the seventeen departments of the lightest emigration represent only 4 per cent of all. Or, reverting to a single com-
parison for final emphasis, the 20,510 exiles of the Bas-Rhin more
than equal the total (20,374) of the first forty departments—
almost half of France—listed in numerical order.

It is at once clear that these enormous differences preclude
the interpretation of the emigration as uniquely a forced flight of
nobility and clergy, for the Jacobins could have had no motive in
applying pressure so unevenly. But our figures will gain in positive
significance if we look at the ranges from a central point. The
median number falls to the Marne with 1,040 émigrés. The forty-
three departments in the range above it supplied 105,030, or 81
per cent, of the expatriates, while the forty-three in the lower range
rendered only 23,029, 18 per cent of the total. Twenty-nine of the
departments in the latter group were inland; nine were on mountainous frontiers; one (the Landes) fronted on the Atlantic; three
faced the Mediterranean; and the island of Corsica makes the total

of forty-three. Most of them enjoyed comparative calm during the Revolution, for in the peaks of the Alps and the Pyrenees, on the great platform of the center, and in much of sunny southern France the storm passed, if not always without devastation, at least without crescendic violence. Apart from the Rhône, with which we shall deal later, and the Gard, a federalist center, in no department of the lower range did the struggles of the period rise to the plane of civil war; again except for the enigmatic Rhône and the federalistic Gard, in none did the Terror take more than a few victims; and only one, the Basses-Pyrénées, was invaded. Sheltered or remote from the bloody arenas of the epochal combat that was the French Revolution, most of these departments saw little to compel emigration.

Antithetic were the circumstances in the exposed or turbulent forty-three departments of the upper range. Their territory comprised not only the Atlantic façade of France and, except for the mountain walls, the land frontiers, but also the principal areas of civil war and foreign invasion. Here we find the Anjou and the Poitou of the Vendean war, the Brittany and the Normandy of endemic *chouannerie*, invaded Flanders, Lorraine, and Alsace, and the great rebellious cities of Bordeaux, Marseille, and Toulon. Here were the storm centers of the Revolution. Here the Terror struck hard, for fourteen thousand of its seventeen thousand victims were executed in these departments. And here, in this theater of merciless conflict between aristocracy and democracy, the bonds of security that tie men to the soil were broken. This was the territory of the great emigration.

The inference seems inescapable. A large part of the emigration was neither voluntary nor, as Taine thought, deliberately forced by the Jacobins. Rather was it a consequence of a great national crisis. Thus far, however, we have been guided only by the light and shade of absolute numbers. Our bar graph (Table IV), which illustrates the relation of the emigration to population, will take us a step further. We now shift the kaleidoscope, for in this table the departments are grouped in regional blocks. Glancing first at the recapitulation, we see that the incidence of the emigration was light in the Center, in the Southwest, and in the Parisian region, rising from a little less than one-fourth of one per cent (.23 per cent) of the population in the first region to a little more than a fourth (.27 per cent, .28 per cent) in the other two. Within the Parisian region there are no startling inequalities, though the weights of Paris and Versailles are apparent in the cases of the Seine and the Seine-et-Oise respectively. In the Center group, the bars for the Côte-d'Or and the Haute-Vienne extend far beyond the others, but both of these departments were atypical. And in the Southwest, the Dordogne and the Lot-et-Garonne,[1] with incidences twice as heavy as the regional average, stand as anomalies. But we need not pause now on these, or a few other exceptions. The sweep of a broad brush stroke through France from the valley of the Aisne to the Pyrenees describes the principal swath of the light emigration, and the same brush stroke would cover much of the territory spared by the furies of the Revolution.

It would also cover most of the South where the index for the region (.41 per cent) is inflated by the 3.48 per cent incidence of the single department of the Pyrénées Orientales, invaded to the very gates of Perpignan. On the other hand, in the North and the Northwest, with incidences of .36 per cent and .38 per cent, the emigration was comparatively uniform. The rich, populous plain of Flanders was the boulevard of the Austrian invasion of 1793, and fertile Normandy was clerical and royalist to the core. The emigration was heavy in the West (.47 per cent), where inextinguishable civil war blazed throughout the Revolution and where the Terror struck with murderous force. Still heavier in the Southeast as a whole (.52 per cent), the enormous contrasts of incidence within the region reflect circumstantial variety, from the quiet isolation of the Alpine peaks to the turgid violence of the great ports of Toulon and Marseille. Finally, the East, where one per

---

[1] André Gain (*La Restauration et les biens des émigrés*, II, 185) ascribes the heavy emigration from these departments to their location in the hinterland of the federalistic Gironde. Neither, however, was deeply involved in federalism, and possibly the emigration from neither department was as heavy as our figures indicate. The data on the Lot-et-Garonne are derived from Gain's hypothesis, and the source materials in the Dordogne are some of the least satisfactory used in compiling our tables.

cent of the population emigrated, touches the ceiling. All of these eastern departments felt the lure of the émigré colonies on the Rhine. Eight of them marched with the frontier; five were invaded, and one of these, the Bas-Rhin, was the scene of a phenomenal panic.

2. Correlation of the Emigration and the Environments

THRICE we have turned the kaleidoscope, and we have seen the pattern of the emigration illustrated in a cartogram, a table, and a graph. The first showed us that its density decreased in recession from the frontiers. The second revealed the correlation of the emigration and the fires of the Revolution. And the third fused and confirmed the other two. Yet we have dealt only in generalities. The conclusions that emerge still are tentative, and the Gulliverian contrasts remain to be explained. One must, of course, allow for imponderables, and it would be both fastidious and futile to seek eighty-seven exact equations of cause and effect. Nevertheless, our conclusions can be advanced from the tentative to the final stage only by a much closer examination of the local emigrations in relation to environmental circumstances.

One more turn of the kaleidoscope, and Table V shows us the departments of revolutionary France scaled and grouped in categories of ascending incidence. Less than one-fourth of one per cent of the population emigrated from the twenty departments of the first category; and, if we neglect the deported clergy, the departures from some of them were so few as to signify scarcely more than normal travel. Most of them were quiet inland departments or were otherwise sheltered. Corsica heads the list with forty-three émigrés—an infinitesimal portion of the population—most of whom followed the English when they evacuated the island in 1795.[2] From the Hautes-Alpes, serene throughout the Revolution, thirty-nine clergymen were forced into exile, and as many nobles, a few bourgeois, and a handful of nondescripts made a total of 105

---

[2] "Département de Liamone. Liste des individus qui ont émigré en suivant les Anglais lors de leur évacuation de la Corse . . .," 10 messidor an V. AD Gironde Q 1477.

emigrants, .09 per cent of the 112,500 inhabitants. For no apparent reason, the incidence of the emigration in tranquil inland districts, such as the Creuse, the Lot, or the Yonne, was a little higher, but the maximum for the group is .18 per cent. Remoteness from the border, immunity from serious disorder, or both, sufficiently explain these low incidences, and when one of the conditioning factors was reversed it was compensated by the other.

There is, however, one glaring anomaly: the Rhône. The great city of Lyon, intensely counterrevolutionary from the beginning of the Revolution, rebelled in the summer of 1793, was besieged by a republican army for three months, and was finally taken on October 9. The repression that followed was one of the most sanguinary and indiscriminate of the Terror, and Lyon is less than fifty miles from the Swiss border. Elsewhere in France similar conditions correlated with the heaviest emigration, and one would expect to find the Rhône in the category of the highest incidence. Yet, if our statistics are correct, there were only 332 émigrés, representing .11 per cent of the population, from this department.[3]

Enigma or paradox? A little of both, perhaps. The lines of class conflict in this great industrial city, where the nobility and the bourgeoisie were united against the revolutionary proletariat, were more sharply drawn than elsewhere.[4] The upper classes controlled the local administrations until the spring of 1793, and they were not keenly interested in detecting emigration. Quite the contrary, Lyon was a haven for refractory clergy and returned émigrés, many of whom doubtless had not been listed as such. As early as October, 1791, the city harbored three thousand nonjurors, and after the fall of the Monarchy Lyon became the open rendezvous for southern conspirators and émigrés transparently masquerading as Swiss citizens.[5] The Jacobins under Chalier seized

---

[3] Even so, our figure (332), based on all available sources (see Bibliography under "Rhône"), is higher than other estimates.

[4] C. Riffaterre, *Le mouvement anti-Jacobin et anti-Parisien à Lyon et dans le Rhône-et-Loire en 1793, 29 mai–15 août* (2 vols.; Lyon et Paris, 1912–1928), II, 6 ff.; Jean Jaurès, *Histoire de la Révolution française* (ed. Mathiez; 8 vols.; Paris, 1922–1924) VII, 68–69.

[5] C. Riffaterre, II, 8, 11–12; S. Charléty, "La journée du 29 mai 1793 à Lyon," *La Révolution française* (1920), XXXIX, 364.

the municipal administration in March, 1793, but their reign lasted less than three months. The anti-Jacobin insurrection of May 29 placed the reactionaries in power, and then crowds of émigrés·and nonjurors flocked into the city.[6] The revolt of Lyon in July attracted still others, and most of the officers of the ‚rebel army, beginning with the commander-in-chief, Perrin de Précy, were erstwhile émigrés.[7]

But Lyon fell. On the night of October 8, the leaders of the rebellion decided to capitulate, and the next morning Perrin de Précy led the elite of his army out of the city. His plan was to cut his way to Switzerland, but the republicans blocked his path and foiled his attempt to turn aside into the mountains of the Forez.[8] He escaped, but his troop was decimated. The chase continued for days, and 1,500 of the rebels were killed or captured in the district of Villefranche alone.[9] Not all of them were émigrés, but it is safe to assume that a fair proportion of them had returned from abroad to defend Lyon. Here, then, are some of the missing émigrés, perhaps unlisted, of the Rhône. Moreover, the fall of the invested city came so suddenly that many others had no opportunity to flee, and thenceforth the avenues of escape were closed. Many of the 1,880 victims of the repression in Lyon were émigrés, though they were condemned for sedition.[10] Thus royalism and clericalism, rebellion and repression, circumstances which elsewhere impelled emigration, constricted it in the Rhône.

Though it contains no such anomaly, the next and largest category—thirty-nine departments with incidences between .20 per cent and .40 per cent—presents far more diversity. In a few of these departments, such as the Corrèze buried in southern central France, there is little evidence of circumstantial compulsion. If

[6] C. Riffaterre, II, 12. "Les auberges sont pleines, il y a beaucoup de ci-devants," wrote Saint-Charles in July, 1793. The banker Couderc reported as early as April, 1792, that there were twenty thousand "étrangers" in Lyon (Ibid., II, 10).

[7] Ibid., II, 12–35. "Les émigrés sont rentrés en foule dans Lyon" (p. 13).

[8] Édouard Herriot, Lyon n'est plus (4 vols.; Paris, 1937–1940), III, 490–504.

[9] Ibid., III, 500.

[10] Donald Greer, The Incidence of the Terror during the French Revolution (Cambridge, 1935), 147.

we regard the group as a whole, however, the causes of higher incidence are discernible. The region surrounding Paris, all of which
falls into this category, was the scene of neither serious disorder
nor severe repression, but it was the orchestra of the theater of
which Paris was the stage. The audience in this orchestra were
opulent and aristocratic, and many of them left their places to
flee from the implications of the drama. In Versailles (Seine-et-
Oise), where the aristocratic quarters were deserted by 1792,
this was especially true. As for Paris itself, the name evokes a
vague notion of a great exodus, and, in fact, the 2,069 émigrés from
the capital place it high in the scale of numerical importance.
But the incidence (.33 per cent) belies the legend of a half-empty
city. Certainly, Paris, like Versailles, had its deserted quarters.
The aristocrats had gone. But so long as life pulsed in Jacobinism,
the Parisians were Jacobins.

The facility of emigration from the Seine-Inférieure and the
Somme, with their Channel coast lines and their fine ports, was
undoubtedly a stimulus. Flight was perhaps a little less easy from
the inland plain of Champagne, but the Aube, the Marne, and the
Haute-Marne were rich departments, dotted with the chateaux of
great nobles and wealthy bourgeois. Obviously money facilitated
flight everywhere, and when other factors were equal there was
a more or less constant relationship between the weight of the
emigration and the wealth of the regions affected. Looking south-
ward from Champagne, the Saône-et-Loire is another typical example. After a blaze of *jacquerie* in 1789, this lush department was
calm enough; nevertheless, a good portion of its aristocracy chose
to depart.

In other departments of this group there were more positive
impulsions. To the east of the Saône-et-Loire, the Ain and the Jura
participated in the federalist effervescence of the summer of 1793,
and that in the Jura subsided only when threatened by the military
of the Convention.[11] On the opposite side of France, Évreux
(Eure) was one of the principal seats of the abortive Norman rising;

[11] Henri Wallon, *La révolution du 31 mai et le fédéralisme en 1793* (2 vols.; Paris, 1886), II, 334.

and in the South Bordeaux (Gironde), Toulouse (Haute-Garonne), Montpellier (Hérault), and Nîmes (Gard) were federalist strongholds. In none of these centers was federalism more than a form of transitory resistance to the democratic republic. The Convention, however, threatened dire retaliation, and the effect, especially where the Terror fulfilled the threat, as in the Gard and the Gironde, was to furnish a decided incentive to emigrate for all those who had taken any part in the movement.

Somewhat more dangerous than the federalism of Languedoc was the royalist insurrection in the Lozère in the spring of 1793. It was intended to explode a general rebellion in the Midi, major military operations were required to defeat it, and the repression that followed was severe.[12] In the Cantal and the Tarn, conscription occasioned riots of considerable proportions. Two thousand persons were involved at Castres (Tarn) on March 16, 1793, and during a similar disturbance at Brassac, pillage was accompanied by seditious cries.[13] Outbreaks of this sort, invariably followed by arrests and executions, decided a certain number of persons to seek refuge on foreign soil. This consequence is even clearer as we approach the regions of civil war. The Indre-et-Loire and the two Charentes were on the outskirts of the Vendean holocaust; the Morbihan was all but involved; and the Sarthe and the Manche were harried by the Vendeans and the republicans alike.

Savoy (Mont-Blanc) presents a very different case. It was one of the annexed departments, and its émigrés were, for the most part, fugitives from "liberation." The French under Montesquiou seized the duchy in September, 1792, against slight resistance. The municipal officers of Chambéry welcomed Montesquiou at the city gates, and the inhabitants, wearing tricolor cockades, feted his troops.[14] On November 21, Doppet, himself a native of the country, submitted to the Convention a Savoyard petition

---

[12] Donald Greer, *The Incidence of the Terror*, 51.

[13] Anacharsis Combes, *Histoire de la ville de Castres et ses environs pendant la Révolution* (Castres, 1875), 120–121.

[14] Ernest Lavisse, ed., *Histoire de France contemporaine depuis la Révolution jusqu'à la paix de 1919* (10 vols.; Paris, 1920–1922), II ("La Révolution, 1792–1799," by Georges Pariset), 27–28.

for union with France, and a week later the Convention proclaimed the annexation of Savoy. Though perhaps this was the desire of the majority of the population, the privileged classes, and especially the clergy, were bitterly opposed to the French conquest, and hundreds of them elected to retire under the flag of the House of Savoy. During the next few months, moreover, the early popular enthusiasm for the Republic cooled, and in the late summer of 1793 the Piedmontese incursion into southeastern Savoy provided another opportunity for the malcontents to escape.[15]

On other soil the enemy invaded France, and wherever the invasion was deep, sustained, or repeated we shall find the index of the emigration rising. The passage of armies, more or less disciplined, occasional pillage, and frequent requisitions were in themselves sufficient to create refugees. And France in revolution was a divided nation. In every region the invaders were hailed when they arrived and followed when they departed by some of the population. The northern frontier was the most exposed: here the Austrians broke through to besiege Lille in the autumn of 1792 and returned to threaten a march on Paris in the summer of the following year. Here, too, the revolutionary tribunal of Joseph Le Bon dealt mercilessly with suspects.[16] The Nord was one of the most patriotic of departments, but its position on a double frontier, the confusion created by the invasions, and the fear of indiscriminate reprisals resulted in at least 2,635 emigrations.[17]

Perhaps more, for in the higher incidence group (.40 per cent to .60 per cent) to which we now turn we find the adjacent Pas-de-Calais, which the Austrians did not penetrate, and the invaded Ardennes and Meurthe. Within sight of the English coast, within

---

[15] *Ibid.*, 144.

[16] The most recent and the best interpretation of Joseph Le Bon's terroristic career is Louis Jacob, *Joseph Le Bon. La Terreur à la frontière* (2 vols.; Paris, 1935).

[17] Nine hundred and seventy-two indemnities were granted in the Nord, and the department is second (the Bas-Rhin, of course, being first) on Gain's list. Yet our figure of 2,635 *émigrés* is derived from a tabulation of apparently comprehensive material (see Bibliography under "Nord"). The fact that the Nord was a rich department and that the peasants, six hundred of whom emigrated, owned 30 per cent of the land (Georges Lefebvre, *Les paysans du Nord pendant la Révolution* [Paris, 1924], 11) may account for the disproportionately large number of indemnities.

a day's march of the Belgian border, the Pas-de-Calais was scarcely less exposed than the Nord, and it was more terrorized by Joseph Le Bon. Furthermore, it was a region of great ecclesiastic property and numerous clergymen from which the clerical emigration appears to have been exceptionally heavy.[18] The Ardennes and the Meurthe were invaded by the Prussians in 1792. The campaign of Valmy, more destructive than the battle, was waged in the Argonne, and Vouziers and Grandpré were traversed by the enemy. To the royalists of the region this invasion borrowed a simulation of legitimacy from the presence of 4,500 émigrés with the Prussian army. Undisciplined, miserably equipped, and despised by the Prussian officers, they were in a plight ridiculous or pathetic, as one might choose to regard it. Still they were Frenchmen ostensibly fighting for the restoration of the type of life that the upper classes desired. As such they drew others with them in retreat.

Our .40 per cent to .60 per cent incidence group, however, is essentially that of the rebellious departments of the West. In much of this country, where the accents of life were both debonair and primitive and where traditional loyalties were very strong, evasion or opposition was the typical reaction to the Revolution. During its early years, the nobility emigrated or conspired at home; the majority of the clergy refused the oath to the Civil Constitution, thus automatically incurring the penalty of exile; and the peasants were passively hostile.[19] The fall of the Monarchy was marked by sporadic disorders, such as the riots at Bressuire (Deux-Sèvres) late in August, 1792. Then, in March, 1793, the attempt to apply conscription provoked other riots at Saint-

[18] From the *district* of Saint-Pol alone 112 clergy emigrated and 138 were deported; total: 250 (G. Sangier, *La Terreur dans le district de Saint-Pol* [2 vols.; Blanquermont, chez l'auteur, 1938], II, 255–260). Since the Pas-de-Calais comprised eight districts there were perhaps a thousand or more ecclesiastic exiles. Only 19 per cent of the clergy took the oath, 930 refusing and thus automatically incurring the deportation sentence (P. Sagnac, "Étude statistique sur le clergé constitutionnel et le clergé réfractaire en 1791," *Revue d'histoire moderne et contemporaine* [1906–1907], VIII, 109–110).

[19] For a good summary of the printed sources on the nonjurors in the Vendée, the Loire-Inférieure, and the Maine-et-Loire see Joseph Dehergne, *Les Vendéens, 1793* (Shanghai, 1939), 235–236.

Florent (Maine-et-Loire) and Machecoul (Loire-Inférieure) which ushered in the tragedy of the Vendean war. Beginning as a small fire, it flamed over the West. After the summer of their victories, the Vendeans were defeated in the autumn of 1793. But they were never conquered. Early in 1794 the republicans under Turreau, and later Vimeux, devastated tracts of their country, burned their homes, massacred their people—and still the war with its nameless atrocities continued. It smoldered during the Directory, and the West was not finally pacified until Bonaparte came.

War, devastation, and terrorism inevitably impelled heavy emigration from this region, and it is certain that the existing records reveal only part of the truth. The southern Loire-Inférieure, the Maine-et-Loire, the Deux-Sèvres, and the Vendée itself formed the *Vendée militaire*, the blood soaked bed of the rebellion. Some districts were rendered uninhabitable: as early as October, 1793, more than a hundred villages had been razed, and in the spring of the following year one could travel miles through the heart of the Vendée without seeing a living soul or a human habitation.[20] All the important towns, except Nantes, were taken by the Vendeans and retaken by the republicans, and the receding Vendean tide carried sympathizers with it. Other people were innocent fugitives from the republican repression. Thousands of rebels and rebel suspects were shot, guillotined, or drowned, making some of the towns of the West veritable charnel houses. The stench of the putrescent corpses of the victims of the Bignon military commission, thinly buried on the outskirts of Nantes, infected the western quarters of the city; dogs dragged human flesh through the streets; and, naturally enough, an epidemic of cholera broke out.[21] Possibly, as Gaston Martin has suggested, the majority of the population of Nantes (and by implication those of other centers of terrorism) were indifferent to these conditions,[22] but certainly many must have fled in horror.

[20] *Ibid.*, 264–267. Émile Gabory, *La Révolution et la Vendée* (3 vols.; Paris, 1925–1928), II, 191–213. For a sympathetic version of Turreau's work, Léon Dubreuil, *Histoire des insurrections de l'Ouest*, II, 8–53.

[21] Gaston Martin, *Carrier et sa mission à Nantes* (Paris, 1924), 336–337.

[22] *Ibid.*, 333ff.

Nor were the war and its terroristic aftermath confined to the *Vendée militaire*. When, in the autumn and winter of 1793, the Vendean trek to Granville carried the war north of the Loire, the Ille-et-Vilaine and the Côtes-du-Nord were among the departments ravaged by the Vendeans and punished by the republicans. These same departments, together with the Orne, Calvados, and Finistère, seethed with *chouannerie*, the Breton and Norman counterpart of the Vendée. Less destructive than the large military operations entailed by the latter, *chouannerie* was even more endemic; and again it was not until Bonaparte treacherously trapped and executed Frotté, the last of the great *chouans*, that these countries relapsed into quasi-quietude.[23] Finally, the influence of geography cannot be ignored in the great cockpit of the West. The Maine-et-Loire and the Deux-Sèvres, though inland departments, are near the coast, and all the others front the sea.

By examining the case of the Doubs, in our next category of departments (.60 per cent to 1.00 per cent), we may glimpse what might have happened in the West had the western sea been a land frontier. Urged by old loyalties and provoked by conscription, the Catholic peasantry of the eastern section of the department rose in insurrection on the last day of August, 1793. The insurgents, numbering two or three thousand, were attacked by national guards from the towns; in the course of a week two-thirds of the rebels were dispersed, and many of them fled across the Doubs to Switzerland. The rest, about five hundred, after a last stand in the village of Bonelège, were driven over the river to Swiss soil. Naturally the insurrection was followed by a hunt for insurgents. Nearly five hundred were arraigned for sedition, but several hundred others escaped by emigrating.[24]

Like the Doubs, the Meuse was on the eastern frontier; it was, moreover, within the shortest radius of the magnetic pole of the emigration in the Rhineland; and, in addition, it was invaded in the late summer of 1792, during the dangerous interlude between

---

[23] L. de La Sciotière, *Louis de Frotté et les insurrections normandes, 1793–1832* (2 vols.; Paris, 1889), II, 467–542.

[24] Jules Sauzay, *Histoire de la persécution révolutionnaire dans le département du Doubs de 1789 à 1801* (10 vols.; Besançon, 1867–1873), IV, ch. 49 (esp. pp. 377–481).

the Monarchy and the Republic. The Meuse as a whole was "patriot," yet there was a strong royalist party which declared against the revolution of August 10.[25] The circumstances of the surrender of Verdun permitted a suspicion of treason, especially as the nobles and the leading bourgeois of the city gave the Prussians a friendly welcome. These royalists had good reason to retire with the enemy, and the later severities of Mallarmé, as representative on mission, gave added motivation for upper-class emigration.

As we turn to the Haut-Rhin, we come upon an old border region of divided allegiance. Alsace had never become completely French in feeling, much less anti-clerical with the Jacobins of the Revolution. The German princes, who in 1789 still possessed certain sovereign rights there, to say nothing of vast properties, commanded loyalties in some cases stronger than those binding the people to France, and many an Alsatian émigré was a follower of his German feudal lord.[26] Religion, too, was an impulsive force. Increasing numbers of the devoutly Catholic peasantry trod the old routes to shrines in Switzerland or Germany, where they received benefit of orthodox clergy. The local authorities at first ignored these diurnal expeditions, but the pressure of the Jacobins soon forced them to close the frontier to the pilgrims and to declare them émigrés.[27] The suppression of the *Conseil souverain* of Colmar, which closed a number of careers and hopes of careers, discontented the bourgeoisie. Many of them, after having formed a disorderly company in the national guard of the town, emigrated when their agitation made continued presence in Alsace dangerous to them.[28] It also appears, though concrete evidence is lacking, that the great panic of December, 1793, in the Bas-Rhin induced a sympathetic movement in upper Alsace.[29]

[25] Ernest Lavisse, ed., *Histoire de France contemporaine*, I ("La Révolution, 1789–1792," by Philippe Sagnac), 427.

[26] Pierre Robin, *Le séquestre des biens ennemis sous la Révolution* (Paris, 1929), 15–23.

[27] Félix Schaedelin, *L'émigration révolutionnaire du Haut-Rhin*, 34–35.

[28] *Ibid.*, 15–16.

[29] M. Schaedelin points out (*ibid.*, 42) that the deputy Barr gratuitously confused the émigrés of the Haut-Rhin and the fugitives from the Bas-Rhin in his report of January, 1795, to the Committees. Nevertheless, an attenuated form of panic is the only plausible reason for the heavy late emigration from the Haut-Rhin.

At the other end of France, in the lower Rhône valley, Avignon and the Comtat Venaissin, Papal territory for five hundred years, witnessed scenes of internecine violence with few parallels during the Revolution. The bloody struggles between the revolutionary party, engendered by the example of France, and the local aristocracy began early in 1790. In June of that year the first blows were struck in Avignon; the disorder rapidly spread over the Comtat; the Papal authority vanished, the vice-legat withdrew behind a barrage of anathema, leaving the province plunged in civil war and anarchy. In the spring of 1791, Avignon sent a troop of some three thousand volunteers ("brave brigands," they were called), led by the notorious Jourdan *coupe-tête*, against conservative Carpentras, the capital of the Comtat proper. Failing to take the place by storm, the "brave brigands" invested it. Meanwhile they ravaged the country, burning country houses, ransoming villages, and killing anyone who came in their way.[30] Finally, the National Assembly intervened, and in September, 1791, Avignon and the Comtat were united with France.

The union did not, however, bring a truce in the local struggle. The massacre of the Glacière (October 16, 1791), in the Palais des Papes, another of Jourdan's exploits, surpassed in sheer horror anything that occurred in France during the Revolution. And despite the Glacière and the continued depredations of Jourdan, the reactionary party survived. It gained temporary ascendancy when federalism swept the South, placing Avignon and other towns of the Vaucluse in federalist hands. General Carteaux with line troops reëstablished the Republic's authority, while Doppet with a band of irregulars took revenge on some of the smaller towns. L'Isle, for example, was sacked and more than a third of its inhabitants were driven into exile.[31] Still the counterrevolution simmered in the country until it provoked a late repression in the summer of 1794. During these tumultuous years there was little security in the Vaucluse for people of any class; every group,

[30] P. Charpenne, *Les grands épisodes de la Révolution dans Avignon et Le Comtat* (4 vols.; Avignon, 1901-1905), I, xxviii.

[31] J. de Joannis, *Le fédéralisme et la Terreur à L'Isle* (Avignon, 1884), *passim*, esp. 167-168 (for an incomplete list of the *émigrés* of L'Isle).

papist, Jacobin, and federalist, had its moment of power, and when the moment passed the group paid toll to the emigration.

Passing from the Vaucluse to Provence, we enter a region of war, treason, and terrorism, and we encounter the last of our categories, that of the heaviest emigration. In the Bouches-du-Rhône, at least, it began early, for two thousand Provençals took passports at Aix in 1790 after the discovery of the royalist conspiracy hatched at Jalès.[32] No doubt some of them returned to conspire again, for Marseille was the cradle of federalism. By the summer of 1792, the mercantile aristocracy had control of this great port, and they used their power to prepare for civil war. The city was already in virtual revolt against the Convention when the coup d'état of June 2, 1793, provided ample pretext for hostilities. A federalist army was assembled in Marseille, and some of these troops marched north into the Vaucluse. At first they even won trifling victories, but Carteaux drove them back, pursued them to Septèmes, just north of Marseille, where, on August 24, he met and routed the main Marseillais army under the Marquis de Villeneuve.

The debacle at Septèmes was known in Marseille in the late afternoon, and in the evening the debris of Villeneuve's army fled through the streets in the direction of Toulon. A local historian has described the ensuing scene as one of sudden confusion quickly followed by desolation. The population rushed from the city "as though Marseille were burning, as though the fields were a place of security," leaving the streets, flanked by abandoned houses, empty and silent.[33] At least two thousand of these fugitives followed Villeneuve to Toulon, and many others scattered over the country, escaped by sea, or reached Italy by land.[34]

The republican repression was comparatively moderate—too moderate, complained Barras, representative on mission in Pro-

---

[32] Emmanuel Vingtrinier, *La contre-révolution, première période, 1789–1791*, II, 266.

[33] Laurent Lautard, *Marseille depuis 1789 jusqu'en 1815* (2 vols.; Marseille, 1844), II, 276.

[34] *Ibid.*, II, 279; F. A. Aulard, *Recueil des actes du Comité de Salut public*, VII, 532–536 (Barras and Fréron to Robespierre, October 20, 1793). The representatives described the Marseille-Toulon road during the panic. It was, they said, jammed with "wagons and carts carrying rich merchants, their wives, and their valuables." Barras and Fréron blamed Carteaux severely for not having cut the retreat of the Marseillais.

vence in the autumn. At all events, his energetic action averted a second revolt in December.[35] Temporarily distracted by the siege of Toulon, Barras, accompanied by Fréron, returned to Marseille early in 1794 to inaugurate such terrorism as even the Convention declined to sanction. To the federalist fugitives now were added some of the Jacobins themselves, whom Barras and Fréron accused of moderatism.[36] At this juncture the two representatives were recalled, but their more austere successor, Maignet, was scarcely less severe. Not until well after Thermidor did a degree of calm return to the Bouches-du-Rhône.

Federalism thus brought disaster to Marseille and the Bouches-du-Rhône, but Toulon, in the adjacent Var, was a still more furious arena. Here the record of the Revolution was a script written in blood. The sanguinary riots of March, 1789, were repeated in November of the same year, in August, 1790, and again in August, 1791. Meanwhile the factional lines became sharp and implacable: on one side were the officers of the naval base and the fleet, the local nobility, and the bourgeoisie; on the other, the working class of the Arsenal and the town. In their struggles brute force was the only arbiter. As the Monarchy crumbled, during the summer of 1792, there were eighteen assassinations in Toulon. The Jacobins controlled the town for the next year, but in July, 1793, federalism broke their hold. This federalism soon became royalism and treason. Toulon revolted; and, when threatened by republican troops approaching from the west and the north, the rebels surrendered the town and the French Mediterranean fleet to the English under Admiral Hood. He was joined by a Spanish fleet of eighteen sail; federalists from all parts of Provence rushed to Toulon; and

---

[35] The abortive December insurrection at Marseille is little known. For the version of Barras and Fréron see Edmond Poupé, *Lettres de Barras et de Fréron en mission dans le Midi* (Draguignan, 1910), 55–57 (Barras to Moyse Bayle, December 4, 1793), 68–81 (Fréron to Moyse Bayle, December 12, 1793). Ricord in his *Rapport sur différentes missions à l'armée d'Italie, deuxième partie* (Paris, an II), 4–5, confirms the Barras-Fréron version. The Archives départementales des Bouches-du-Rhône (L111 129) contain other revealing documents concerning the affair.

[36] AN, AF11 90/662 (Barras and Fréron to Fouquier-Tinville, January 26 (?), 1794); Edmond Poupé, 142–143 (Barras to Moyse Bayle, January 20, 1794).

later the Piedmontese and the Neapolitans sent troops to assist in the defense of the place.[37]

The republicans at once established a siege, but Toulon, garrisoned by an allied army and open to the sea, was nearly impregnable. More than three months elapsed before the French were able to wrest the heights of Le Caire, which commanded the harbors, from the allies. Then, however, Bonaparte's guns made the water untenable for enemy ships, and Hood decided to evacuate. "Nothing," wrote Barras, who participated in the attack of December 16, "can save Toulon from the national vengeance."[38] No one in Toulon had any illusions on that score. On the evening of the seventeenth, when the allied troops began to embark, a panic broke out among the townspeople. All night and all of the following day and into the night again a frantic throng, estimated by a contemporary at twenty thousand people, milled about the water front seeking escape on the ships.[39] Hours of nocturnal confusion, frenzy in the stark light of a flawless winter day while the republicans bombarded the town from the outlying forts, aftermath on the night of the eighteenth in the glare of the burning Arsenal, fired by the English—such were the elements of the scene. Some of the terrorized people were drowned, some were trampled to death; others swam to the ships, and hundreds reached them in small boats. Conservative estimates place the number of those who thus escaped at seventy-five hundred.[40] This figure includes

[37] The best works on the occupation and the siege of Toulon are Paul Cottin, *Toulon et les anglais* (Paris, 1898), and J. Holland Rose, *Lord Hood and the defense of Toulon* (Cambridge, 1922).

[38] F. A. Aulard, IX, 507–509 (Barras to the Committee of Public Safety, undated).

[39] For the panic scenes, Louis Richaud, *Mémoires . . . sur la révolte de Toulon et l'émigration. Annotés et publiés par R. Busquet, B. Roberty, et A. J. Parès* (Paris, 1930), 98ff. (Excellent; Richaud was one of the fugitives); Z. Pons, *Mémoires pour servir à l'histoire de la ville de Toulon en 1793* (Paris, 1825); and Paul Cottin, 318–322.

[40] At least two thousand refugees were embarked in English ships, three thousand in Spanish ships, fifteen hundred in French war vessels, five hundred in French merchantmen, and four hundred in Neapolitan ships (Louis Honoré, "L'émigration dans le Var," *Bulletin de la Société d'études de Draguignan* [1923], XXXIV, 45; Paul Cottin, 321; J. Holland Rose, 77–78; and Arthur Chuquet, *Dugommier* [Paris, 1904], 108–109). But these are minimum estimates. Louis Honoré (*loc. cit.*, p. 13) believes that the real total was over ten thousand. E. Coulet ("Les fugitifs de Toulon et les

neither those who slipped through the republican lines, nor the later fugitives from the merciless repression directed by Barras and Fréron, nor the emigrants from other communes of the Var. Furthermore, contemporaries asserted that the emigration and the Terror together melted the population of Toulon to one-third of its normal size.[41]

In the autumn of the preceding year Nice had witnessed a similar, though less dramatic, panic. In September, 1792, General Anselme, commanding a French army in the Var, was ordered to attack this Piedmontese possession, which, for the rest, was the refuge of a large colony of French émigrés. Anselme had only about six thousand men, but he made a great display of artillery on the banks of the Var and circulated terrifying rumors, while Admiral Truguet with the French Mediterranean fleet threatened Nice by sea. The Piedmontese commander, fearing both siege and blockade, abandoned the place on September 28. The sudden attack, the unexpected evacuation, the precipitous flight of the French émigrés, and Anselme's propagated rumors spread winged terror in the city. Many of its inhabitants fled with the military. Under an autumn rain, a crowd of perhaps ten thousand refugees, laden with such possessions as they could carry, took the road to Piedmont.[42] They were fired on once, apparently by the Piedmontese themselves, but most of them reached the frontier two days later.

Meanwhile Nice was in the throes of disorder. The riffraff of the town began to pillage on the night of September 28, after the withdrawal of the Piedmontese authorities, and the arrival of Anselme's undisciplined troops the following evening completed

---

anglais dans la Méditerranée," *Bulletin de la Société d'études de Draguignan* [1929], XXXVII, 22–29) enumerates more than ten thousand fugitives disembarked by the Allies and the French rebels in Italy, on the island of Elba, and in Spain. And Ramsay Weston Phipps (*The Armies of the First French Republic* [4 vols.; Oxford, 1936], III, 120) gives a precise figure of 14,877. Moreover, Fréron (Edmond Poupé, 96) and Richaud (*op. cit.*, 104), both of whom were present, estimated twelve thousand fugitives.

[41] Edmond Poupé, 129–132 (Barras to Moyse Bayle, January 8, 1794).

[42] Georges Doublet, "L'émigration française à Nice de 1789 à 1792," *Nice historique* (1928), XXXI, 7–13, 59–64, 122–135, 190–200; (1929) XXXII, 1–19.

the picture of chaos. Churches, public buildings, shops, wealthy residences were looted.[43] The orgy continued for several days, until, in fact, it was checked by Barras, whom Anselme appointed president of the Provisional Administration. But if Barras stopped the pillage, his administration did not endear the Republic to the inhabitants of Nice. He set out to revolutionize the county, and his methods provoked protests that reached Paris. Three deputies were sent to investigate, and one of them, none other than Collot d'Herbois, reported to the Convention that Barras and his colleagues "did not govern, they tyrannized."[44] This opinion was general at Nice, and the deputies Grégoire and Jagot, who later organized the county as the department of the Alpes-Maritimes, concluded that Barras' administration "left in this country a memory charged with malediction."[45] Little wonder, then, that the emigration from Nice continued after the French occupation.[46]

Shifting the scene from the Alpine to the Pyrenean frontier, we are in another war zone. The Convention declared war on Spain on March 7, 1793. Here the enemy took the offensive. Within a month the Spaniards were well into Roussillon (Pyrénées-Orientales), familiar soil for them, since it was more Catalan than French. Moreover, the invading army comprised three corps of French émigrés, a large proportion of whom were natives of the department, and these early expatriates were joined by other malcontents as the invasion progressed.[47] At first the Spaniards encountered little opposition, and occasional treason facilitated their advance. In July, however, they failed in an attack on

[43] Joseph Combet, *La Révolution dans le comté de Nice et la principauté de Monaco, 1792-1800* (Paris, 1925), 56-57.

[44] Collot d'Herbois, *Rapport à la Convention nationale au nom des commissaires envoyés à l'armée du Var et dans le pays de Nice* (Paris, s.d. [1793]), 4-5.

[45] Antoine Emanuel, "Le séjour de Barras à Nice. Son action politique et sociale," *Nice historique, année* 1911, p. 181.

[46] A supplementary list issued by the *district de Menton* on April 3, 1794, gives 705 names (Joseph Combet, 239). The figure 3,000, which we have used in our tables to represent the emigration from the Alpes-Maritimes, is a minimum. According to a local scholar (E. Tisserand, *Histoire de la Révolution française dans les Alpes-Maritimes* [Nice, 1878], 469) the total was "from 4,000 to 5,000 émigrés."

[47] P. Torreilles, *Perpignan pendant la Révolution, 1789-1800* (2 vols.; Perpignan, 1896-1897), II, 154-157.

Perpignan, and on September 17 the battle of Peyrestortes again saved the departmental capital. After the war had languished during the winter, General Dugommier with reinforcements from Toulon expelled the Spaniards in the spring of 1794.[48]

During this year of invasion Roussillon was one of the most chaotic regions of France. The Spaniards pillaged and ravaged, the French irregulars looted and extorted, and the French conscripts were scarcely better behaved.[49] Parts of Roussillon became a no-man's land whence the people disappeared or where they lived furtively, like wild animals. The threats of the republican authorities, whose position was desperate, turned the fears of the suspects into terror and few of them remained to face any charges.[50] The *levée en masse* was a lamentable failure, for a great many of the conscripts either ignored the call to arms or deserted by the hundred, in either case automatically becoming fugitives from the Republic.[51] And as the conflict moved back and forth the inhabitants fled, some with and some from the Spaniards. A contemporary, writing of the flight from Rivesaltes, which the enemy captured on September 8, described the roads crowded with "entire families" of refugees; on the other hand, the Spaniards, as they retired from Peyrestortes to the lines of the Tech, were followed by a horde of peasants and village artisans.[52] There is, then, nothing accidental in the fact that 90 per cent of the emigrants from the Pyrénées-Orientales were from the two districts of Prades and Ceret, which had borne the brunt of the invasion, while Perpignan, with more population, supplied only 10 per cent.[53]

Turning to the Mayenne and the Moselle, we discover conditions much like those we have already described in connection with neighboring departments. The Mayenne, perhaps the most

[48] Pierre Vidal, *Histoire de la Révolution française dans le département des Pyrénées-Orientales* (3 vols.; Perpignan, 1885–1889), III, 1–257.

[49] P. Torreilles, II, 158–167.

[50] *Ibid.*, II, 157–158.

[51] *Ibid.*, II, 145–147.

[52] *Ibid.*, II, 167ff.; Pierre Vidal, II, 236, 345.

[53] AD Pyrénées-Orientales, Q 734 (lists of *émigrés*); cf. P. Torreilles, II, 168.

royalist of the Breton departments, was invaded by the Vendeans in their *outre*-Loire campaign of the winter of 1793; Laval was twice occupied by the rebels; and, finally, but certainly not least among the cogent factors, this department, the home of the famous Jean Cottereau, was the incubator of *chouannerie*.[54] And if the incidence of the emigration, higher than that for the Vendée itself, still seems incongruous, it is derived from intact records, an assurance lacking in the Vendée and several other western departments.[55] Even in the Moselle the sources do not reflect the total emigration, yet the index is higher than that of the Meuse, where circumstances were similar. Both departments were exposed to the magnetic attraction of the émigré camps on the Rhine, both were invaded, and both harbored royalists who were sucked into the Prussian retreat. Here, as elsewhere, caprice made the margin of difference.

The great flight of December, 1793, from the Bas-Rhin, the phenomenal climax of the emigration, was the issue of a complex of factors. The peasantry of Alsace, German in speech, royalist in ideology, and devout in religion, were lost for the Revolution when the throne and the altar fell. "The only thing to do," wrote J. B. Lacoste, "is to guillotine a fourth of the inhabitants of this province, to save only those who have taken an active part in the Revolution, and to drive out the rest."[56] The remark, of course, was typical Jacobin fanfare, and so, too, was much of the spectacular melodrama performed by the local terrorist, Euloge Schneider. Nevertheless, all this trumpeting struck fear into the countrysides. Schneider was credited with the most heinous crimes, and rumors circulated to the effect that the French intended to massacre all the men who could not be used in the army, to burn their homes, and to make a desert of the country.[57] The Alsatians

---

[54] Charles Le Goffic, *La chouannerie, blancs contre bleus, 1790–1800* (Paris, 1930), 44; Léon Dubreuil, I, 312, 320.

[55] AD Mayenne, Q 103–106. (See Bibliography under "Mayenne" for details of the lists.)

[56] Quoted by Marcel Marion, "Les fugitifs alsaciens sous la Révolution," *Revue historique* (1923), CXLII, pt. 1, p. 210.

[57] *Ibid.*, 212.

were people of mixed blood and culture, and now, with 92 per cent of their clergy condemned to exile,[58] with their king dead under the guillotine, and with the shadow of the Jacobin terror upon them, they were poised on the brink of panic.

Then came the Austrian invasion of the autumn of 1793. On October 13 Wurmser carried the lines of Wissembourg, a few days later he entered Haguenau, and by mid-November the northern half of the Bas-Rhin was in enemy hands. These invaders, however, were received as friends. Wurmser himself was a Strasbourger, and with his army was a contingent of émigrés under Condé. The latter were greeted with cries of "Vive le Roi" in Haguenau; in some rural communes the people turned out with white flags to meet the Austrians; and presently, like harbingers of the old regime, some of the early Alsatian émigrés, nobles, priests, or bourgeois, reappeared in their home communes.[59] Apparently the people of Alsace had reason to believe that Austria and the counterrevolution had triumphed.

Their illusion was brief, their disillusionment terrifying. Before the echoes of their welcome to the Austrians had died, the French counteroffensive had begun. Late in November the republicans under Pichegru and Hoche rallied their forces; they attacked in December, Haguenau fell on the twenty-sixth, and by the end of the year not an Austrian soldier remained in Alsace. The population fled before the advancing republicans. As early as November 19, when the French approached Bouxwiller, five hundred persons of the commune were reported in flight, a few days later the exodus from other rural communes began, and during the next month panic created a tidal wave of fugitives driven in front of the advancing French.[60] Men, women, and children of all classes,

---

[58] Philippe Sagnac, "Étude statistique sur le clergé constitutionnel et le clergé réfractaire en 1791," *Revue d'histoire moderne et contemporaine* (1906–1907), VIII, 109–110; R. Reuss, *La grande fuite de décembre 1793 et la situation politique et religieuse du Bas-Rhin de 1794 à 1799*, 2.

[59] Henri Carré, "Le journal d'émigration de Louis, Marquis Aymer de la Chevalerie," *Bulletin de la Société des antiquaires de l'Ouest, 3e série* (1933), IX, 862; R. Reuss, 1ff.

[60] Marcel Marion, *loc. cit.*, pp. 210–228; R. Reuss, 5ff.

of all creeds, of all cults, were seized and carried willy-nilly in this wave of fear. Louis d'Aymer, one of the fugitives, later described the figures of the scene in the town of Haguenau on a cold, foggy winter night, from the peasants with their household goods heaped in carts and their stock driven ahead of them to ladies of the upper classes, walking in the mud up to their knees, their feet bare and bloody.[61] Similar scenes occurred in other towns during the last days of December as the tidal wave swept through the districts of Haguenau and Wissembourg. A population was in flight, leaving behind it a path of desolation.[62]

3. Exceptions and Conclusions

WE HAVE now viewed the emigration in relation to local circumstances, and we have unveiled a recurrent set of coincidences. True, we have been obliged to select the cogent from the maze of facts which form the history of the Revolution in the provinces, and here and there our choices may be challenged. True, too, in a few cases there seems to have been no correlation of environment and emigration, no nexus of cause and effect. For instance, the Côte-d'Or, one of the richest departments of Burgundy, was near the frontier, and Dijon was the seat of a wealthy *parlement*; yet these inherent facts scarcely explain why the department had the highest incidence in a group that included the Loire-Inférieure and the Côtes-du-Nord. Mode, caprice, psychological climate, or other nebulae, might be invoked in explanation, but our interpretations will be better without rationalizations.

For certain broad conclusions are clear. From every part of France, certainly from every district and probably from most of the communes, there was some emigration. Generally, and despite the

---

[61] Henri Carré, *loc. cit.*, pp. 827–828.

[62] An English woman, the Baroness de Bode, married to an Alsatian seigneur, described the scene as follows: "All that part of Alsace was in the greatest desolation; all ran away that could. The press was so violent to get over the Rhine that it was impossible all could do so, and mothers with their children in their arms threw themselves into the river and drowned themselves rather than fall into the hands of those unmerciful monsters" (William S. Childe-Pemberton, *The Baroness de Bode* [London, 1900], 156; quoted in French translation by R. Reuss, 10).

influence of circumstantial environments, the incidence of the movement tended to increase on a radius from the center of the country to the borders. Hence a portion of the lay emigration was "voluntary" in the sense that the emigrants deliberately chose expatriation to the risk or the loss that was implied in readjustment to the new order in France. This was especially true in the quiet departments, and, as we have seen, these same departments were those of early and aristocratic emigration. And since the exodus from the quiet regions was on the whole light or moderate, the "voluntary" émigrés were distinctly in the minority. Too many unknown and unknowable factors are involved to permit an accurate statistical expression of this minority. Of the lay émigrés, however, it seems that not more than one-fourth belonged to the group of "flagrant deserters from their natural post of duty."

The rest were voluntary émigrés by legal fiction only. For in at least half of France circumstances varied from impelling to compulsory, and as they varied so varied the degrees of human volition present in the acts of expatriation. To recall as examples some of the salient conditions, the quasi-certainty of reprisals impelled federalists to emigrate, the havoc of the civil wars in the West created a mass of homeless fugitives, the Provençal rebels were swept in front of the advancing army of Carteaux, the panic-stricken people of Toulon tumbled pell-mell into boats in the glare of the burning Arsenal and to the sound of bursting bombs, and the powerful undertow of receding invasions dragged thousands into exile. Most of these people actually had little choice. Probably the majority of them were not even active counterrevolutionaries. They were inhabitants of storm centers, and they departed not like reasoning humans but like animals driven by elemental forces. No one plotted to ostracize them, any more than they planned to emigrate. They were the victims not of a Jacobin plot, not of their own actions, but of a cyclonic disturbance in the life of their nation.

CHAPTER IV

THE SOCIAL INCIDENCE

1. The Legend of the White and the Black

ONE OF THE legends of the emigration depicts a galaxy of aristocrats and prelates posed at the bar of History. An outraged Condé raises a belligerent sword, a Champion de Cicé pronounces solemn anathema, a Talleyrand smiles ironically, a Chateaubriand chants the nostalgic strain,

"Ma soeur, qu'ils étaient beaux les jours
De France . . ."

These figures, and thousands like them, were incontestably real. The emigration drained France of her elite. Cancel a few names, some of which were of victims of the guillotine, and d'Hozier's *Armorial* becomes a list of émigrés. The legend errs not in commission but in omission. The brilliant company of aristocrats obscures the presence of a dense throng of drab figures. But they, too, were émigrés—the émigrés of the Third Estate. The revolutionaries took cognizance of them, listed them, seized their possessions, later offered many of them an amnesty, and the Restoration indemnified those whose property had been confiscated. Yet the legend has lost none of its impact. Except to a few specialists the word "émigrés" still suggests nobles and churchmen.

The longevity of this myth is, of course, explicable. In the first place, there is a psychological trap. It is easy, hence habitual, to accept great names as symbols of groups; it is difficult, thus repellent, to discern the character of anonymous crowds. Everyone knows that Talleyrand emigrated, and therefore is predisposed to believe that thousands of Talleyrands emigrated. But who has heard of Joseph Deplacker, a Flemish potter who crossed the frontier into the Austrian Netherlands in June, 1793?[1] Talleyrand *is* a prototype, but so is Joseph Deplacker, and the group coefficient of the latter is at least equal to that of the former.

In the second place, the legend has been furbished by both conservative and liberal historians. To the former, to Taine and his school especially, the emigration was an intended consequence of a subversive plot to rid France of her best people. Republican historians, such as Mathiez or Vingtrinier, disagreed with Taine as to the cause of the emigration, but they regarded it as a phase of the counterrevolution involving principally the upper classes. Neither Taine nor Mathiez quite ignored the mass of obscure emigrants, but both relegated them to an indistinct background. To place the masses in the shadows was to garble the total significance of the emigration. Yet there they remained, partly because the inaccessibility and the imperfection of the source material repelled scholars trained to believe that no conclusion is valid without exactitude in minutiae. The emergence of the truth was thus frustrated, for so long as the social incidence of the emigration was vaguely and uncertainly known the legend of a movement confined to lily-white aristocrats and black-gowned priests was in reprieve.

Now, however, the reprieve is at an end. The deficiencies in the sources, which we have already discussed, render forever impossible a social classification of all the émigrés. But certainly a sampling which includes more than three-fourths of them is an adequate basis for conclusions, and our tables of the social incidence comprise 97,545, or 78 per cent of the total number (129,099). Nor is it remotely plausible that the inclusion of the remaining 22 per cent would reverse the class proportions we have derived. On the contrary, a miracle of complete social classification probably would increase the percentage representing the Third Estate, especially in the artisan and peasant classes, while correspondingly reducing that of the other two orders.[2]

[1] "Premier supplément à la liste générale des émigrés . . . du Nord," 28 ventôse an VII. AD Nord, L 1079.

[2] The evidence, though inferential, is virtually conclusive. Numbers, geography,

At all events, of our tabulated émigrés 51 per cent were members of the Third Estate, 25 per cent were clergy, and 17 per cent were nobles (Table I). With the 7 per cent of unidentifiables carried in our tables we shall deal later, but even were it assumed that virtually all of them belonged to the privileged classes (the opposite is far more likely), the unprivileged still would predominate. The ratio of commoners to clergy is two to one, of plebeians to nobles three to one. And the émigrés, far from being all of the privileged orders, form a cross section of social France at the end of the eighteenth century.

The use of "estates" as social compartments, however, gives only the crudest picture of the society of the emigration. The distinction was legal, or political, rather than social. As descriptive of the French social order it had always been somewhat inaccurate; by the end of the eighteenth century it had lost all social validity, and was nothing more than a consecrated anachronism. Of course the clergy was a sacerdotal corporation—within which the hierarchical gamut was enormous. Certain exclusive privileges distinguished the nobility as a body, but from the petty *noblesse de cloche* to the great *noblesse de cour* was a vast distance in the social scale. And the development of capitalism had so fractioned the Third Estate that to conceive even the urban classes as a single, united, or homogeneous group is to ignore class lines more real than those which delineated the "estates" themselves. Nor did the society of the old regime possess the rigidity implicit in the term "estates." There was no caste system. Property, not birth, ulti-

---

and local circumstances imply that the emigration from Finistère, the Côtes-du-Nord, and the Loire-Inférieure was of the same social texture as that of other western departments—predominantly plebeian. Our incomplete data for Calvados and the Sarthe point unmistakably in the same direction. The reverse probably was true for the Seine-et-Oise, which stands high, no. 78, in the scale of indemnity averages (André Gain, *La Restauration et les biens des émigrés*, II, 202), and for the Ain, another department of high average indemnities (no. 79 in the scale). The Pas-de-Calais, with 930 nonjurors and 250 clerical émigrés and *déportés* from the single district of Saint-Pol (see above, p. 48, n. 18) may well have been the department of heaviest ecclesiastic emigration. But in general, as our tables show, where the index of the emigration was high the Third Estate predominated, and most of the departments omitted from our social classification were seriously affected by the emigration.

mately denominated social status, and the "moyens de parvenir" were many and various.

An ideal classification of the émigrés, then, would reflect a fluid, complex society quite unlike the rigid, simple structure evoked by the terminology of estates. Unfortunately the sources do not reveal all the finer distinctions. Obviously the First Estate presents the least difficulty, since, on the whole, it is easy enough to separate the upper clergy from the lower, the secular from the regular. As for the Second Estate, it too often happened that nobles were listed merely as nobles, without further qualification. The great names, it is true, have a lustre of their own; most of the parliamentarians are distinguishable; and the rank of officers indicates, roughly at least, their place in the social hierarchy. For statistical purposes, however, only the broadest distinctions—military and civilian groups, territorial (*noblesse d'épée*) and official (*noblesse de robe*) categories—can be drawn. In part for these reasons, in part because the nobility and the clergy did constitute legally privileged orders, we have retained them as social corporations in our tables, reserving for discussion their internal divisions.

But the "Third Estate," except as a term of political parlance, is quite meaningless. It comprised the vast majority of the nation and is divisible into four distinct classes.[3] First in rank and power was the *grande bourgeoisie*, in the less connotative English equivalent, the upper middle class—professional men, high functionaries, rich merchants, financiers, wealthy property owners. The *petite bourgeoisie*, or lower middle class, was less clearly delineated. It was a social midway, essentially the class of the shopkeepers, the "white-collar" employees, and other townsmen living on small incomes. The group captioned "working class" in our tables was more heterogeneous. It comprised a great miscellany of manual producers and a variety of social dregs as well. The majority of its members were artisans, but some of them, living in the country, owning or farming land, were more precisely peasant-artisans. Except for the textile workers, however, most of them earned the

---

[3] For further discussion of these classes see Donald Greer, *The Incidence of the Terror during the French Revolution*, 89–95.

greater part of their living by their trades, and, moreover, they usually were described as artisans on the émigré lists. The fourth class was that of the peasants, among whom there were important economic differences. The upper crust of the peasantry represented comparative wealth, the lower depths sheer destitution.[4] Yet as a group the peasant class had more social cohesion than any other of the old regime.

In thus classifying the émigrés of the Third Estate, vocation is our principal key. Use of it entails difficulties, some of which are inherent in the sources, and some of which are inseparable from any method of social sorting. The government employees who drew up the lists were subject to idiosyncrasies such as vague diction, baffling brevity, and the use of colloquialisms. For instance, in Roussillon (and nowhere else) a candle-maker was a "man-gonnier"; a peasant landowner, a "pagès."[5] Or, in the way of vagueness, the description "veille Marie, valet (sic) de charrue" may place "old Mary" as a peasant woman, no matter what surname she bore, and to the same class we may safely ascribe Jacqueline Mallesys, "fille de peine" in a rural commune of Hazebrouck (Nord);[6] but hundreds of emigrants appear in the sources simply as "fille" or "garçon"—words often used to abbreviate "fille de peine" or "garçon de ferme."[7] Many émigrés described as "tailleurs" were not tailors but stonemasons (tailleurs de pierre), and the qualifications "militaire" or "deserteur" may mean anything from common soldier to marshal of France. And one could multiply these examples. We have been obliged to base a certain number of classifications on dubious or fragmentary descriptions, yet in most of these cases the names, the residences,

---

[4] Georges Lefebvre, La grande peur de 1789 (Paris, 1932), ch. 1. On the rural proletariat during the Revolution, see Edmond Soreau, "La Révolution et le prolétariat rural," Annales historiques de la Révolution française (1932), IX, 28–36, 116–127, 325–335; (1933), X, 25–48.

[5] For aid in ascertaining the meaning of many of these terms I am indebted to M. Pierre Xavier Pams, Chevalier of the Legion of Honor, of Perpignan.

[6] "Premier supplément à la liste générale des émigrés . . . du Nord," 28 ventôse an VII. AD Nord, L 1079.

[7] Especially numerous in the lists for Alsace, Flanders, and Brittany.

the amount of property (if any), and sometimes the parentage of the emigrants corroborate our assumptions.

There were, moreover, marginal vocations and marginal groups. Not sharp, clear lines but frontier zones separated the classes from one another in eighteenth-century society. The doctors, for instance, were definitely of the *haute bourgeoisie*, but what of the dentists? Some of them were well-to-do, but their craft was not yet a profession. Again, if the veterinarians ("artiste vétérinaire," as embellished by some of the clerks of the period) were lower middle class, as we have decided, to what category did the gelders (*chatreurs*) belong? Or, to consider a specific case, Jean Grozholz was an Alsatian of some importance:[8] he was a public executioner, but whose social equal was he? Occasionally, too, there were differences within vocations. The great brewers of Lille, for example, certainly were bourgeois, but the brewers of small beer in the Flemish villages usually were peasants. The *procureurs* in the *parlements* were generally rich men, while some of the advocates barely made a living.[9] Thus a few arbitrary classifications impose themselves. Still, we have resolved these equivocal cases in accord with the standards of the old regime, and such incongruities as may appear in our classification are reflected from the social pattern of the age.

2. *The Ubiquity and the Ubieties of the Social Incidence*

WITH the bases of classification thus established we may examine the social incidence of the emigration (Table I). The first facts are, in themselves, striking. Of the 97,545 socially classified émigrés the 24,596 clergy, representing one-fourth ($25\frac{1}{4}$ per cent) of the total, constituted the largest group. *Second* in numerical importance were the 18,910 peasants, approximately one-fifth ($19\frac{1}{2}$ per cent) of the classified emigrants. *Third* in order came the 16,431 nobles, only one-sixth ($16\frac{3}{4}$ per cent) of the tabular total—only a fraction

[8] "Liste supplétive des émigrés du district de Wissembourg," 16 messidor an III. AD Bas-Rhin, Q unclassified.

[9] Henri Sée, *La vie économique et les classes sociales en France au XVIIIe siècle* (Paris, 1924), 186.

higher than the working class, whose 13,953 members amounted to one-seventh ($14\frac{1}{4}$ per cent) of the émigrés. The *haute bourgeoisie* supplied one-ninth (11 per cent), in numbers, 10,792; and the gamut ends with the 6,012 representatives of the lower middle class, a scant sixteenth ($6\frac{1}{4}$ per cent) of the figurants of our table.

Whatever qualifying light the analyses to follow may shed on the social incidence of the emigration, these figures have absolute significance. They put an end to the myth of the white and the black. The nobility and the clergy combined represented only 42 per cent of the émigrés; the bourgeois more than equaled the nobles; and the two laboring classes outnumbered the nobility two to one. French society, from its crest to its base, participated in the movement. Every class, every condition, and (with an anticipatory glance at the vocational incidence) every profession, trade, and craft contributed its quota. And the prototype émigré was *not* Talleyrand, the priest-noble, but a composite figure, priest-noble-bourgeois-artisan-peasant, with shades of the nondescript for seams.

At once, however, one may suspect our variegated totem of being a caricature. Is its garish glitter a varnish over other significance? Perhaps; at all events, it must be subjected to a careful analysis. First and obviously, the social incidence of the emigration means literally the proportion of each class that emigrated. Concerning this problem, however, the most that we can hope to attain is a quasi-hypothetical solution, for we must use two sets of estimates. On the one hand, we must assume that the group percentages of our socially classified émigrés hold for the ensemble—for example, that $25\frac{1}{4}$ per cent, or 32,597, of the 129,099 emigrants were clergy. Likewise computed, there were 21,624 nobles, 14,201 bourgeois, 8,069 shopkeepers and petty employees, 18,397 manual producers and miscellaneous poor, and 25,174 peasants.

On the other hand, we must accept rather vague conjectures concerning eighteenth-century demography. Apparently, at the end of the century, the nobility of all ranks, from petty to illustrious, numbered between four hundred and five hundred thousand. Estimates of the clergy have varied widely, but the total, including the regulars, both monks and nuns, appears to have been about two hundred thousand. Concerning the professional, shopkeeping, and artisan classes there is still less certainty. The upper middle class, as defined for our tabular category, was not much more numerous than the nobility, comprising perhaps a little over half a million persons; the lower middle class was at least twice as large, say a million and a quarter members; some three million persons constituted the proletariat; and, finally, the great majority of the French, about twenty million, were peasants.[10]

Accepting these estimates at their face value, we may now compute the literal social incidence of the emigration. It was highest for the clergy, though still not as high as the relevant martyrology implies. Sixteen per cent of the French clergy were indicted as emigrants, though, as we shall see, the majority of them were deportees. Five per cent of the nobility, a much smaller proportion than that usually imagined, departed; and of the *haute bourgeoisie*, which tended to merge with our inclusive noble class, three per cent emigrated. Here, parenthetically, is further light on the mythical numerical predominance of the upper classes in the emigration. The absence of one-sixth of the clergy (and a much higher percentage of the secular clergy), of one-twentieth of the nobility (including virtually all of the illustrious families), of a liberal sprinkling of lawyers, doctors, bankers, and wholesalers left conspicuous vacancies in society. But when we look from the upper to the lower reaches of the social order, the incidence of the emigration drops sharply. Only three-fourths of one per cent of the lower middle class, only one-half of one per cent of the laboring class, and only one-eighth of one per cent of the peasantry left France. The absence of these obscure people, flecks of grey in a grey sea,

10 Cf. Donald Greer, 106–107. Most modern scholars (for example, Henri Sée, *La France économique et sociale au XVIIIe siècle* [Paris, 1925], 55) estimate about 130,000 clergy, the figure given by Moheau, *Recherches et considérations sur la population de la France en 1789* (ed. Gonnard; Paris, 1912), 61. But according to other eighteenth-century authorities the total was higher. Bonvalet-Desbrosses estimated 208,800. Moreover, Marcel Marion (*Dictionnaire des institutions de la France au XVIIe et XVIIIe siècle* [Paris, 1923], 97) concludes that the secular clergy alone numbered 90,000. In the light of these figures it seems probable that the total of regular and secular clergy was not less than 200,000.

was scarcely noticed except in the few departments whence they emigrated en masse.

Coming now to a different analysis of our statistics (Table VI), it was precisely the mass migrations from a few departments that caused the lower classes to predominate among the émigrés. The Bas-Rhin alone weighs heavily, perhaps to the degree of distortion, in all of our tabular totals. Its 20,510 emigrants amount to 21 per cent of the classified total; *but* its 9,601 peasants constitute 51 per cent of all peasant emigrants, its 6,051 proletarians 43 per cent of the working class, and its 2,113 *petits bourgeois* 35 per cent of the lower middle class. Now omit the Bas-Rhin, and the index for the clergy rises five per cent, that for the nobility four per cent, while that for the proletariat sinks four per cent, that for peasantry seven per cent. Leave out of account, in addition to the Bas-Rhin, the Var and the Pyrénées-Orientales, the two other departments of most pronounced mass migration, and the percentages signifying the privileged orders rise, those representing artisans and peasants fall, about two per cent in each case. And if we exclude the six departments of the heaviest emigration, those considered above plus the Bouches-du-Rhône, the Mayenne, and the Moselle, the percentages of clergy and nobility again increase, four and three points, those of artisans and peasants decrease two and three points respectively.

Encroachments such as these could be pushed to any depth—to the zone of absurdity, or beyond. But the results already obtained are abundantly significant. A final glance at Table VI will reveal that by deducting the émigrés of six departments we have reversed the social pattern of the emigration. Now the *privilégiés* form a clear majority of 63 per cent. The *haute bourgeoisie* remains virtually constant, but the three lower classes have diminished to a total of 18 per cent. Though this last proportion is larger than the legend of the white and the black admitted, it is certain that the emigration from the greater part of France was essentially clerical and aristocratic.

Even so, its social texture presents a puzzle in contrasts, some of them so bold that they must be dismissed as inexplicable on any other ground than that of deficiencies in the sources. Conversely, there is little close uniformity anywhere, not even within distinct geographic regions, such as Burgundy. In one department, or in one district, we shall find towering percentages of nobles, or of peasants; in the adjacent circumscription the exact reverse will be true. One is immediately tempted to conclude that the animus of the emigration was inchoate impulse, and perhaps, in the end, we shall concede a strip of the terrain to imponderables. Table VII, however, is devised to aid us in understanding the quilt-like variations. Here the departments are reassembled in seven categories determined by circumstantial environments. The first four include the territory where the internal struggle of the Revolution raged in different forms; the fifth embraces the invaded regions, the sixth relatively quiet sections; and Paris merits unique consideration.

In the civil war theater of the West (Region I) the pattern of the emigration was a replica of political demography. The middle classes of the towns, liberal before and Jacobin during the Revolution, scarcely figured in the exodus, and many of those who did emigrate were chaff blown by the storm. On the other hand, the clergy of these regions, fanatic in their zeal, the nobility, ardent in their royalism, and the peasants, firm in their devotion to throne and altar, fought the Revolution and never yielded their principles. To these classes belonged the majority of the western émigrés. The clergy composed the largest class, 35 per cent of the regional total. Most of them were deportees, technically at least, for the proportion of nonjurors was higher in the West (virtually unanimous in certain departments) than in any other large region of France.[11] The nobility, with 23 per cent of the categoric ensemble, ranked second. Angevin, Poitevin, and Breton nobles were among the first to flock to the standards of the Princes on the Rhine,

[11] Philippe Sagnac, "Étude statistique sur le clergé constitutionnel et le clergé réfractaire en 1791," *Revue d'histoire moderne et contemporaine* (1906–1907), VIII, 97–115. This article has been severely criticised—and then cited!—by almost every writer on the subject, including Mathiez. See also the works on the western clergy and the Church given under departmental captions in the Bibliography. It seems certain that well over three-fourths of all the western clergy refused the oath.

and those who remained in their provinces fled after the Vendean defeats. Third came the peasants, 20 per cent of the émigrés of the group; and in this region the artisan emigrants (10 per cent) were, for the most part, village artisans, assimilable to the peasantry. The Vendean troops were drawn from the rural masses, and when they were defeated, their homes burned, their fields devastated, they sought refuge where they could. Some escaped to Guernsey and Jersey, some to England, a few elsewhere.[12] Many of them remained hidden in their own country or nearby districts, but whenever and wherever the revolutionary authorities were able to carry on their functions these absentees were listed as émigrés.

The emigrants from the cockpits of the Southeast (Region II) were equally representative of the seditious factions. The revolts of Lyon, Avignon, Marseille, and Toulon were the work of the middle classes.[13] The nobility and the clergy supported them, and once the die of rebellion was cast they were able to enlist or to enforce the armed participation of many workers and some peasants. When the rebellions were crushed, most of the rebel leaders and thousands of the rank and file fled; and other thousands of men, women, and children, guilty only of residence in rebel territory but terrified by the menace of republican revenge, were pulled into the debacle. In the Bouches-du-Rhône, where the mercantile aristocracy was especially compromised, 40 per cent of the émigrés were of the *haute bourgeoisie*, 18 per cent of the tradesmen class. In the Rhône, where the revolt was born of an alliance between the merchant princes of the city and the local nobility, the society of the former supplied 33 per cent of the emigrants, that of the latter 27 per cent. In the Var, where the

---

[12] Regis de L'Estourbeillon, *Les familles françaises à Jersey pendant la Révolution* (Nantes, 1886), *passim*; Charles Hettier, *Relations de la Normandie et de la Bretagne avec les îles de la Manche pendant l'émigration* (Caen, 1885), *passim*; Émile Gabory, *L'Angleterre et la Vendée* (2 vols.; Paris, 1930–1931), I, ch. 1; and Jules Bertaut, "Les émigrés français à Londres," *Le monde nouveau* (1923), VII, 183–194.

[13] Cf. Donald Greer, 101–103. For the most recent account of federalism in the Var and the revolt of Toulon see Edmond Poupé, *Le département du Var, 1790–an VIII* (Cannes, 1933), 199–319.

closing scene of the rebellion was an epic panic, 26 per cent of the fugitives were proletarians and 37 per cent belonged to the combined middle classes. The recapitulative percentages for the region are still more significant: the upper middle class led with 29 per cent; the lower middle class (15 per cent) was almost twice as large as in any other of our seven groups; and the working class represented 20 per cent of the total. As far as numbers are concerned the aristocratic and clerical emigration was heavy enough, and over a thousand peasants were listed in the Var and the Bouches-du-Rhône; but these classes formed small proportions of the total, in order 10 per cent, 9 per cent, and 8 per cent.

In the departments of southern federalism (Region III) the social aspects of the emigration were nearly identical with those for our sixth category, the quiet sections. Federalism was an ephemeral threat, dangerous but soon lifted. Except where royalism or foreign aid vitalized it, as at Lyon or Toulon, it lacked the impulsion necessary to carry into civil war. It involved only small upper-class groups, and it received scarcely any support from the masses. But upper-class opposition to the Jacobin Republic was widespread, and therefore the repression of federalism, though it augmented the volume of the emigration, produced no distinctive social configuration. Only 11 per cent of the émigrés of the category were members of the lower classes, 13 per cent were bourgeois, and 22 per cent were nobles. The clergy (42 per cent) formed the largest group. The proportion of nonjurors was high in the Gard, the Hérault, and the Haute-Garonne;[14] and in the Gironde, where it was much lower,[15] the clergy constituted 28 per cent of the exiles.

The three departments of our next group (Region IV) disclose some of those contrasts which cursorily belie the correlation of the counterrevolution and the emigration. In the Haute-Loire, the Lozère, and the Doubs, insurrections involving approximately

---

[14] About 70 per cent in the Haute-Garonne. AD Haute-Garonne, Q 60 ff. 58 per cent in the Hérault, and 64 per cent in the Gard, according to Philippe Sagnac, *loc. cit.*, pp. 109–110.

[15] 41 per cent. *Ibid., idem.*

the same number of combatants occurred;[16] all three were occasioned by conscription; all three were repressed with about the same degree of severity.[17] Now the emigration from the two mountainous departments of southern central France was small in volume and prevailingly aristocratic and ecclesiastic in character. Indeed 79 per cent of the emigrants of the Lozère, 72 per cent of those of the Haute-Loire, were *privilégiés*. But in the Doubs, not only was the emigration heavy, but it also represented essentially the agrarian masses. Six hundred and eighty-four peasants, thirty-five per cent of the departmental emigrants, went into exile, and the Doubs ranks fourth in the scale of peasant emigration among the departments of our tables. Furthermore, a large proportion of the two hundred and ninety-four working class emigrants (15 per cent of the local total) belonged to the border-line class of artisan-peasants. Yet it is easy to see why similar circumstances corresponded to dissimilar consequences in these three departments. Geography was the intervening factor. The defeated peasants of rugged central France, with little hope of gaining foreign soil, hid in their own mountains; the insurgents of the Doubs, vanquished in their last stand on the river frontier, crossed to Switzerland.[18]

In the fifth of our composite regions, the turmoil of war and invasion created veritable *déracinés* of all classes. Fifty-eight per cent of the emigrants from the invaded departments were peasants or artisans, and only twenty-three per cent enjoyed privileged status. True, the single department of the Bas-Rhin burdens the recapitulative percentages; but, even without the Bas-Rhin, plebeians predominated among the émigrés of these departments. In some of them the proportion of peasants was very high—20 per cent in the Moselle, 23 per cent in the Nord, 44 per cent in the Pyrénées-Orientales. The working class, too, was well represented —12 per cent, 14 per cent, 16 per cent in the Aisne, the Ardennes,

---

[16] Donald Greer, 50–52.

[17] *Ibid.*, 146.

[18] Jules Sauzay, *Histoire de la persécution révolutionnaire dans le département du Doubs de 1789 à 1801*, IV, ch. 49.

and the Moselle respectively. On the other hand, in the Meurthe, and especially in the Meuse, the nobility and the clergy were in the majority, but, for that matter, the suction of the receding invasions was socially indiscriminate.

Nowhere else, however, were the consequences of invasion so catastrophic as in the Bas-Rhin. The early emigration from this department was sluggish, aristocratic, and ecclesiastic. The first printed list for the district of Strasbourg, not issued until January, 1793, contained the names of only 166 emigrants, and of these 71 were nobles and 27 were clergy.[19] During the following month Haguenau and Wissembourg published "general lists" totaling 184 inscriptions, in majority persons of the privileged orders.[20] The fall of the Gironde, in June, 1793, the fury of the Jacobins of Strasbourg during the summer, and, in the autumn, the departmental tour of Euloge Schneider with his itinerant revolutionary tribunal and his guillotine on wheels, stimulated the movement, but by November not more than a thousand persons had emigrated. Then, suddenly, the curtain rose on a scene of lurid tumult. In an atmosphere already charged with terrorism came the rapid Austrian invasion, hurled back within a month by the French counteroffensive. A frenzy of fear gripped the people of the war districts and compelled them to flee. Haguenau and Wissembourg were nearly depopulated; other parts of the Bas-Rhin were less seriously affected, but few villages were quite immune.

This stampeded herd was social France in miniature. It comprised people of all classes, callings, and cults. Priests and nobles, who predominated among the earlier émigrés, were sparse in the throng. Bourgeois were more numerous—a hundred rich merchants and *rentiers*, seventy-five state functionaries, fifty doctors and surgeons, as many lawyers, a number of musicians, artists, sculptors,

---

[19] "État général des émigrés du district de Strasbourg," 15 janvier 1793. AD Bas-Rhin, Q unclassified.

[20] "État général des émigrés du district de Haguenau," 7 février 1793; "État général des émigrés du district de Wissembourg," 19 février, 1793. AD Bas-Rhin, Q unclassified. Cf. on the question of the early emigration from the Bas-Rhin, Pierre Haas, "L'émigration et le partage des communaux à Schwabwiller en 1793," *Revue d'Alsace* (1937), LXXXIV, 430-435.

a fair representation of all the professions.[21] Represented by still larger numbers was the lower middle class. Among the fugitives were three hundred tailors, a hundred millers, about the same number of butchers, of bakers, of miscellaneous shopkeepers, of hotel and cabaret keepers, and (surprisingly enough) of school-teachers. Present, too, were mercers and grocers, pastry-cooks and confectioners, midwives and governesses, dancing teachers and fencing masters, and samples of the entire hierarchy of employees.

The multitude, however, was composed mainly of peasants and artisans. Almost half of the fugitives (47 per cent) were tillers of the soil, fleeing with their wives, sons, and daughters, their serv-ants, stock, farm implements, and household belongings. Among the artisans the largest group was that of the weavers—over six hundred men, more than one hundred women. Next in numerical importance were the masons and stonecutters, a total of some seven hundred persons. Other large aggregations, scaling into the hun-dreds, were those of the shoemakers, the carpenters, joiners, and turners, the blacksmiths and wheelwrights, the metalsmiths, the servants, and the day laborers. Near and falling away from the one hundred mark, the miscellany embraced all sorts of craftsmen, high and low: skilled artisans, locksmiths, for example; domestic workers, such as basket-weavers; fishermen of the Rhine; and practitioners of dubious callings, such as poaching and smuggling.

Regarded from the point of view of cults, the Alsatian emigra-tion was equally comprehensive. The Catholic world of the prov-ince delegated its leading personage, the Cardinal-Bishop de Rohan, of diamond-necklace notoriety, and, of course, the majority of the emigrants were members of his flock. But the Protestant and Jewish faiths were also well represented, from their priesthoods to their dregs. About thirty of the Protestants were pastors; most of the others were artisans or shopkeepers. As for the Jews, among the several rabbis was a Guggenheim;[22] among the Jewish merchants

[21] These and the following statistics concerning the vocational incidence of the emigration from the Bas-Rhin are derived from the lists given in the Bibliography under "Bas-Rhin."

[22] Described as follows: "Guggenheim, sa femme, 1 fils, rabin." ("Liste supplétive des émigrés du district de Haguenau," 4 messidor an II. AD Bas-Rhin, Q unclassified.)

was the Dreyfus family[23] (and, by ironic coincidence, the name Drumont follows next on the list!); a family of six Jewish artisans bore the name Hittler;[24] and at least one of the race was described simply as a "begging Jew."[25] In the social spectrum of the emigration from the Bas-Rhin no nuance was lacking.

Thirty-seven departments, more than half of those (70) embraced in our table, appear in our next category (Region VI). We have qualified them as "quiet." This term does not mean necessarily that they were immune to the "spontaneous anarchy" of the summer of 1789, or free from sporadic riots, such as those provoked by requisitioning, or unvisited by terroristic representatives on mission. It does mean that here the design of daily living was less disturbed than elsewhere, that the routines of life were reshaped without being broken by the impact of the Revolution, that in some remote countrysides the people may have been only dimly aware that France was in revolution. The emigration from these departments, then, was not the result of tangible local provocations. Of course, it still was the consequence of the Revolution, of the multiform insecurities, of the dangerous climate of the period. Yet most of the laymen who emigrated from the quiet regions were neither greatly menaced, nor forced by panic, nor driven by other chimeras. They were not fugitives. They were émigrés in the literal sense of the word, for they deliberately chose between expatriation and life under the pall of the Revolution.

As such they hold especial interest for us. Two qualities characterize them as a group. First, they were comparatively few. In only seven of the thirty-seven departments did the number, in-

[23] Twelve members, all men. ("Liste supplétive des émigrés du district de Wissembourg," 16 messidor an III. AD Bas-Rhin, Q unclassified.)

[24] One listed simply as "Hittler"; the first names of the others were Catherine, Mathieu, Mathieu, Joseph, and Céleste. ("Liste supplétive des émigrés du district de Wissembourg," 7 brumaire an IV. AD Bas-Rhin, Q unclassified.) Since the Alsatian émigrés scattered through southern Germany, and since the distance from the Rhine to the Austrian frontier was not great, the hypothesis that Adolph Hitler may have been a descendant of an Alsatian Jew is at least interesting.

[25] Listed as "Loewel, Mayer, juif mendiant." ("Liste supplétive des émigrés du département du Bas-Rhin," 30 germinal an V. AD Bas-Rhin, Q unclassified.)

cluding the clergy, exceed one thousand,[26] and the regional total
(26,881, again including the clergy) represented but 27 per cent
of the classified emigrants. Second, apart from the clergy (40 per
cent of the total), most of whom were nonjuring deportees, the
nobility formed by far the largest class—26 per cent of the category as a whole, 42 per cent of the laymen. As usual, the upper
middle class held its own (11 per cent of the total, 19 per cent of
the laymen). But the three lower classes together amounted to
only 12 per cent of the ensemble, 20 per cent of the lay émigrés.
From a number of these tranquil departments only a handful
of non-nobles emigrated. As examples, the contingent from the
Creuse was confined to three bourgeois chatelains, four lawyers,
a merchant, a mason, and nine peasants; that from the Cher, to
twenty-seven bourgeois of various professions, one wigmaker,'one
day laborer, one glazier, and one gamekeeper. From some of the
rich departments, such as the Côte-d'Or or the Oise, upper middle
class emigration was quite heavy; in one or two cases (e.g., the
Vosges) even peasant emigration was considerable; and the pattern
of the emigration from the Haut-Rhin, the circumstances of which
we have already discussed, was that of a storm center rather than
of a quiet sector. On the whole, however, it is again clear that the
voluntary emigration from regions where there was little direct
compulsion was essentially aristocratic.

Paris, which defies assimilation to any of the other six categories,
presents amazing paradoxes. Though the department comprised
a small farming zone around the city, no peasant was listed; though
Paris had the largest working class population of any city in France,
only sixteen artisans and nine shopkeepers were inscribed; though
the bourgeoisie of Paris was the most powerful of the country,
only ninety-three of the class were indicted as émigrés. So in-

[26] The seven exceptions are the two rich Burgundian departments of the Côte-
d'Or (1,781 émigrés) and the Saône-et-Loire (1,052 émigrés); the Marne (1,040
émigrés), another rich department; Mont-Blanc (1,806 émigrés, 1,033 of whom were
clergy), annexed during the Revolution; the Haut-Rhin (2,746 émigrés), on the
frontier and rocked by events in the Bas-Rhin; the Seine-Inférieure (2,038 émigrés),
clerical and royalist, and infected with *chouannerie*; and the wealthy Channel department of the Somme (1,286 émigrés, of whom more than half, 52 per cent, were clergy).

credible are these figures that we must concede a probable discrepancy in the source material.[27] But allowance for a wide margin of error still would leave the Third Estate in a very small minority. Moreover, the extremely high average of the indemnities granted in the Seine in 1825 clearly implies that few poor people emigrated from the capital.[28] As for the *privilégiés*, the clergy numbered at least four hundred and sixty-two, but the nobility dwarfed all other classes. Nine hundred and forty-two nobles (46 per cent of the Parisian exiles) emigrated; and, in contrast to the probabilities elsewhere, many, perhaps most of the five hundred and forty-seven unidentifiables were almost certainly of the same social status. The Parisian list reads like a Gotha of the most illustrious families. Few, if any, of the great clans of France were absent from the roll. The Broglies, the Choiseuls, the Bourbon-Condés, the Richelieus, the Grammonts, the La Rouchefoucaulds, the La Tremoilles, the Luxembourgs, the Polignacs, the Rochechouarts . . .[29] the mere names would cover pages. For these people, the elite of the French nobility, the citadel of the Revolution became uninhabitable at an early date. But even during the Terror, it seems, Paris held its artisans, its shopkeepers, and its bourgeois.

The conclusions to be drawn from the foregoing examination of categories are too patent to require much emphasis. Incontestably the variety of the social pattern of the emigration, the puzzle in contrasts, corresponded to the variety of circumstances in revolutionary France. Despite a number of exceptions, the correlations are too constant to permit any other interpretation. In this new light the emigration appears as a much more complex phenomenon than lately supposed. A welter of circumstances, political, moral, and geographic, operated singly, in conjunction with one another,

[27] Our data for the Seine are derived from the sources indicated in the Bibliography under the departmental caption. Possibly an intensive study of the dossiers in the Archives départementales de la Seine would render more accurate statistics. These dossiers were in considerable disorder when the author attempted to use them.

[28] The Seine stands near the top, no. 76, in André Gain's table of the average value of the indemnities.

[29] "Liste par ordre alphabétique des émigrés . . . de Paris," Paris, an II. AD Pyrénées-Orientales, Q 730; and André Gain, *La Restauration et les biens des émigrés*, II, 210–211.

or in mutual opposition to create respectively impulsions, imperatives, or frustrations. The consequence was the social variegation of the emigration.

3. The Vocational Incidence

OUR general conception of the flight from France is now fixed, but we may amplify it by a brief study of the social anatomy of each of the several classes of emigrants (Table VIII). First in official rank, in numerical importance, and in the scale of the social incidence was the clergy. A great many of the ecclesiastics were literally ostracized, and though we have until now more or less ignored the distinction between émigrés and deportees, it was basic. There were four main categories of deportees: nonjurors who departed in compliance with the law of August 26, 1792; forcibly deported *réfractaires*; clerics of any sort, jurors or nonjurors, secular or regular, deported in consequence of denunciations by six citizens; and others deported by order of representatives on mission, or, after the coup d'état of the eighteenth of Fructidor, by decree of the Directory. The first group was by far the largest, comprising fully two-thirds of all the clergy carried on the emigration lists;[30] the second group, though next in importance, included at most three or four thousand ecclesiastics, and for most of these deportation actually consisted in detention in the environs of Rochefort or Bordeaux;[31] the last two groups were very small in France

---

[30] Concurring in the estimate of André Gain, *Liste des émigrés, déportés et condamnés ... de la Moselle*, II, 740. There is, however, some evidence that in certain regions at least the early ecclesiastic emigration was somewhat heavier than has been believed. See E. Sevestre, *Les problèmes religieux de la Révolution et de l'Empire en Normandie*, II, 793; and Élie Rossignol, *Les prêtres du Tarn persécutés pendant la Révolution*, 17–18.

[31] For lists of the forcibly deported clergy, based on archive sources, see Abbé Manseau, *Les prêtres et religieux déportées sur les côtes et dans les îles de la Charente-Inférieure* (2 vols.; Lille, 1886), II, 223–497. The total, including the clergy deported to Bordeaux (the title of the work is misleading on this point), is 3,693. Of these less than 300 (288 French clergy) were subsequently deported to French Guiana. Cf. Pierre Lemonnier, *Martyrologe de la déportation ecclésiastique à Rochefort-sur-Mer, 1794–1795* (Paris, 1917), *passim*; A. C. Sabatié, *La justice pendant la Révolution. La déportation révolutionnaire du clergé français* (2 vols.; Paris, s.d. [1917]), *passim*; and Jacques Herissay, *Les prêtres pendant la Terreur. Les pontons de Rochefort, 1792–1795* (Paris, 1925), *passim*. For the Fructidorian deportations see below, p. 102.

as a whole, though in certain departments they formed sizable parts of the local totals.[32] In addition to the banished clergymen, other clerics, under no legal compulsion, emigrated. The anti-Catholic and finally anti-Christian Republic of the Jacobins was intolerable to any priesthood. Indeed, the de-Christianizers scourged the clergy from some departments.[33] And, naturally, priests and monks were caught like others in the currents of panic that carried so many laymen into exile.

So much for the distinction. But how many of the ecclesiastic exiles were émigrés, and how many were deportees? Few of the official lists differentiate the two groups clearly or accurately, and the most intensive research by local scholars has produced only approximately exact results. Yet our information is sufficient to make it quite certain that the deportees were in the majority. In the Gard they constituted 91 per cent of the total,[34] in the Gers 90 per cent,[35] in Savoy 87 per cent.[36] Elsewhere their preponderance was less overwhelming—71 per cent in the Moselle,[37] 67 per cent in the Bouches-du-Rhône;[38] and in some of the theaters of turmoil, the Pyrénées-Orientales, for instance,[39] the deportees were in the minority. For France as a whole, however, the ratio of

[32] In the Meuse, for example, Mallarmé, representative on mission, ordered the deportation of 120 ecclesiastics, both constitutional and refractory (Jean Dubois, *Liste des émigrés . . . de la Meuse*, 11).

[33] Fouché in the Nièvre and in the Rhône, Couthon in the Puy-de-Dôme, Carrier in the Loire-Inférieure, Barras in the Bouches-du-Rhône, etc. Or, to cite a specific instance, on July 22, 1794, Hentz and Goujon, representatives on mission in the Moselle and the two Rhenish departments, ordered the arrest of *all priests*, including constitutionals, in the three departments (Félix Schaedelin, *L'émigration révolutionnaire du Haut-Rhin*, 36–37).

[34] François Rouvière, *Histoire de la Révolution française dans le Gard* (4 vols.; Nîmes, 1887–1889), II, 504–523; III, 445–464 (lists).

[35] AD Gers, Q 336 (lists); cf. P. Lamazoude, *La persécution contre le clergé du département du Gers sous la Révolution française* (Auch et Paris, 1879), 111ff.

[36] François Descostes, *Les émigrés en Savoie, à Aoste et dans le pays de Vaud, 1790–1800*, 40–175 (lists).

[37] André Gain, *Liste des émigrés . . . de la Moselle*, II, 739.

[38] Paul Moulins, *Documents relatifs à la vente des biens nationaux. Département des Bouches-du-Rhône* (4 vols.; Marseille, 1908–1911), I, xii.

[39] AD Pyrénées-Orientales, Q 734, and Q 532–729 (dossiers). About 100 deportees in a total of 482 clerical exiles. According to Philippe Sagnac, *loc. cit.*, pp. 109–110, there were only 61 nonjurors in the department in the spring of 1791.

deportees to émigrés appears to have been about five to one.[40] In other words, of our 24,596 classified clergy, 20,497 were deportees and 4,099 were emigrants. And if, as we have computed, the clerical exodus from all France totaled approximately 32,000, about 26,560 of these were banished while about 5,440 emigrated.[41]

The question of the rank and the order of the clergy can be dealt with more precisely. True, it is impossible to break down the entire classified First Estate, but our sources do permit an analysis of 20,791. As upper clergy we have classed bishops, other episcopal ◦dignitaries, such as grand vicars and canons, and abbots and priors. So defined, 2,298 or 11 per cent of the analysis group were of the upper hierarchy; the rest—18,493 priests, vicars, monks, and nuns

---

[40] Cf. André Gain, *Liste des émigrés . . . de la Moselle*, II, 740.

[41] Corroborative evidence supports these figures. First, the number of French clergy in foreign countries during the Revolution about equals our estimate of the total of clerical exiles (see below, pp. 94–95). Second, the number of deportees should approximately equal the number of nonjurors. True, the question of the division of the clergy is complicated and controversial. While the Pope, with Avignon at stake, delayed his condemnation of the Civil Constitution the French clerics had to decide for themselves, and, as all the monographs insist, a large number of the original jurors retracted after the papal briefs of March 18 and April 13, 1791. On the other hand, a certain number of priests took the oath belatedly, after the announcement of the deportation law (for cases, see Émile Queruau-Lamerie, *Le clergé du département du Maine-et-Loire pendant la Révolution*, 246; and E. Sevestre, *Les problèmes religieux de la Révolution en Normandie*, II, 793). Others retracted their retractions, and—complication of complications!—a few took the oath, retracted, took the oath again, and again retracted (for cases, see Émile Queruau-Lamerie, 124, 233–234). Finally, numerous clergy, including many regulars, *not* subject to the oath nevertheless swore it. In Paris, for instance, only 428 of the 628 jurors were required to take the oath (Augustin Sicard, *Le clergé de France pendant la Révolution* [2 vols.; Paris, 1927], II, 191). These difficulties in the way of an accurate estimation of jurors and nonjurors armed the critics of Sagnac's "Étude statistique . . ."—but in the end Sagnac's critics came very near to agreement. Pierre de La Gorce (*Histoire religieuse de la Révolution française* [5 vols.; Paris, 1909–1923], I, 398–399) decided that between 52 per cent and 55 per cent of the clergy refused the oath; Albert Mathiez (*Rome et clergé français sous la Constituante* [Paris, 1911], 468) concluded that about half of the secular clergy were nonjurors. Accepting Mathiez's estimate, there were about 30,000 *réfractaires* (60,000 priests subject to the oath). The law exempted from deportation the aged and the infirm, a provision which may have covered as many as 20 per cent (6,000) of the nonjurors. But some jurors and other clerics not subject to the oath were deported in consequence of denunciations or orders of representatives on mission. If we deduct the exempted and add the others, the number would be somewhere near our estimate of 26,560.

—were so-called lower clergy. Nearly the same percentages signify the proportions of the seculars (90 per cent) and the regulars (10 per cent). To determine precisely the incidence of the exodus for each of these categories probably is impossible, but it was very high, and in fact approached 100 per cent for the upper clergy;[42] it was much higher for the secular than for the regular, few of whom were affected by the deportation laws; and it was almost negligible for the nuns. Indeed, the very small number of nuns listed as émigrées (213) confronts us with a minor enigma. Nuns were numerous, aggregating perhaps 50,000, in eighteenth-century France,[43] and that so few of them emigrated seems incredible. We are forced to conclude that many emigrant sisters never were listed as such. When their orders were dissolved and their houses closed, they dispersed. Many of them returned to their families, some drew together in communal groups in the cities, but others disappeared, no doubt beyond the frontiers.[44] According to the letter of the law, these nuns should have been inscribed as émigrées, but since they had been evicted from their convents the authorities often carelessly or benignly (even the Jacobins were human!) assumed that they had gone to their homes.

The nobility, like the clergy, contributed sizable contingents to the emigration in all the departments. If we fix our attention on

---

[42] Only six old-regime bishops subscribed to the Civil Constitution. They were Talleyrand (Autun), Jarente (Orléans), Savine (Viviers), Gobel (Paris), Loménie de Brienne (Sens), and Du Bourg Miroudot (Babylone).

[43] The Abbé Expilly (*Dictionnaire géographique, historique et politique des Gaules et de la France* [6 vols.; Paris, 1762–1770], II, 365) estimated 80,000 nuns. His figure appears to have been much too high. Actually the religious orders were in decline during the eighteenth century, and Henri Sée (*La France économique et sociale au XVIIIe siècle*, 55) estimated only 60,000 *monks and nuns*.

[44] Victor Pierre, *Religieuses françaises en exil, 1791–1803* (Paris, 1903; first appeared in *Revue des questions historiques*, January, 1903), *passim*. "On peut dire que, proportionnellement au grand nombre des religieuses existant alors en France, celles qui se décidèrent à émigrer ne forment qu'une exception . . ." (p. 8). But in the course of his article, M. Pierre casually enumerates 120, including 36 from the single convent of Bellecourt at Lyon. See also François Rousseau, *Moines bénédictins martyrs et confesseurs de la foi pendant la Révolution* (Paris, 1926), 211ff.; and J. Peter and C. Poulet, *Histoire religieuse du département du Nord pendant la Révolution, 1789–1802* (2 vols.; Lille, 1930–1933), I, 243–246.

numbers rather than percentages, it is at once plain that the incidence of the clerical and aristocratic emigration was less variable than that of other classes. In only a few departments were less than one hundred clerics or nobles listed; no single department (with the possible exception of Paris) furnished as many as one thousand noble emigrants; and in only one (Mont-Blanc) can we be certain that the ecclesiastics exceeded that number.[45] Were we to study the inter-quartile range of figures for these classes, thus sloughing off the extremes, we should discover a remarkable constancy. Once more one must infer that the local circumstances which determined the patterns of the emigration as a whole affected the privileged classes less than others. The compulsion of law, of course, was a stabilizing element in the clerical emigration, but the evidence that there were more voluntary émigrés among the nobles than in any other group is now conclusive.

The procession of aristocrats was headed by the court nobility for whom even the France of the Estates General was contaminated, but they were followed by rank upon rank of provincial nobles. Especially conspicuous were the parliamentarians, whose pre-revolutionary pseudo-liberalism had turned into bitter reaction. Of the 2,000 members of the sovereign courts 872 (more than a third) emigrated.[46] Far more numerous than the parliamentarians, however, were the officers, who constituted 35 per cent (5,695) of the noble émigrés. Yet it is worth noting that even the noble emigration was predominately civilian, that 45 per cent (7,358) of the noble exiles were described as having no vocation other than that of living nobly. Nor were the women quite as numerous as is implied in the anecdotal versions of the emigration; they formed only 15 per cent (2,506) of the class total.

[45] Perhaps the Pas-de-Calais was another exception. See above p. 48, n. 18.

[46] Among them were 57 members of the *parlement* of Paris, 58 of the *parlement* of Dijon, 44 of the *parlement* of Toulouse, 42 of the *parlement* of Bordeaux, 40 of the *parlement* of Aix, 33 of the *parlement* of Besançon, and 104 of the *parlement* of Rouen, as well as smaller numbers from all the other *parlements* and *cours souveraines*. These figures, derived from my own tabulations, differ slightly from those given by Henri Carré, *La fin des parlements, 1788–1790* (Paris, 1912), 271–276. His total, however— "about one-third of the personnel of the courts," in other words about 800—corresponds to mine.

Our table of the vocational incidence discloses a much more detailed view of the émigrés of the Third Estate. Here the items speak for themselves, and we need do no more than italicize the salient facts. The upper middle class emigrants represented the official, the professional, and the business strata of French society. Almost a thousand (979) important functionaries emigrated. Two hundred and thirty of them were described merely as "administrators." For the most part they were federalist refugees; to the same group belonged the mayors (83), the municipal officers (38), and the secretaries of local administrations (55). Receivers (221), controllers (46), and inspectors (54) likewise bulked large in the total of functionaries: doubtless many of them were fugitives from the Nemesis of old regime grudges. The largest bourgeois category, however, was that of the professional men. Of these there were 2,683, almost two-thirds of whom (1,741) were lawyers or magistrates. Eighteenth-century France was a lawyer-ridden country, and the lawyers were inveterate politicians. Doctors and surgeons formed the second largest professional group (587), while delegations from the other professions were smaller. The world of business and finance contributed 896 emigrants, the majority of whom (645) were wholesale merchants. Less specifically described were 934 persons entered on the lists as "bourgeois" or "rentiers"; and twice as large (1,818, 17 per cent of the upper middle class) was the item composed of bourgeois officers. Finally, 1,525 or 14 per cent of the class were women.

In the lower middle class we encounter more diversity of vocation. About six hundred (564) of these emigrants were petty civil servants—clerks, scribes, supervisors. But the majority of the *petits bourgeois* were tradespeople. Those engaged in the clothing trades were in the plurality (706), and those in the food trades (589) ranked second. By far the largest single occupational group was that of the tailors (661), but the delegations of butchers, of bakers, of eating-house keepers, and of wig-makers also rose into three figures. In general, there was a fairly constant relationship between the number of persons engaged in any given occupation and the size of the corresponding item in our table, but doubtless the economic stress of the period affected certain vocations, wig-making, for example, more than others. The miscellany which concludes the catalogue of the class embraces a surprising number (248) of schoolteachers, a large representation of millers (165), as well as people of rarer occupations—three organists, for instance, and a handful of traveling salesmen. Many of the women either shared their husbands' work or were in business independently. Ninety-seven were qualified as "merchants," fifty-four as hotel or cabaret keepers, thirty-seven as butchers, twenty-seven as bakers, sixteen as hairdressers. In all, the women aggregated 19 per cent (1,135) of the lower middle class.

Passing to the vocational catalogue of the working class, we discover a complete array of the manual skills of the old regime, from the highest to the lowest, and, in addition, samplers of the jetsam of the social order. Every niche in this façade of proletarian France is filled. There are the aristocrats of the crafts—goldsmiths, glass blowers, armorers; there are the great fraternities of the builders, the textile workers, the metalsmiths; there is a mass of day laborers, another of servants; there is a panel of street merchants, from fish vendors to ragpickers; and in the lower depths of the scene are beggars, vagabonds, fools, bandits, convicts, and prostitutes.[47] The dust of a legend had concealed this façade; now it emerges in bold relief.

To enumerate its figures in detail would be to repeat the items of our table, but here at least emphasis demands some measure of reiteration. The builders alone—carpenters, masons, roofers—numbered 1,343; the textile workers, in majority weavers, were not far behind (1,104); the single craft of the shoemakers was represented by 677 emigrants, and the blacksmiths and wheelwrights totaled 353. Other large groups were those of the carters

---

[47] Examples: From the Lot, one Pascal, "vagabond," and a "gueux de profession," name illegible ("Relevé général des émigrés . . . du Lot," ms., 4 octobre 1793. AD Lot, Q 1); from Mont-Terrible, Joseph Tuiller, "imbécile" ("Liste générale des émigrés . . . du Mont-Terrible," 21 ventôse an II. AD Gironde, Q 1477); and from the Haut-Rhin, two convicts, fugitives from the prisons of the province (Félix Schaedelin, 89). The other convicts in our tables escaped from the galleys at Toulon during the fire set by the English as they evacuated the city in December, 1793.

and drivers (113), the earthenware workers (136), the garment makers, such as hatters and glovers (162), some of whom, incidentally, were quite wealthy, the leather workers (154), including tanners, harness-makers, saddlers; or, as single trades, the coopers (161) and the locksmiths (96). Hailing principally from coastal towns were fishermen (133), seamen (103), and dockyard workers (75), such as sail-makers and calkers.[48] And from everywhere in France came servants, the entire *valetaille* of an aristocratic society —coachmen, cooks, footmen, bodyguards—a regiment of 1,295. Apart from these principal groups, there were émigrés of many obscure or lowly vocations. As random examples, we find in our façade two cork-makers, two gelders, four chimney sweeps, four executioners, three grave diggers, three tobacco cutters. But even a list of oddities would be long, so comprehensive was the representation of the French masses.

Women were especially numerous, forming a total of 2,886 or 21 per cent of the class, and the crafts and conditions they represented were scarcely less diverse than those of the men. There were many (189) women textile workers—weavers, spinners, stocking-makers; a band of fifty seamstresses, a dozen washerwomen, a few wool carders, and over a hundred women who worked by the day. As one might expect, the largest single group (393) was that of the servants. Nor was the dross of society absent from the feminine emigration. Three women were described as beggars, and along with half a dozen "filles publiques" we have presumed to class a "vivandière de mauvaise vie."[49] Amazing but authentic, these scattered cases again prove that the social incidence of the emigration was ubiquitous.

Superficially, at least, the most uniform class of emigrants was the peasantry. But within the class there were cleavages which our sources dimly reveal. The amounts of property confiscated, ranging

[48] For example, 24 calkers and 14 sail-makers from Toulon alone (Louis Honoré, "L'émigration dans le Var," *Bulletin de la Société d'études . . . de Draguignan* [1923], XXXIV, 5-781, *passim*).

[49] André Gain, *Liste des émigrés . . . de la Moselle*, II, 760. There were also three women beggars ("mendiantes") from the Moselle.

from large holdings (in the Nord, for instance) to none at all (numerous cases in the Bas-Rhin) indicate that some of the peasants were comparatively wealthy, while others were poor or destitute. Broadly, then, both the landed peasantry and the rural proletariat participated in the emigration, and probably the latter group was the larger. Our data are too imprecise for a statistical analysis, but the predominance of the poorer peasantry is suggested by the low average indemnities accorded in the Bas-Rhin and the Pyrénées-Orientales,[50] the two departments of the heaviest peasant emigration. The feminine element, 25 per cent (4,687) of the class total, constituted a larger proportion than in any other class—an effect of the mass migrations produced by panic.

As for the émigrés of our last class, the 6,851 unidentifiables, we can only speculate concerning their social status. Yet it is plausible to assume that most of them were of humble rank. One indicative circumstance is that wherever the number of these nondescripts was high the proportion of lower class emigrants was suspiciously low. For example, in the Basses-Pyrénées, an invaded department, the unidentifiables amounted to 30 per cent of the émigrés, while the three lower classes aggregated only 19 per cent; and, a still more striking case, in the Charente, more than a little disturbed by the violence in the West, only $1\frac{1}{2}$ per cent of the emigrants were described as *petits bourgeois*, artisans, or peasants, but 37 per cent defy classification. For the rest, people of any local importance—nobles, clergy, doctors, lawyers, merchants—were more frequently identified in the emigration records than those of little or no social standing. And the lower ones goes in the social scale, the more numerous become the omissions of vocations or qualities. The obscure waif, propertyless and perhaps homeless, was of little interest to anyone. However, it is probable that fewer women than men in the no-status category were of the masses, for in general women of all classes were sketchily identified in the records.

[50] André Gain, *La Restauration et les biens des émigrés*, II, 202. The Bas-Rhin had the lowest average (3,458 francs) in France; the Pyrénées-Orientales was third from the bottom (13,731 francs).

Each of the constituent classes, then, formed an intricate pattern, but if the emigration was socially complex, it was predominantly civilian in composition. The military emigration, so conspicuous from first to last, at Coblenz, at Valmy, at Quiberon, at Ghent, comprised only ten per cent of the total volume. The myth of the red and the black thus may be laid to rest along with that of the white and the black. Of our classified émigrés, only 9,750 were officers, soldiers, or sailors (see Table I). The officers, of course, were in the majority (7,513 or 77 per cent), and the majority of the officers (5,695 or 76 per cent) were nobles, but 1,818 (24 per cent) of the commissioned men were bourgeois or recently ennobled. Common soldiers and sailors, however, constituted an important minority, almost one-fourth (2,237 or 23 per cent) of the classified military. Some of them, especially noncommissioned officers (for instance, those of the Dauphin-Cavalerie, stationed in the Haut-Rhin)[51] were influenced by their superiors, and in a few cases the latter were able to lead entire regiments into exile.[52] But most of the emigrant soldiers and sailors were spontaneous deserters or fugitives from conscription. Desertion from the revolutionary armies reached incredible proportions. Of 2,879 conscripts who set out from the Morbihan for Flanders in the autumn of 1793, 300 deserted at once, 1,200 disappeared before the troop reached Tours, and others decamped later.[53] By Prairial of the Year III virtually all of the volunteers of the Lozère had deserted.[54] And fugitive conscripts from frontier departments such as the Doubs, where conscription provoked the insurrection of August, 1793, or the Pyrénées-Orientales, where the attempt to enroll men synchronized with the Spanish invasion, were very numerous. Even quiet interior departments were not immune:

---

[51] L. Hartmann, *Les officiers de l'armée royale et la Révolution*, 436.

[52] Félix Schaedelin, 87.

[53] R. R. Palmer, *Twelve who ruled. The Committee of Public Safety during the Terror* (Princeton, 1941), 212.

[54] Gustave Vallée, *La conscription dans le département de la Charente, 1789–1807* (Paris, 1936), 12. By the end of the Year III the Army of Italy had lost two-thirds of its effectives through desertion. (François Vermale, "La désertion dans l'armée des Alpes après Thermidor," *Annales révolutionnaires* [1913], VI, 511).

for example, fourteen of the conscripts of the Tarn disappeared rather than accept military servcie.[55]

Finally, it is noteworthy that the emigration was overwhelmingly masculine. Eighty-five per cent (83,289) of our classified emigrants were men (Table I). Moreover, the majority of the émigrées hailed from a dozen exposed or turbulent departments. Were these regions to be excluded from our table, the percentage of women would sink about nine or ten points. Thus the compulsion of circumstances affected the feminine more than the masculine emigration, particularly among the lower classes, since very few peasant or artisan women emigrated from tranquil districts.

Perhaps still other views of the revolutionary emigration are implicit in the material of our tables, and those who seek may find. But the patterns we set out to discover are now amply clear. So, too, are the conclusions which impose themselves. In its ensemble the society of the emigration was a comprehensive representation of social France. It was also a mirror of political demography, for regionally its texture was determined by the environments of the Revolution. The inferences follow inescapably. Most of the nobles who left France were deliberate expatriates; most of the clergy were ostracized; and most of the men and women of the masses were fugitives driven by fear, despair, or panic.

[55] AD Tarn, Q 451–452 (lists). Specific examples are numerous: Gabriel Roche, a peasant of the Corrèze, deserted while en route to join the Army of the Rhine (Victor Forot, *Les émigrés corrèziens avec la nomenclature et la valeur de leurs biens séquestrés*, 173); Tarrion, cook by profession in the Côte-d'Or, mounted chasseur in the army, decamped with his "horse, arms and baggage" ("Dixième liste [des émigrés de la Côte-d'Or]," 29 frimaire an II. AD Côte-d'Or, Q 515).

CHAPTER V

CONCLUSION

1. The Émigrés Abroad

THE ODYSSEYS of the emigration lie beyond the scope of our study. Some of the emigrants traveled far in the world—to Africa, to Asia, to the United States. The American contingent, augmented by the Creoles driven out of Santo Domingo by the black rebellion, was quite large, well over ten thousand. They began to arrive in 1792, and in the following years "thousands upon thousands of Frenchmen crowded into the American seaboard towns."[1] But this immigration was not confined to the East. One group formed a project to found a new city, Gallipolis, on the Ohio, and some six hundred of them not only reached the Ohio wilderness but survived in it.[2] They were people of humble rank, and a fair proportion of the émigrés in the East were artisans and shopkeepers. The majority of those from metropolitan France, however, were aristocrats. Among them were some notable figures— Talleyrand, Chateaubriand, the Duc de Chartres (future Louis Philippe), and if the impress of America is not discernible in the cynic it is clear enough in the poet and in the king.

Most of the émigrés, however, clustered around France. Nice, until its conquest by the French, harbored several thousand of

[1] Frances S. Childs, *French Refugee Life in the United States, 1790–1800* (Baltimore, 1940), 10. Cf. Henri Carré, "Les émigrés français en Amérique, 1789–1793," *Revue de Paris, année* 1898, vol. III, pp. 311–340.
[2] Marcus Hansen, *The Atlantic Migration* (Cambridge, 1941), 57–58. Cf., principally for the émigrés in the state of New York, Thomas Wood Clarke, *Émigrés in the Wilderness* (New York, 1941), *passim*, esp. 28–84.

them, and when Anselme's descent upon the county drove them out they went to Italy, there joining many of their compatriots.[3] Switzerland, from the first, was a *terre d'élection* for the émigrés. Perhaps 5,000 of them gathered in the canton of Fribourg,[4] and the records of Lausanne reveal that at least 1,165 resided in the city between 1794 and 1797.[5] The Rhineland was full of them: more than 20,000 crowded into Coblenz and Mannheim; at least another 5,000 dispersed in Franconia and Bavaria;[6] and, though Prussia banned them, they congregated in other parts of Germany, especially in Hamburg.[7] Many of the émigrés of northern and eastern France went first to the Austrian Netherlands,[8] whence, of course, they were compelled to flee again when the French arrived in 1793. But England was the principal refuge for the emigrants of the Channel region, receiving thousands of them.[9] Nor were the Channel Islands neglected. Between 3,500 and 4,000 took refuge in Jersey,[10] and, though not so many went to Guernsey,

[3] Georges Doublet, "Marins et magistrats provençaux émigrés à Nice lors de la Révolution," *Mémoires de l'Institut historique de Provence* (1924), I, 136–150; "Émigrés provençaux à Nice, 1789–1792," *ibid.* (1925), II, 80–94; (1927) IV, 152–162; (1928) V, 226–238; "L'émigration française à Nice de 1789 à 1792," *Nice historique* (1928), XXXI, 7–13, 59–64, 122–135, 190–200; (1929) XXXII, 1–19.

[4] Tobie de Raemy, *L'émigration française dans le canton de Fribourg, 1789–1798* (Fribourg, 1935), 77–78; Comte de Sainte-Colombe, *Catalogue des émigrés français à Fribourg en Suisse de 1789 à 1798* (Lyon, 1884), *passim* (a list of 264 names; obviously incomplete).

[5] François Descostes, *Les émigrés en Savoie . . .*, 267–347 (lists).

[6] Pierre de Vaissière, *À Coblence ou les émigrés français dans les pays rhenans de 1789 à 1792* (Paris, 1924), *passim*; René Bittard des Portes, *Histoire de l'armée de Condé, 1791–1801* (Paris, 1896), appendix and *passim;* Wilhelm Wühr, *Die Emigranten der Französischen Revolution im bäyerischen und frankischen Kreis. Mit dem Verzeichnis aller im Gebiet des rechtsreinischen Baherns festgestellten Emigranten* (Munich, 1938), 259–581 (lists).

[7] "Les émigrés à Hambourg," *Feuilles d'histoire* (1911), V, 519–520.

[8] Félix Magnette, *Les émigrés français aux Pays-Bas, 1789–1794* (Brussels, 1907), *passim*; Ferdinand Courtoy, "Les émigrés français dans le Namurois, 1789–1794," *Annales du Cercle archéologique de Namur* (1923), LX, 245–288; "Les émigrés à Bruxelles," *Revue des documents historiques* (1880), II, 81–86.

[9] Émile Gabory, *L'Angleterre et la Vendée*, I, ch. 1, and *passim*; Jules Bertaut, "Les émigrés français à Londres sous la Révolution," *Le monde nouveau* (1923), VII, 183–184.

[10] Regis de L'Estourbeillon, *Les familles françaises à Jersey pendant la Révolution*, 2, 4–5, 268–480.

four companies of émigré troops were formed there.[11] Spain was an asylum for many of the exiles of the Southwest; the Spanish authorities at Puigcerda, on the frontier opposite Cerdagne, recorded the entrance of 1,284, and they represented but a small part of the influx.[12] Completing the cordon, the French consuls in Minorca and Majorca in 1797 and 1798 reported that 243 of the expatriates had resided in the islands.[13]

Vague or fragmentary though these estimates are, they give some support to our conclusion that the revolutionary emigration involved about 130,000 persons. In regard to the clergy we can go a step further, for the number of French priests in foreign lands during the period has been rather accurately determined. There were 10,000 in the British Isles (including those in Jersey and Guernsey),[14] 7,000 in Spain,[15] about 4,000 in Italy (including 2,000 in the Papal States),[16] 6,000 in Switzerland,[17] about 5,000 in Germany (including many driven from the Low Countries by the French invasions),[18] and perhaps 1,000 elsewhere (including

---

[11] Charles Hettier, *Relations de la Normandie et de la Bretagne avec les îles de la Manche pendant l'émigration*, 238–271.

[12] "Tableau alphabétique des noms d'émigrés pris sur le registre espagnol de Puigcerda . . . dressé par les authorités espagnols au passage des émigrés entrés en Espagne par la Cerdagne," s.d. AD Pyrénées-Orientales, Q 740.

[13] "Liste des émigrés et prêtres réfractaires qui ont résidé aux îles de Minorque et Marjorque tirés de la correspondence des consuls de la République pendant les années V et VI," Ventôse an VII. AD Indre, Q 553.

[14] F. X. Plasse, *Le clergé français réfugié en Angleterre* (2 vols.; Paris, 1886), II, 408–443 (lists) and *passim*. Cf. Ernest Daudet, *Histoire de l'émigration pendant la Révolution française*, I, 288 (for an estimate of 12,000).

[15] J. Contrasty, *Le clergé français exilé en Espagne, 1792–1802* (Toulouse, 1910), 96–98.

[16] E. Audard, *Les actes des martyrs et des confesseurs de la foi pendant la Révolution* (3 vols.; Tours, 1920–1923), I, appendix. Cf. J. Contrasty, 98; and Victor Pierre, *Le clergé français dans les États pontificaux* (Paris, 1902, first appeared in *Revue des Questions historiques*, January, 1902), *passim*.

[17] L. Jérôme, *Collectes à travers l'Europe pour les prêtres français déportés en Suisse pendant la Révolution, 1794–1797* (Paris, 1897), 7, 381; Tobie de Raemy, 77 (2,000 to 3,000 at Fribourg alone); Victor Pierre, *L'émigration française à Fribourg* (Paris, 1896; first appeared in *Revue des Questions historiques*, January, 1896), 10.

[18] Victor Pierre, *Le clergé français en Allemagne* (Paris, 1899; first appeared in *Revue des Questions historiques*, January, 1898), *passim*; J. Contrasty, 98; Wilhelm Wühr, 259–581; and A. Frézet, "Liste des prêtres français réfugiés à Liége en 1793

a few in the United States).[19] This total of clerical immigrants thus reaches 33,000 and approximately correlates with our estimation of 32,000 clerical emigrants. And since the equation is demonstrable for the clergy, it is fair to assume that it exists for the other classes of émigrés, and hence for the ensemble.

Leaving aside the question of totals, scraps of information in hand fit into the patterns that have emerged from our tabular analyses. For example, 76½ per cent of the 1,806 emigrants of Savoy (Mont-Blanc) belonged to the privileged orders, 21 per cent to the Third Estate, and of the 239 known Savoyard immigrants at Lausanne 71½ per cent were *privilégiés*, 19½ per cent commoners.[20] Another instance: in the Pyrénées-Orientales, a department of heavy Third Estate emigration, peasants and artisans comprised 55 per cent of the total, the middle classes 15 per cent; of the lay immigrants recorded in the registers of the Spanish authorities at Puigcerda, facing the departmental frontier, 70 per cent were peasants or artisans, 15 per cent bourgeois.[21] Or to single out one group: we have seen that the vocational incidence of the emigration was high in the serving class, and there were 154 French servants (65 men and 89 women) in the canton of Fribourg alone.[22] Again, citing a different sort of case, the émigrés captured and executed at Quiberon in 1795 were by no means all nobles; on the contrary, of the 748 victims of the military commission 280 (37½ per cent) were peasants or workmen and 54 (7 per cent) were bourgeois,[23] and these proportions relate to the demography of the western emigration. Still other data, less conclusive or more general in bearing, could be invoked. For instance, in the Balearic Islands, where one might expect to find only noble or ecclesiastic refugees,

---

et 1794," *Revue d'histoire de l'église de France* (1934), XX, 230–242 (815 priests were at Liége).

[19] C. Moreau, *Les prêtres français émigrés aux États-Unis* (Paris, 1856), *passim*.

[20] François Descostes, 332–347 (lists).

[21] AD Pyrénées-Orientales, Q 740 ("Table alphabétique . . . ," as cited above, note 12).

[22] Tobie de Raemy, 76–77.

[23] Thomas de Closmadeuc, *Quiberon, 1795* (Paris, 1898), 575–597 (list) Cf. Le Garrec, Chanoine, *Les vrais martyrs de Quiberon* (Vannes, 1935), *passim*.

at least 17 per cent (42) of the French immigrants of the period were of the Third Estate.[24] Straws in the wind these few cases may be, but they all point in the same direction: all that we can learn about the émigrés abroad confirms what we have learned about them within France.

How these exiles lived abroad does not concern us, but how many of them died abroad is relevant. Again, however, we have only straws in the wind to guide us. It is known that 4 per cent (217) of the émigrés of the Var and approximately the same proportion (164, or just under 4 per cent) of those of the Moselle died on foreign soil, but in both cases the casualties were probably twice the recorded number.[25] Furthermore, the death rate among the clergy as a whole certainly was much higher. Well over a thousand technical deportees perished in the prison ships at Aix and at Blaye and in the prisons of Bordeaux;[26] and perhaps four or five times as many died in exile.[27] To adduce one example, only 316 or 65 per cent of the proscribed priests of the Pyrénées-Orientales survived to return to France.[28] In the light of these indications one might hazard the guess that 10 per cent of all the exiles died abroad.

2. The Return of the Émigrés

THE revolutionary emigration was unique in that the vast majority of the émigrés returned to France. The reflux began immediately

---

[24] AD Indre, Q 553 ("Liste des émigrés . . . qui ont résidé aux îles de Minorque et Majorque . . .," as cited above, note 13).

[25] Louis Honoré, "L'émigration dans le Var . . . ," *Bulletin de la Société d'études . . . de Draguignan* (1923), XXXIV, 147–149, André Gain, *Liste des émigrés . . . de la Moselle*, II, 769–772.

[26] Abbé Manseau, *Les prêtres et religieux déportés sur les côtes et dans les îles de la Charente-Inférieure*, II, 223–497 (lists); A. C. Sabatié, *La justice pendant la Révolution. La déportation révolutionnaire du clergé français*, II, 327–348 (lists).

[27] The martyrologies are too numerous to cite and too unscientific to serve as a basis for statistics. Among the leading works are those cited in the Bibliography under "Clergy" (pp. 139–140). In addition, many of the local studies, such as Émile Querrau-Lamerie, *Le clergé du département du Maine-et-Loire pendant la Révolution*, indicate the fate of the clergy for specific regions.

[28] Philippe Torreilles, *Histoire du Clergé dans le département des Pyrénées-Orientales pendant la Révolution française* (Perpignan, 1890), 580. Abbé Torreilles, however,

after Thermidor. The penal legislation still was intact; indeed the law of November 15, 1794, was a revised and much improved edition of that of March 28, 1793.[29] But, as Doulcet de Pontécoulant, returning in August, wrote, "The fall of the tyrant was feted as the signal of deliverance."[30] The poor, the ignorant, and the bold—peasants of Alsace, workmen of Provence, bourgeois and nobles of Normandy—returned first. Some came openly, some in disguise, some equipped with forged papers, and all were favored by the confusion and complaisance of the Thermidorian administration. As the number of returned exiles increased, they established agencies in the cities, such as Paris, Lyon, Marseille, Orleans, and Caen, for the manufacture of spurious evidence of non-emigration, ranging from hospital receipts to certificates of residence and passports.[31] Quantity production of the last soon brought the price down to ten francs each and made them available to almost anyone. Many of the forgeries were extremely crude, with all the visas in the same handwriting and the same ink[32] but they appear to have been generally accepted by the Thermidorian authorities.

So, fraud and complaisance first breached the barriers against the émigrés, but soon the legal bars themselves were lowered. On December 19, 1794, the Convention authorized emigrant naval officers and sailors to return provided that, once repatriated, they embark immediately on fighting ships of the Republic. Less than a month later (January 11, 1795) the assembly offered an amnesty to manual workers, peasants or artisans, who had emigrated after

believed that there were nearly a thousand clerical émigrés or déportés from the department.

[29] Marcel Ragon, La législation sur les émigrés, 1789–1825, 249–276 (text).

[30] Comte de Pontécoulant, Souvenirs historiques et parlementaires (4 vols.; Paris, 1861–1865), I, 284.

[31] AD Deux-Sèvres, L 72 (The Departmental Directory to the cantonal administrations, 22 ventôse an V); Archives des Affaires étrangères. France et divers pays d'Europe. Mémoires et documents, no. 518, p. 175 (evidence that some French consuls abroad falsified passports); Charles Ballot, Le coup d'état du 18 fructidor an V (Paris, 1906), 45.

[32] Marc Bouloiseau, Le séquestre et la vente des biens des émigrés dans le district de Rouen, 1792–an X, 264–265.

May 1, 1793, on condition that they regain French soil before March 21 (1 Germinal an III). In principle this measure pardoned over forty thousand persons; in practice only a small portion of them were able to take advantage of it. The time limit, sixty-eight days, was too short. What happened in the case of the émigrés of Alsace is important, though possibly not altogether typical. Dispersed in southern Germany, they received news of the amnesty tardily, or not at all. En route for France they were delayed by German authorities. Some of them reached the Rhine after the expiration of the time limit. Others arrived at Germersheim only to find that the crossing point designated by the French had been changed to Kehl; after going to Kehl they were told to go to Huningue; and when they reached Huningue it was too late. Still others, the majority, it seems, did congregate opposite Huningue a few days before March 21. But their only means of crossing the Rhine was in small boats; the boatmen demanded high prices; and once across the river, the French officials turned some of them back because they could not prove their status as manual workers.[33] The result was that relatively few of them reentered France before the prescribed date. In the department of the Bas-Rhin the number may have exceeded a thousand; in the Haut-Rhin, with its smaller volume of emigration, the records show that 223 persons benefited from the amnesty.[34] Nor does it appear that the proportion of beneficiaries was higher elsewhere. In the Pyrénées-Orientales, for example, with its mass of exiled laborers, only 316 were repatriated in virtue of the amnesty.[35]

Nevertheless, many manual workers, ignorant or defiant of the temporal limitation, returned later, in the aura of the law, as it were, and despite official fulminations the authorities were lenient. They were also liberal in issuing certificates of vocation to bour-

[33] Marcel Marion, "Les fugitifs alsaciens sous la Révolution," *Revue historique* (1923), CXLII, 217.

[34] Félix Schaedelin, *L'émigration révolutionnaire du Haut-Rhin*, 43. He adds: "Il y eu assurément beaucoup plus."

[35] "Liste des individus inscrits sur la liste des émigrés qui ont été admis par les administrations de district ou de département à jouir de la faveur des lois des 22 nivôse et 4e jour complémentaire an III," ms., s.d. AD Pyrénées-Orientales, Q 746.

geois, or even to nobles and priests, who suddenly discovered for themselves manual callings.[36] Such free interpretation compensated for the restrictive features of the amnesty. Nor was official conciliation yet at an end. On April 11, 1795, the Convention repealed the decrees outlawing federalists and specifically authorized them to return to their homes. Émigrés of all classes posing as federalists now rushed upon France. The abuses of the pardon were so flagrant that on June 10 the Convention attempted to restrict it to bona fide federalists, and on September 6 the assembly excluded from its benefits the rebels of Toulon. But leniency and its abuse had already enabled thousands of émigrés to reenter France. In the Var, at least, most of the unprivileged emigrants had returned by September, 1795.[37] Moreover, the fugitives from a large section of the West were briefly favored by the pacifications of La Jaunaye and Mabilais, which accorded them virtual pardon. True, the peace was soon broken and the treaties lapsed, but meanwhile there was an influx of émigrés in the region of the Vendean war. For other regions the evidence is scant, but probably a heavy proportion of all the Third Estate exiles had come home by the end of 1795 in virtue of or in defiance of the laws.

The returning émigrés who dispensed with all legal, or pseudo-legal, formalities were outlaws. Yet grace to the tolerance of the authorities, many of them could live unmolested in their own communes. Others resided under assumed names in the cities or wandered uneasily from place to place, and a few became "chauffeurs"—that is, gentlemen highwaymen. Some joined the *chouan* bands in the West or enrolled in the "Companies of Jesus" or "Companies of the Sun," instruments of the White Terror in the Southeast. For example, two refractory priests, Jauffret and Martinet, and a lay émigré, Lieutaud, were leaders of the notorious band of Aubagne (Bouches-du-Rhône), which spread its criminal exploits from the Rhône to Nice.[38] Another band, with its head-

---

[36] Louis Honoré, *loc. cit.*, pp. 80–88; Félix Schaedelin, 43; Marcel Marion, *loc. cit.*, p. 219; and most of the other local monographs on the emigration.

[37] Louis Honoré, *loc. cit.*, pp. 86–87.

[38] Paul Gaffarel, "La bande d'Aubagne," *Annales de Provence* (1920), XVII, 75–76.

quarters at Pourrières, in the Var, comprised close to a thousand émigrés,[39] and still other "companies" existed throughout the Rhône valley from Marseille to Lyon. Their depredations equaled in quality if not in quantity the atrocities of the Red Terror. "They killed patriots as they killed thrushes in the fields," remarked Durand de Maillane, "whenever and wherever they came across them."[40]

Complete reaction, such as even the Thermidorians had not permitted, now threatened France, and even they recoiled. The captured participants in the Quiberon expedition of July, 1795, were punished with a ruthlessness that matched that of the heroic days of the Republic. The perpetual banishment of the émigrés and the *réfractaires*, without any more exceptions, was embodied in the Constitution of the Year III (1795); they were excluded from the general amnesty of October 26, 1795, and their relatives were barred from public office. The National Convention, republican even in its degeneration, wrote its testament in these acts of definitive ostracism.

Legal barriers, however, were of little avail when confided to apathetic authorities. During the early years of the Directory the reflux of the emigration continued, rising to flood tide in 1797. This strong sweep was in part consequence, in part cause of the royalist reaction which threatened the Republic in the Year V of its existence. On December 2, 1796, the law of October 25, 1795, the last rampart built by the Convention against the émigrés, was modified, and on June 27, 1797, after the anti-republican victory in the elections of the spring, its repressive articles were repealed. Though still proscribed, the exiles were emboldened. Crowds of clergy flocked back to France. A single ship from Ragusa debarked one hundred and fifty at Marseille; eight hundred at one time returned by way of Jersey from England; hundreds embarked for France at Cadiz, Santander, and Leghorn; throngs crossed the

---

[39] *Ibid.*, 85; Louis Honoré, *loc. cit.*, pp. 91–93.

[40] Quoted by Albert Mathiez, *After Robespierre: The Thermidorian Reaction* (Eng. tr.; New York, 1931), 196. Mathiez insisted (ch. 11, esp. p. 180) that the relaxation of the legislation concerning the émigrés was the principal cause of the White Terror.

Pyrenees from Spain into the department of the Ariège.[41] By midsummer between twelve and thirteen thousand deportees had reentered the country.[42] Finally, on August 24, the Councils repealed en bloc the legislation affecting nonjurors, recalled them to France, and restored to them full political and civil rights. This measure, it is true, had little effect, for its abrogation only twelve days after its passage was a part of the coup d'état of the eighteenth of Fructidor. By then, however, perhaps half of the banished clergy had returned.

As for the lay émigrés, they returned in hordes. "From every side," wrote Sotin, Minister of Police in 1797, "émigrés of both sexes precipitated themselves onto the territory of the Republic as they rushed to Coblenz in 1790 and 1791."[43] Seventeen thousand of them had obtained provisional cancellation, and no one knows how many more returned surreptitiously. They virtually monopolized certain cafés in Paris; they appeared in bands in Rouen; they owned, so to speak, the keys to Lyon. No one molested them. "You are in no more danger here," wrote one of them from Lyon to a friend still abroad, "than in your own room."[44] Some of them dared to bargain with the authorities for their cancellation, which would enable them to recover their unsold property. For instance, Robert Bigot, the son of a parliamentarian of Rouen, offered the proper officials in the Ministry of Police forty thousand francs; they asked eighty thousand.[45] The number and the audacity of the émigrés within France was an ill omen for the Republic, and apparently it was understood, for not one sale of national property was recorded between March and September, 1797.[46]

---

[41] Antoine Bernard, "Le 18 fructidor à Marseille et dans les Bouches-du-Rhône," *La Révolution française* (1901), XLI, 198; Albert Meynier, *Les coups d'état du Directoire. Le dix-huit fructidor an V* (Paris, 1928), 95.

[42] Albert Mathiez, "Le coup d'état du 18 fructidor," *Annales historiques de la Révolution française* (1929), VI, 527.

[43] Charles Ballot, 161.

[44] Victor Pierre, *La Terreur sous le Directoire. Histoire du persécution politique et religieuse après le coup d'état du 18 fructidor* . . . (Paris, 1887), 105.

[45] Marc Bouloiseau, *Le séquestre et la vente des biens des émigrés*, 270.

[46] Albert Mathiez, "Le coup d'état du 18 fructidor," *Annales historiques de la Révolution française* (1929), VI, 526.

The sands were running out when the coup d'état of the eighteenth of Fructidor not only saved the Republic but also abruptly reversed the flux of the emigration. The law passed by the rump legislature on the following day was a reversion to the spirit of '93. It revived the proscriptive legislation, ordered the departure from France within fifteen days of the *réfractaires* and the émigrés who had not obtained definitive cancellation, authorized the Directory to deport priests who disturbed the peace, and established military commissions to pass mandatory death sentence on the recalcitrant. The government demanded literal enforcement of the law, which meant, of course, that innocent persons erroneously listed as émigrés but not definitely canceled were liable to death if they did not emigrate.[47] Likewise menaced were the manual workers amnestied but not canceled in 1795, and, sure enough, Sotin ordered their arrest in Alsace, Flanders, and Provence, where they were most numerous.[48] Furthermore, during the next eighteen months, the Directory, in virtue of its power to deport clergy, condemned 1,701 French priests to exile.[49] At the same time, the military commissions instituted in Paris and in the principal provincial cities rendered 160 death sentences.[50] The "Fructidorian Terror," then, was not merely an emulative gesture. Quite the contrary, it precipitated a reemigration of vast proportions. As divers examples, 300 provisionally canceled émigrés quickly left the Haut-Rhin;[51] over a hundred were proscribed in the single district of Rouen;[52] and the flight from Provence, where 15,000 persons, many of whom were returned émigrés, went from Mar-

---

[47] Marc Bouloiseau, *Le séquestre et la vente des biens des émigrés*, 271, points out that Fructidor thus created new émigrés.

[48] Victor Pierre, *La Terreur sous le Directoire*, 106.

[49] *Ibid.*, 459–461. Of the 1,701 sentenced, 705 were not deported; 323 were sent to Guiana, 607 to the island of Ré, and 66 to the island of Oleron. In addition to the French clergy, 8,225 Belgian priests and 2 from the Rhineland were sentenced, though the vast majority of them (7,847) were not deported. Cf. for slightly different figures; Victor Pierre, *La déportation ecclésiastique sous le Directoire . . .* (Paris, 1896), pp. xxxi–xxxii, 461–481.

[50] Victor Pierre, *La Terreur sous le Directoire*, pp. xxiv, 164.

[51] Félix Schaedelin, 58.

[52] Marc Bouloiseau, *Le séquestre et la vente des biens des émigrés*, 271.

seille in a few days,[53] was enormous. Comprehensive statistics are not available, but if the Fructidorian repression did not empty France of émigrés, it at least drove them to cover.

Yet this repression, like those of other years, waned in a few months, and by 1799 the émigrés again were slipping into the country. The current was especially noticeable after the coup d'état of the thirtieth of Prairial an VII (June 18, 1799), which further discredited the Directory. Once more the émigrés invaded Provence, cried "à bas les Jacobins" in the streets of Rouen, and disported themselves in the select Parisian cafés. By midsummer counterrevolutionary anarchy was rampant in the West and the South, and the Republic *in extremis* turned at bay. On July 12, 1799, the Councils adopted the Law of Hostages. The relatives of émigrés and ex-nobles were accused of complicity in the disorders; from these groups hostages were to be taken in each troubled department; and for each patriot or functionary assassinated, four hostages were to be deported. Unenforced, the Law of Hostages was hardly more than a gesture, an enervated expression of the republican will to survive. But if the Jacobins of 1799 were not the Jacobins of 1793, they alone, in a situation rapidly degenerating into disaster, placed the safety of the Republic above all other considerations.

Then Bonaparte came, and the fateful dusk of the nineteenth of Brumaire settled over the last session of the Legislative Councils at Saint-Cloud. To the émigrés the omen was unmistakable. They poured over all the frontiers. "They are returning," wrote an official of the Bas-Rhin, "with all the trust and candor of innocence." When arrested they asked to be taken to Bonaparte. "He will see that we are good citizens," they said.[54] Their faith was not misplaced. The consular decree of March 3, 1800, closed the lists as of December 25, 1799, thus implicitly abrogating the legislation prohibiting emigration. The ban on the exiles remained in force; indeed, the Constitution of December 13, 1799, repeated

[53] Antoine Bernard, *loc. cit.*, pp. 200–201.
[54] Marcel Marion, "Les fugitifs alsaciens sous la Révolution," *Revue Historique* (1923), CXLIII, 225.

almost word for word the clauses of the Constitution of 1795 banishing the émigrés. But who now feared the withering laws? So, at the turn of the century the tide of the emigration turned for the last time, and very likely the great majority of the émigrés were in France by the autumn of 1800.

Still, however, they were outside the law. Only persons who had proved, often by fraud, to the facile satisfaction of the authorities that they had not emigrated had obtained cancellation. Of the two steps entailed, provisional cancellation by local administrations and its confirmation by the central government, the second was the more difficult. Very few definitive cancellations were accorded during the Convention: 25 in the Indre-et-Loire[55] (551 émigrés), 44 in the Pyrénées-Orientales[56] (3,854 émigrés), 156, a somewhat larger proportion, in Paris[57] (2,069 émigrés). The Directory proceeded faster, but by 1799 the ban had been lifted in only about 13,000 cases. The incidence of this dubious justice was very uneven, scaling downward from a fourth to a twentieth of local emigration totals. In the Ardennes the canceled and the amnestied represented 25 per cent (360) of the local émigrés,[58] in the Charente 12 per cent (74),[59] in the Pyrénées-Orientales 9 per cent (360),[60] in the Indre-et-Loire 7 per cent (41),[61] in the Ille-et-Vilaine 5 per cent (112).[62] The average of these five departments was 11 per cent, according approximately with the proportion of one-tenth (13,000) for the country as a whole.

[55] "État nominatif des noms . . . des individus portés sur la liste . . . des émigrés . . . qui ont été rayés définitivement," s.d. AD Indre-et-Loire, Q unclassified.

[56] "Liste des émigrés . . . des Pyrénées-Orientales qui ont obtenu des arrêts [de radiation] . . .," 11 prairial an II. AD Pyrénées-Orientales, Q 746.

[57] "Noms des individus . . . de la Seine qui ont été rayés définitivement de la liste des émigrés," s.d. [1795], BN, 8° La[34] 28.

[58] "Tableau contenant les noms des personnes qui ont obtenu du Directoire exécutif les arrêts de radiation de la liste des émigrés," s.d. [1799?]. AD Ardennes, Q 625.

[59] "Liste alphabétique des émigrés [de la Charente] rayés ou amnistiés," ms., s.d. [an X?]. AD Charente, Q[xx] 1.

[60] AD Pyrénées-Orientales, Q 746 (Divers lists and dossiers. See Bibliography under "Pyrénées-Orientales").

[61] AD Indre-et-Loire, Q unclassified (dossiers).

[62] E. Tanguy, "L'émigration dans l'Ille-et-Vilaine et la vente des biens nationaux de 2e origine," *Annales de Bretagne* (1906), XXI, 162.

The legal repatriation of the émigrés, then, was essentially Bonaparte's work. The commission which he established in March, 1800, to expedite cancellations struck twelve hundred names from the rolls. His partial, and, incidentally, unconstitutional amnesty of October 20, 1800, readmitted the peasants, the artisans, the deported clergy, most of the women of all classes, and all children under sixteen—fifty-two thousand persons, according to Bonaparte himself. So to the general amnesty of April 26, 1802 (the senatus-consulte of 6 floréal an X). The exceptions, not to exceed one thousand in all, covered the notorious leaders of the military emigration, rebel chieftains, the Bourbons and their agents, and the prelates who rejected the Concordat. All the others were offered complete repatriation provided that they pledged loyalty to Bonaparte's government.

Thus, after a decade of proscription, was the slate wiped clean. And thus, after a decade of struggle, did the last republican rampart fall. We now know that the majority of the émigrés were victims of circumstance; to the obviously innocent among them the Thermidorian Convention had beckoned briefly to return. We know, too, that the minority represented the France of the reaction; with them neither the Convention nor the Directory had compromised, and when Bonaparte threw open the flood gates his star had eclipsed the Republic.

3. The Slough of a Revolution

In sharp silhouettes statistics have told us what they could of the emigration—its volume, its incidences, its modalities. From these have emerged our interpretations, necessarily products of circumstantial evidence rather than direct testimony. The hard material of statistics mutes the human voices of the past. The émigrés have not been heard. Nor can there be any question now of evoking their clamor. Yet concerning one basic matter, that of motivation, we shall consult them briefly and they shall tell us in accents of disdain, fanaticism, or fear why they emigrated. The Marquis d'Autichamp, an officer in the royal army, deserted and emigrated after the fall of the Bastille because, he said, it was impossible to remain longer in the King's service "without debasing and dishonoring oneself."[63] The Abbé Pelletier, a nonjuror of the Indre, preferred deportation in 1792 to "an eternity of damnation."[64] Joseph Barry, a carter of Toulon, fled in December, 1793, because "the bombs were raining down"; Raymond Roque, a retail merchant, sought escape "from the fire which raged in part of the city"; and Amiel Mathieu, a ship's captain, joined in the flight simply "par l'effet de la frayeur."[65] The nobleman who abhorred the Revolution, the priest who would not compromise with heresy, the townsmen of a bombed and burning city represented thousands of their kind.

Other Frenchmen emigrated for miscellaneous reasons, different from any we have mentioned. The economic crisis that preceded and accompanied the Revolution influenced the movement in a number of ways. In frontier districts, such as Alsace, people crossed the border to sell their produce for better money than the assignats or to buy in the well stocked shops where no *maximum* drove commodities from the market.[66] When they attempted to return, as most of them did, they often found the frontier closed. Some of the numerous artisans thrown out of work by the crisis emigrated in quest of a livelihood. As early as November, 1789, for instance, two silk workers of Lyon recommended their "rare talents"—"the best mottlers that there are in England and in France"—to the municipal council of Barcelona, where, they wrote, they intended to establish themselves.[67] Necessity aside, many workmen, accustomed to seasonal tours, attached no importance to crossing frontiers, perhaps even ignored their exact location. This was especially true of the itinerant artisans of the border regions. Such, no doubt, were the two Jewish peddlers who appeared at Lausanne in July, 1794, and to the same category belonged the band of roving knife grinders executed for emigration in the Pas-de-Calais during

[63] L. Hartmann, *Les officiers de l'armée royale et la Révolution*, 119.

[64] AD Indre, Q 775 (dossier).

[65] Louis Honoré, *loc. cit.*, pp. 404, 50, 501, respectively.

[66] Félix Schaedelin, 35.

[67] Joseph Calmette, "Émigrants lyonnais à Barcelone en 1789," *Annales du Midi* (1926), XXXVIII, 431-433.

the Terror.[68] And ever present, even in the great drama, were the lesser vicissitudes of life: an "imbecile" of Porrentruy disappears in the mountains, a prostitute of the Var accompanies her patron of the moment to Genoa, a Breton fisherman is blown onto the English coast, a young man of twenty-two leaves his home in the Saône-et-Loire because a certain demoiselle swears that she is "grosse de ses oeuvres," and has the law on him. . .[69]

Finally, in some cases emigration was a rationalization of suppressed desire. For many a young noble, head over heels in debt and perhaps "en délicatesse" (as André Gain put it) with his family, emigration offered an escape from *de grands ennuis*. With a light pocketbook and a light heart he rode to the frontier, like young Lochinvar out of the West, leaving behind him the clamor of his creditors and the wrangle of his family. Moreover, since Henri Baldensperger has illuminated the relationship between the emigration and romanticism, one might ask if incipient romanticism was not one of the concealed springs of the emigration. At all events, the lure of travel and the urge of adventure mingled with other motivations. To many upper-class Frenchmen, cosmopolitan by education, the charms of the Old World beckoned, and some of them imagined that "the New World was what the philosophers had taught them to desire."[70] To impulses of this sort some would have yielded, revolution or no revolution.

Yet all these other reasons, from grim to trivial, only embellish the statistical evidence adduced by our study. In its essential significance the emigration was the slough of a great revolution. The French nation, shaken from base to crest, cast off one hundred and thirty thousand of its human constituents. The early tremors dislodged a portion of the nobility and a few others; half of the

---

[68] François Descostes, 282, 306.

[69] Respectively, AD Gironde, Q 1477 ("Liste . . . des émigrés . . . du Mont-Terrible"); Louis Honoré, *loc. cit.*, pp. 60, 645; A.D. Finistère, Q unclassified (dossier); and Paul Montarlot, "Les émigrés de Saône-et-Loire," *Mémoires de la Société éduenne* (1928–1931), XLVI, 153–154. According to the documents produced by the young man in question, one Charles Vitte, he did not actually emigrate, having gone no farther than Chateau Chalon in the Jura.

[70] Frances S. Childs, 1–2.

clergy were excised before being rejected; and the climacterics of '93 hurled thousands of the common people into exile. They were the emigrants, the deportees, and the fugitives of the French Revolution. Some went in quest of arms and allies to turn against their country; others were legally forced to ask asylum; and still others sought a refuge from turmoil. All of them answer to the general appellation of *émigrés*—émigrés of hatred, émigrés of faith, émigrés of fear, and mixed in the crowd were émigrés of hunger, of accident, of pleasure, and, humanly, émigrés without reason.

TABLE I
GENERAL TABLE OF THE EMIGRATION

Department	*Clergy*		*Nobility*		*Upper Middle Class*		*Lower Middle Class*		*Working Class*		*Peasants*		*No Status Given*		*Totals*
	No.	*%*	*No.*	*%*	*No.*	*%*	*No.*	*%*	*No.*	*%*	*No.*	*%*	*No.*	*%*	
Ain															660
Aisne	368	*32½*	329	*29¼*	105	*9¼*	62	*5½*	141	*12½*	44	*4*	79	*7*	1128
Allier	70	*20½*	128	*37¾*	59	*17¼*	3	*1*	7	*2*	4	*1¼*	69	*20¼*	340
Alpes, Basses-	205	*40½*	119	*23¼*	57	*11¼*	9	*1¾*	22	*4¼*	2	*½*	96	*18¾*	510
Alpes, Hautes-	39	*37¼*	39	*37¼*	13	*12¼*	0	*0*	0	*0*	0	*0*	14	*13¼*	105
Alpes-Maritimes															3000
Ardèche	122	*27*	184	*40¾*	49	*10¾*	4	*1*	14	*3¼*	7	*1½*	71	*15¾*	451
Ardennes	339	*2[illegible]*	251	*21*	128	*10½*	56	*4½*	170	*14¼*	173	*14½*	84	*7*	1201
Ariège	277	*57¼*	54	*11½*	29	*6*	4	*1*	59	*12½*	35	*7¼*	22	*4½*	480
Aube	157	*21½*	229	*31½*	133	*18¼*	53	*7½*	36	*5*	80	*11*	40	*5½*	728
Aude	507	*66¾*	125	*16¼*	19	*2½*	4	*½*	14	*2*	4	*½*	86	*11¼*	759
Aveyron	274	*46*	177	*29½*	19	*3¼*	5	*¾*	12	*2*	13	*2½*	97	*16¼*	597
Bouches-du-Rhône	480	*9¼*	360	*7*	2049	*40*	945	*18½*	819	*16*	472	*9¼*	0	*0*	5125
Calvados	114	*38¾*	75	*25½*	10	*3½*	9	*3*	36	*12¼*	42	*14¼*	8	*2¾*	2080[a]
Cantal	402	*56¾*	241	*34*	37	*5¾*	4	*½*	11	*1½*	1	*¼*	13	*1¾*	709
Charente	173	*27¼*	191	*30¼*	25	*4*	5	*¾*	5	*¾*	0	*0*	234	*37*	633
Charente-Inférieure															1335
Cher	92	*38½*	102	*42¾*	27	*11¼*	1	*½*	3	*1¼*	0	*0*	14	*5¾*	239
Corrèze	316	*39¼*	236	*29¼*	104	*13*	4	*½*	19	*2¼*	43	*5¼*	85	*10¼*	807
Corse (Dep. de Liamone)	4	*9¼*	29	*67¼*	6	*14*	0	*0*	2	*4¾*	0	*0*	2	*4¾*	43
Côte-d'Or	346	*19½*	449	*25¼*	424	*23¾*	136	*7½*	150	*8½*	46	*2½*	230	*13*	1781
Côtes-du-Nord															2575
Creuse	135	*48¼*	101	*36*	8	*3*	0	*0*	1	*¼*	9	*3¼*	26	*9¼*	280
Dordogne															2000
Doubs	521	*27*	216	*11¾*	88	*4½*	39	2	294	*15¼*	684	*35½*	88	*4½*	1930
Drôme															632
Eure	52	*24½*	40	*19*	15	*7*	12	*5¾*	23	*11*	41	*19½*	28	*13¼*	1112[b]

TABLE I—(*Continued*)

Department	*Clergy*		*Nobility*		*Upper Middle Class*		*Lower Middle Class*		*Working Class*		*Peasants*		*No Status Given*		*Totals*
	No.	*%*	*No.*	*%*	*No.*	*%*	*No.*	*%*	*No.*	*%*	*No.*	*%*	*No.*	*%*	
Eure-et-Loir															760
Finistère															2086
Gard	336	52¾	68	10¾	78	12½	14	2¼	31	4¾	20	3	91	14¼	638
Garonne, Haute-	525	45½	300	26	92	8	21	1¾	65	5½	6	½	148	12¾	1157
Gers	262	43	197	32¼	51	8¼	4	¾	22	3½	14	2¼	61	10	611
Gironde	331	28	360	30¼	196	16½	53	4½	79	6¾	34	3¾	133	11¼	1186
Hérault	338	51¼	81	12¼	94	14¼	34	5¼	37	5½	29	4½	46	7	659
Ille-et-Vilaine	758	36¼	793	38½	43	2	30	1½	71	3½	71	3½	306	14¾	2072
Indre	57	20½	117	42¼	39	14	6	2¼	7	2½	3	1	48	17½	277
Indre-et-Loire	285	51¾	160	29	24	4½	6	1	4	¾	2	½	70	12¾	551
Isère	320	50¾	142	22½	50	8	4	½	2	¼	0	0	114	18	632
Jura	131	30¼	138	32	87	20	2	½	20	4½	2	½	53	12¼	910[c]
Landes	383	65¼	119	20¼	32	5½	3	½	4	¾	4	¾	41	7	586
Loir-et-Cher	111	29	137	35½	47	12½	3	¾	5	1¼	0	0	82	21¼	385
Loire															105
Loire, Haute-	110	40½	85	31½	17	6¼	3	1	10	3¾	23	8½	23	8½	271
Loire-Inférieure															1750
Loiret															520
Lot	130	22¾	187	33	65	11½	12	2	19	3¼	7	1¼	149	26¼	569
Lot-et-Garonne															1610
Lozère	209	61¾	59	17½	21	6¼	4	1¼	7	2	22	6½	16	4¾	338
Maine-et-Loire	609	37	483	29½	109	6¾	34	2	152	9¼	235	14¼	21	1¼	1643
Manche	812	40½	394	19½	83	4¼	24	1¼	239	12	358	17¾	95	4¾	2005
Marne	350	33¾	269	25¾	110	10½	33	3¼	43	4¼	65	6¼	170	16¼	1040
Marne, Haute-	283	37¼	189	25	97	12¾	31	4	47	6¼	21	2¾	91	12	759
Mayenne	589	18¼	294	9	25	¾	100	3	628	19¼	1454	44¾	163	5	3253
Meurthe	519	33½	292	19	186	12	11	¾	150	9¾	386	25	0	0	1544
Meuse	488	29¾	594	36¼	266	16¼	47	2¾	151	9¼	37	2¼	57	3½	1640
Mont-Blanc (Savoie)	1033	57¼	349	19¼	283	15½	55	3	37	2	16	1	33	2	1806

Morbihan	741	*54¾*	136	*10*	97	*7¼*	66	*4¾*	108	*8*	145	*10¾*	60	*4½*	1353
Moselle	982	*25½*	697	*18¼*	480	*12½*	263	*6¾*	614	*16½*	791	*20½*	0	*0*	3827
Nièvre	123	*35¾*	183	*53¼*	11	*3¼*	0	*0*	5	*1½*	3	*¾*	19	*5½*	344
Nord	738	*28*	374	*14½*	436	*16½*	188	*7¼*	277	*10½*	600	*22¾*	22	*¾*	2635
Oise	238	*32½*	162	*22*	142	*19½*	7	*1*	25	*3½*	6	*¾*	152	*20¾*	732
Orne	267	*47¼*	97	*17¼*	101	*18*	19	*3¼*	22	*4*	39	*7*	19	*3¼*	1870[d]
Pas-de-Calais															2260
Puy-de-Dôme . . .															840
Pyrénées, Basses- . .	137	*30½*	66	*14¾*	27	*6*	16	*3½*	45	*10*	25	*5½*	133	*29¾*	449
Pyrénées, Hautes- .	228	*58½*	50	*12¾*	15	*3¾*	5	*1¼*	4	*1*	34	*8¾*	55	*14*	391
Pyrénées-Orientales .	482	*12½*	252	*6½*	385	*10*	209	*5½*	431	*11¼*	1677	*43½*	418	*10¾*	3854
Rhin, Bas-	936	*4½*	499	*2½*	993	*5*	2113	*10¼*	6051	*29½*	9601	*46¾*	317	*1½*	20510
Rhin, Haut- . . .	855	*31¼*	323	*11¾*	224	*8¼*	93	*3¼*	686	*25*	407	*14¾*	158	*5¾*	2746
Rhône	98	*29½*	91	*27½*	111	*33½*	13	*4*	10	*3*	1	*0*	8	*2½*	332
Saône-et-Loire . . .	437	*41½*	375	*35¾*	144	*13½*	25	*2½*	27	*2½*	13	*1¼*	31	*3*	1052
Saône, Haute- . . .	443	*49¾*	219	*24¾*	136	*15¼*	12	*1¼*	41	*4¾*	20	*2¼*	18	*2*	889
Sarthe	95	*29*	115	*24¼*	87	*18¼*	9	*2*	59	*12½*	97	*20½*	12	*2½*	1090[e]
Seine	462	*22¼*	942	*45½*	93	*4½*	9	*½*	16	*¾*	0	*0*	547	*26½*	2069
Seine-et-Marne . . .	177	*28½*	166	*26¾*	50	*8*	14	*2¼*	7	*1*	7	*1*	202	*32½*	623
Seine-et-Oise															1598
Seine-Inférieure . .	335	*38¾*	290	*33½*	74	*8¼*	31	*3½*	29	*3¼*	16	*2*	90	*10½*	2038[f]
Sèvres, Deux- . . .	169	*33*	235	*46*	45	*8¾*	10	*2*	20	*4*	32	*6¼*	0	*0*	1200[g]
Somme	666	*51¾*	221	*17¼*	142	*11*	54	*4¼*	32	*2½*	71	*5½*	100	*7¾*	1286
Tarn	546	*64½*	131	*15½*	20	*2¼*	6	*¾*	29	*3½*	12	*1½*	102	*12*	846
Var	335	*6½*	374	*7*	1131	*21¼*	808	*15¼*	1407	*26¼*	535	*10*	741	*14*	5331
Vaucluse	311	*24½*	223	*17½*	196	*15¼*	107	*8½*	227	*17¾*	33	*2½*	178	*14*	1275
Vendée	500	*43¾*	409	*35¾*	21	*1¾*	23	*2*	62	*5½*	127	*11¼*	0	*0*	1142
Vienne															1710
Vienne, Haute- . . .															1165
Vosges	204	*36*	156	*27½*	56	*10*	9	*1½*	23	*4*	99	*17½*	20	*3½*	567
Yonne	129	*27¼*	163	*34½*	76	*16*	14	*3*	28	*6*	10	*2¼*	52	*11*	472
TOTALS	24596	*25¼*	16431	*16¾*	10792	*11*	6012	*6¼*	13953	*14¼*	18910	*19½*	6851	*7*	129099[h]

TABLE I—(*Continued*)

RECAPITULATION OF THE CLASSIFIED ÉMIGRÉS BY ESTATES

	First Estate (Clergy)	Second Estate (Nobility)	Third Estate (Commoners)	No Status Given	Total
Number	24596	16431	49667	6851	97545
Per cent	25	17	51	7	100
Per cent neglecting no status given	27	18	55	—	100

THE MILITARY EMIGRATION

OFFICERS						SOLDIERS and SAILORS		TOTAL MILITARY	
Nobles		Bourgeois		Total					
No.	% of Officers	No.	% of Officers	No.	% of Military	No.	% of Military	No.	% of Émigrés
5695	75½	1818	24½	7513	77	2237	23	9750	10

REPARTITION OF THE SEXES

	Clergy		Nobility		Upper Middle Class		Lower Middle Class		Working Class		Peasants		No Status Given		Totals	
	Men	Wo.	Men	Wo.	Men	Wo.	Men	Wo.	Men	Wo.	Men	Wo.	Men	Wo.	Men	Wo.
Number	24344	252	13925	2506	9267	1525	4877	1135	11067	2886	14223	4687	5586	1265	83289	14256
Per cent	99	1	84¾	15¼	85¾	14¼	81	19	79¼	20¾	75¼	24¾	81½	18½	85½	14½

aClassified, 294. Unclassified, 1786. In this instance and in the six following instances of partial social classification, the class percentages are based on the classified total.

bClassified (*District d'Evreux only*), 211. Unclassified. 901.

cClassified, 433. Unclassified. 477.

dClassified, 564. Unclassified. 1306.

eClassified, 474. Unclassified. 615.

fClassified (*District de Rouen only*), 865. Unclassified. 1163.

gClassified, 511. Unclassified. 689.

hClassified, 97,545; 78 per cent of the gross total. Unclassified, 31,554; 22 per cent of the gross total. The class percentages are based on the classified total.

TABLE II
THE TEMPORAL INCIDENCE
PART 1. CATEGORY 1
DEPARTMENTS WHERE THE PREPONDERANCE OF THE EMIGRATION
OCCURRED PRIOR TO JAN. 1, 1793

Department	Periods of Emigration		Total Émigrés	Social Repartition			
	1789– 1792	1793– 1799		Clergy	Nobility	Third Estate	No Status Given
Alpes, Basses- . .	323	187	510	205	119	90	96
Alpes, Hautes- . .	95	10	105	39	39	13	14
Aube	629	99	728	157	229	302	40
Aude	650	109	759	507	125	41	86
Charente	484	149	633	173	191	35	234
Cher	192	47	239	92	102	31	14
Côte-d'Or	1119	662	1781	346	449	756	230
Creuse	249	31	280	135	101	18	26
Eure	800	312	1112	(For partial classification v. T.I)			
Gard	412	226	638	336	68	143	91
Garonne, Haute- .	700	457	1157	525	300	184	148
Indre	232	16	277[a]	57	117	55	48
Indre-et-Loire . .	416	135	551	285	160	36	70
Landes	423	163	586	383	119	43	41
Loir-et-Cher . . .	250	135	385	111	137	55	82
Lozère	228	110	338	209	59	54	16
Meuse	954	686	1640	488	594	501	57
Oise	631	101	732	238	162	180	152
Pyrénées, Hautes-	332	59	391	228	50	58	55
Saône, Haute- . .	689	200	889	443	219	209	18
Seine-et-Marne .	500	123	623	177	166	78	202
Seine-et-Oise . .	1174	424	1598	(Not classified)			
Seine-Inférieure (Dist. de Rouen only)	570	130	865[b]	335	290	150	90
Tarn	701	145	846	546	131	67	102
TOTALS	12,753	4,716	17,663[c]	6,015	3,927	3,099	1,912
Per cent	$72\frac{1}{4}$	$26\frac{3}{4}$	100	$40\frac{1}{4}$	$26\frac{1}{4}$	$20\frac{3}{4}$	$12\frac{3}{4}$

[a]Including 29 for whom no date of emigration determined.
[b]Including 165 for whom no date of emigration determined.
[c]Including 194 for whom no date of emigration determined. The total number of socially classified émigrés here represented is 14,953, and this figure is the denominator of the class percentages.

PART 1. CATEGORY 2

DEPARTMENTS WHERE THE PREPONDERANCE OF THE EMIGRATION OCCURRED AFTER JAN. 1, 1793

Department	*Periods of Emigration*		*Total Émigrés*	*Social Repartition*			
	1789–1792	*1793–1799*		*Clergy*	*Nobility*	*Third Estate*	*No Status Given*
Ardèche	154	243	451[d]	122	184	74	71
Ardennes	485	716	1,201	339	251	527	84
Bouches-du-Rhône	1,125	4,000	5,125	480	360	4,285	0
Doubs	678	1,252	1,930	521	216	1,105	88
Jura	300	610	910	(For partial classification v. T.I.)			
Mayenne	889	2,364	3,253	589	294	2,207	163
Morbihan	496	857	1,353	741	136	416	60
Moselle	1,500	2,327	3,827	982	697	2,148	0
Pyrénées-Orientales	700	3,154	3,854	482	252	2,702	418
Rhin, Bas- . . .	811	19,699	20,510	936	499	18,758	317
Rhin, Haut- . . .	900	1,846	2,746	855	323	1,410	158
Var	545	4,786	5,331	335	374	3,881	741
TOTALS	8,583	41,854	50,491[e]	6,382	3,586	37,513	2,100
Per cent	17	83	100	12¾	7¼	75¾	4¼

[d]Including 54 for whom no date of emigration determined.
[e]Including 54 for whom no date of emigration determined. The total number of socially classified émigrés here represented is 49,581, and this figure is the denominator of the class percentages.

RECAPITULATION

Categories	*Periods of Emigration*				*Total*
	1789–1792		*1793–1799*		
	No.	*%*	*No.*	*%*	
Preponderance prior Jan. 1, 1793	12,753	*72¼*	4,716	*26¾*	17,663
Preponderance after Jan. 1, 1793	8,583	*17*	41,854	*83*	50,491
TOTALS	21,336	*31¼*	46,570	*68¼*	68,154[f]

Categories	*Social Repartition*							
	Clergy		*Nobility*		*Third Estate*		*No Status Given*	
	No.	*%*	*No.*	*%*	*No.*	*%*	*No.*	*%*
Preponderance prior Jan. 1, 1793	6,015	*40½*	3,927	*26¼*	3,099	*20¾*	1,912	*12¾*
Preponderance after Jan. 1, 1793	6,382	*12¾*	3,586	*7¼*	37,513	*75¾*	2,100	*4¼*
TOTALS	12,397	*19¼*	7,513	*11½*	40,612	*63*	4,012	*6¼*

[f]Including 248 for whom no date of emigration determined. The total number of socially classified émigrés here represented is 64,534, and this figure is the denominator of the class percentages.

PART 2

PREPONDERANCE PROBABILITIES FOR THE DEPARTMENTS NOT INCLUDED IN PART 1

CATEGORY 1		CATEGORY 2		CATEGORY 3	
Probable Preponderance Prior to Jan. 1, 1793		Probable Preponderance After Jan. 1, 1793		Doubtful Departments	
Department	*Émigrés*	*Department*	*Émigrés*	*Department*	*Émigrés*
Ain	660	Calvados	2,080	Aisne	1,128
Allier	340	Corse (Liamone)	43	Charente-Inférieure	1,335
Alpes-Maritimes	3,000	Côtes-du-Nord	2,575	Hérault	659
Ariège	480	Finistère	2,086	Meurthe	1,544
Aveyron	597	Gironde	1,186	Orne	1,870
Cantal	709	Ille-et-Vilaine . .	2,072	Pas-de-Calais . .	2,260
Corrèze	807	Loire	105	Somme	1,286
Dordogne	2,000	Loire-Inférieure .	1,750	Vienne	1,710
Drôme	632	Manche	2,005	Vienne, Haute- .	1,165
Eure-et-Loir . .	760	Maine-et-Loire .	1,643		
Gers	611	Nord	2,653	TOTAL	12,957
Isère	632	Pyrénées, Basses-	449		
Loire, Haute- . .	271	Rhône	332		
Lot	569	Sarthe	1,090		
Lot-et-Garonne .	1,610	Sèvres, Deux- . .	1,200		
Loiret	520	Vaucluse	1,275		
Marne	1,040	Vendée	1,142		
Marne, Haute- . .	759				
Mont-Blanc (Savoie)	1,806	TOTAL	23,686		
Nièvre	344				
Puy-de-Dôme . .	840				
Saône-et-Loire . .	1,052				
Seine (Paris) . . .	2,069				
Seine-Inférieure[g]	1,173				
Vosges	567				
Yonne	472				
TOTAL	24,320				

[g]Exclusive of the District de Rouen.

TABULAR RECAPITULATION

Category	Number of Departments	Number of Émigrés
Preponderance prior to January 1, 1793 . . .	23	17,663
Probable preponderance prior to January 1, 1793	26	24,320
Preponderance after January 1, 1793	12	50,491
Probable preponderance after Janaury 1, 1793	17	23,668
Doubtful departments	9	12,957
TOTALS	87	129,099

TABLE III. NUMERICAL CATEGORIES   117

TABLE III

THE GEOGRAPHIC INCIDENCE

NUMERICAL CATEGORIES

LESS THAN 500 ÉMIGRÉS

Department	Location	Circumstances	Émigrés
Corse (Liamone)	Island, Mediterranean . . . . Invaded		43
Loire	Southeast, interior		105
Hautes-Alpes	Southeast, Italian frontier		105
Cher	Center, interior		239
Haute-Loire	South, interior . . . . Insurrection . . .		271
Indre	Center, interior		277
Creuse	Center, interior		280
Lozère	South, interior . . . . Insurrection . . .		338
Rhône	Southeast, interior . . . . . . Civil war		332
Nièvre	Center, interior		344
Allier	Center, interior		340
Loir-et-Cher	Center, interior		385
Hautes-Pyrénées	Southwest, Spanish frontier		391
Basses-Pyrénées	Southwest, Spanish frontier . . Invaded		449
Ardèche	South, interior . . . . Camp de Jalès . .		451
Yonne	Center, interior		472
Ariège	Southwest, Spanish frontier		480

Number of departments: 17		Number of émigrés	5,302

FROM 500 TO 1000 ÉMIGRÉS

Basses-Alpes	Southeast, Italian frontier		510
Loiret	Parisian region, interior		520
Indre-et-Loire	Center, interior		551
Vosges	East, interior		567
Lot	Southwest, interior		569
Landes	Southwest, Atlantic		586
Aveyron	Southwest, interior . . . . . . Serious riots . .		597
Gers	Southwest, interior		611
Seine-et-Marne	Parisian region, interior		623
Drôme	Southeast, interior		632
Isère	Southeast, Italian frontier		632
Charente	West, interior		633
Gard	South, Mediterranean . . . . Federalist revolt .		638
Hérault	South, Mediterranean . . . . Federalist revolt .		659
Ain	Southeast, Swiss frontier . . . Federalist revolt .		660
Cantal	Center, interior . . . . Serious riots . . .		709
Aube	East, interior		728
Oise	Parisian region, interior		732
Aude	South, Mediterranean		759
Haute-Marne	East, interior		759
Eure-et-Loir	Parisian region, interior		760
Corrèze	Center, interior		807
Puy-de-Dôme	Center, interior . . . . Serious riots . . .		840

TABLE III (*Continued*)

Department	Location	Circumstances	Émigrés
Tarn	South, interior	Serious riots . . .	846
Haute-Saône . . .	East, Swiss frontier		889
Jura	East, Swiss frontier	Federalist revolt .	910

Number of departments: 26   Number of émigrés: 17,727

FROM 1000 TO 2000 ÉMIGRÉS

Department	Location	Circumstances	Émigrés
Marne	East, interior		1,040
Saône-et-Loire . .	Southeast, interior		1,052
Sarthe	West, interior	Civil war	1,090
Eure	Northwest, English Channel . .	Federalist revolt .	1,112
Aisne	Parisian region, Belgian frontier		1,128
Vendée	West, Atlantic	Civil war	1,142
Haute-Garonne . .	South, Spanish frontier	Federalist revolt .	1,157
Haute-Vienne . .	Center, interior		1,165
Gironde	Southwest, Atlantic	Federalist revolt .	1,186
Deux-Sèvres . . .	West, Atlantic	Civil war	1,200
Ardennes	East, Belgian frontier	Invaded	1,201
Vaucluse . . .	Southeast, interior	Annexed; civil war	1,275
Somme	North, English Channel		1,286
Charente-Inférieure	West, Atlantic	Civil war	1,335
Morbihan	West, Atlantic	Civil war	1,353
Meurthe	East, interior	Invaded	1,544
Seine-et-Oise . .	Parisian region, interior		1,598
Lot-et-Garonne .	Southwest, interior		1,610
Meuse	East, German frontier	Invaded	1,640
Maine-et-Loire . .	West, interior	Civil war	1,643
Vienne	West, interior	Civil war	1,710
Loire-Inférieure .	West, Atlantic	Civil war	1,750
Côte-d'Or	Center, interior		1,781
Mont-Blanc(Savoie)	Southeast, Swiss-Italian frontier	Conquered, annexed	1,806
Orne	Northwest, interior	Chouannerie . .	1,870
Doubs	East, Swiss frontier	Major insurrection	1,930
Dordogne	Southwest, interior		2,000

Number of departments: 27   Number of émigrés: 38,604

FROM 2000 TO 3000 ÉMIGRÉS

Department	Location	Circumstances	Émigrés
Manche	Northwest, English Channel . .	Civil war	2,005
Seine-Inférieure .	Northwest, English Channel . .	Chouannerie . .	2,038
Seine (Paris) . . .	Parisian region, interior		2,069
Ille-et-Vilaine . .	West, English Channel	Civil war	2,072
Calvados	Northwest, English Channel . .	Federalist revolt .	2,080
Finistère	West, Atlantic	Chouannerie . .	2,086
Pas-de-Calais . .	North, English Channel		2,260
Côtes-du-Nord . .	West, English Channel	Civil war	2,575
Nord	North, North Sea, Belgian frontier	Invaded	2,635
Haut-Rhin . . .	East, German-Swiss frontier		2,746

Number of departments: 10   Number of émigrés: 22,566

TABLE III. NUMERICAL CATEGORIES   119

TABLE III (*Concluded*)

3000 OR MORE ÉMIGRÉS

Department	Location	Circumstances	Émigrés
Alpes-Maritimes	Southeast, Mediterranean, Italian frontier	Conquered, annexed	3,000
Mayenne	West, interior	Civil war	3,253
Moselle	East, German frontier	Invaded	3,827
Pyrénées-Orientales	South, Mediterranean, Spanish frontier	Invaded	3,854
Bouches-du-Rhône	Southeast, Mediterranean	Civil war	5,125
Var	Southeast, Mediterranean	Civil war	5,331
Bas-Rhin	East, German frontier	Invaded	20,510

Number of departments: 7   Number of émigrés: 44,900

RECAPITULATION

Category	Departments Number	Per Cent	Émigrés Number	Per Cent
Less than 500 émigrés	17	20	5,302	4
From 500 to 1000 émigrés	26	30	17,727	$13\frac{3}{4}$
From 1000 to 2000 émigrés	27	31	38,604	30
From 2000 to 3000 émigrés	10	11	22,566	$17\frac{1}{2}$
3000 or more émigrés	7	8	44,900	$34\frac{3}{4}$
TOTALS	87	100	129,099	100

TABLE IV
THE GEOGRAPHIC INCIDENCE
REGIONAL CATEGORIES

Per Cent of Population That Emigrated

Region and Department	.05	.10	.15	.20	.25	.30	.35	.40	.45	.50	.55	.60	.65	.70	.75	
PARISIAN REGION																
Aisne	xxxxx	xxxxx	xxxxx	xxxxx	x											
Eure-et-Loire	xxxxx	xxxxx	xxxxx	xxxxx	x											
Loiret	xxxxx	xxxxx	xxx													
Oise	xxxxx	xxxxx	xxxxx													
Seine (Paris)	xxxxx	xxxxx	xxxxx	xxxxx	xxxxx	xxx										
Seine-et-Marne	xxxxx	xxxxx	xxxxx													
Seine-et-Oise	xxxxx	xxxxx	xxxxx	xxxxx	xxxxx	xxxxx	xxx									
NORTH																
Nord	xxxxx	xxxxx	xxxxx	xxxx												
Pas-de-Calais	xxxxx	xxxxx	xxxxx	xxxxx	xxxxx	xxxxx	xxxxx	xxxxx								
Somme	xxxxx	xxxxx	xxxxx	xxxxx	xxx											
EAST																
Ardennes	xxxxx	xxxxx	xxxxx	xxxxx	xxxxx	xxxxx	xxxxx	xxxxx	x							
Aube	xxxxx	xxxxx	xxxxx	xxxxx	xxxxx	x										
Doubs	xxxxx	xxxxx	xxxxx	xxxxx	xxxxx	xxxxx	xxxxx	xxxxx	xxxxx	xxxxx	xxxxx	xxxxx	xxxxx	xxxxx	xxxxx	to .89xx
Jura	xxxxx	xxxxx	xxxxx	xxxxx	xxxxx	xx										
Marne	xxxxx	xxxxx	xxxxx	xxxxx	xxxx											
Marne, Haute-	xxxxx	xxxxx	xxxxx	xxxxx	xxxxx	xxx										
Meurthe	xxxxx	xxxxx	xxxxx	xxxxx	xxxxx	xxxxx	xxxxx	xxxxx	x							
Meuse	xxxxx	xxxxx	xxxxx	xxxxx	xxxxx	xxxxx	xxxxx	xxxxx	xxxxx	xxxxx	xxxxx	x				
Moselle	xxxxx	xxxxx	xxxxx	xxxxx	xxxxx	xxxxx	xxxxx	xxxxx	xxxxx	xxxxx	xxxxx	xxxxx	xxxxx	xxxxx	xxxxx	to 1.10xx
Rhin, Bas-	xxxxx	xxxxx	xxxxx	xxxxx	xxxxx	xxxxx	xxxxx	xxxxx	xxxxx	xxxxx	xxxxx	xxxxx	xxxxx	xxxxx	xxxxx	to 4.56xx
Rhin, Haut-	xxxxx	xxxxx	xxxxx	xxxxx	xxxxx	xxxxx	xxxxx	xxxxx	xxxxx	xxxxx	xxxxx	xxxxx	xxxxx	xxxxx	xxxxx	to .90xx

Table of French departments with frequency bars (represented by x marks):

Department	Frequency bar	Total
Saône, Haute-	xxxxx xxxxx xxxxx xxxxx xxxxx	
Vosges	xxxxx xxxxx xxxxx xxx	
SOUTHEAST		
Ain	xxxxx xxxxx xxxxx xxxxx xx	
Alpes, Basses-	xxxxx xxxxx xxxxx xxxxx xxxxx xxx	
Alpes, Hautes-	xxxxx xxxx	
Alpes-Maritimes	xxxxx xxxxx xxxxx xxxxx xxxxx xxxxx xxxxx xxxxx	to 1.26xx
Bouches-du-Rhône	xxxxx xxxxx xxxxx xxxxx xxxxx xxxxx xxxxx xxxxx	to 1.80xx
Corse (Liamone)	xxx	
Drôme	xxxxx xxxxx xxxxx xxxxx xx	
Isère	xxxxx xxxxx xxxx	
Loire	xxx	
Mont-Blanc (Savoie)	xxxxx xxxxx xxxxx xxxxx xxx	
Rhône	xxxxx xxxxx x	
Saône-et-Loire	xxxxx xxxxx xxx	
Var	xxxxx xxxxx xxxxx xxxxx xxxxx xxxxx xxxxx xxxxx	to 1.96xx
Vaucluse	xxxxx xxxxx xxxxx xxxxx xxxxx xxxxx xx	
SOUTH		
Ardèche	xxxxx xxxxx xxxxx xx	
Aude	xxxxx xxxxx xxxxx xxxxx	
Gard	xxxxx xxxxx xxxxx x	
Garonne, Haute-	xxxxx xxxxx xxxxx xxxx	
Hérault	xxxxx xxxxx xxxx	
Loire, Haute-	xxxxx xx	
Lozère	xx	
Pyrénées-Orientales	xxxxx xxxxx xxxxx xxxxx xxxxx xxxxx	to 3.48xx
Tarn	xxxxx xxxxx xxxxx xx	
CENTER		
Allier	xxxxx xxxxx xxx	
Cantal	xxxxx xxxxx xxxxx xxxxx xxxxx xx	
Cher	xxxxx xxxxx	

TABLE IV—(Continued)

Per Cent of Population That Emigrated

Region and Department	.05	.10	.15	.20	.25	.30	.35	.40	.45	.50	.55	.60	.65	.70	.75
Corrèze	xxxxx	xxxxx	xxxxx	xxxxx	xxxxx	xxx									
Côte-d'Or	xxxxx	xxxxx	xxxxx	xxxxx	xxxxx	xxxxx	xxxxx	xxxxx	xx						
Creuse	xxxxx	xxxxx	xxx												
Indre	xxxxx	xxxxx	xxx												
Indre-et-Loire	xxxxx	xxxxx	xxxxx												
Loir-et-Cher	xxxxx	xxxxx	xxx												
Nièvre	xxxxx	xxxxx	xxxxx												
Puy-de-Dôme	xxxxx	xxxxx	xxxxx	xx											
Vienne, Haute-	xxxxx	xxxxx	xxxxx	xxxxx	xxxxx	xxxxx	xxxxx	xxxxx	xxx						
Yonne	xxxxx	xxxxx	xxxxx												
SOUTHWEST															
Ariège	xxxxx	xxxxx	xxxxx	xxxx											
Aveyron	xxxxx	xxxxx	xxxxx	xxx											
Dordogne	xxxxx	xxxxx	xxxxx	xxxxx	xxxxx	xxxxx	xxxxx	xxxxx	xxxx						
Gers	xxxxx	xxxxx	xxxxx	xxxxx	xxx										
Gironde	xxxxx	xxxxx	xxxxx	xxxxx	xxx										
Landes	xxxxx	xxxxx	xxxxx	xxxxx	x										
Lot	xxxxx	xxxxx	xxxxx												
Lot-et-Garonne	xxxxx	xxxxx	xxxxx	xxxxx	xxxxx	xxxxx	xxxxx	xxxxx	xxxxx						
Pyrénées, Basses-	xxxxx	xxxxx	xx												
Pyrénées, Hautes-	xxxxx	xxxxx	xxxxx	xx											
WEST															
Charente	xxxxx	xxxxx	xxxxx	x											
Charente-Inférieure	xxxxx	xxxxx	xxxxx	xxxxx	xxxxx	xxx									
Côtes-du-Nord	xxxxx	xxxxx	xxxxx	xxxxx	xxxxx	xxxxx	xxxxx	xxxxx	xxxxx	x					
Deux-Sèvres	xxxxx	xxxxx	xxxxx	xxxxx	xxxxx	xxxxx	xxxxx	xxxxx	xxxxx						
Finistère	xxxxx	xxxxx	xxxxx	xxxxx	xxxxx	xxxxx	xxxxx	xxx							

Ille-et-Vilaine . . . . . . xxxxx xxxxx xxxxx xxxxx xxxxx xxxxx xx
Loire-Inférieure . . . . . xxxxx xxxxx xxxxx xxxxx xxxxx xxxxx xxxxx xx
Maine-et-Loire . . . . . . xxxxx xxxxx xxxxx xxxxx xxxxx xxxxx xxxxx   to 1.06xx
Mayenne . . . . xxxxx xxxxx xxxxx xxxxx xxxxx xxxxx xxxxx xxxxx xxxxx
Morbihan . . . . xxxxx xxxxx xxxxx xxxxx xxxxx xxxx
Sarthe . . . . xxxxx xxxxx xxxxx xxxxx xxx
Vendée . . . . xxxxx xxxxx xxxxx xxxxx xxxxx xx
Vienne . . . . xxxxx xxxxx xxxxx xxxxx xxxxx xxxxx xxxxx x

NORTHWEST
Calvados . . . . xxxxx xxxxx xxxxx xxxxx xxxxx x
Eure . . . . xxxxx xxxxx xxxxx xxxxx xxxxx xx
Manche . . . . xxxxx xxxxx xxxxx xxxxx xxx
Orne . . . . xxxxx xxxxx xxxxx xxxxx xxxxx xxxxx xx
Seine-Inférieure . . . . xxxxx xxxxx xxxxx xxx

REGIONAL RECAPITULATION

Per Cent of Population That Emigrated

Region and Department	.05	.10	.15	.20	.25	.30	.35	.40	.45	.50	.55	.60	.65	.70	.75		to 1.00xx
PARISIAN REGION .	xxxxx	xxxxx	xxxxx	xxxxx	xx												
NORTH	xxxxx	xxxxx	xxxxx	xxxxx	xxxxx	x											
EAST	xxxxx	xxxxx	xxxxx	xxxxx	xxxxx	xxxxx	xxxxx	xxxxx	xxxxx	xxxxx	xxxxx	xxxxx	xxxxx	xxxxx	xxxxx		to 1.00xx
SOUTHEAST . . .	xxxxx	xxxxx	xxxxx	xxxxx	xxxxx	xxxxx	xxxxx	xxxxx	xxxxx	xx							
SOUTH	xxxxx	xxxxx	xxxxx	xxxxx	xxxxx	x											
CENTER	xxxxx	xxxxx	xxxxx	xxxxx	xxx				x								
SOUTHWEST . . .	xxxxx	xxxxx	xxxxx	xxxxx	xx												
WEST	xxxxx	xxxxx	xxxxx	xxxxx	xxxxx	xxxxx	xxxxx	xxxxx	xx								
NORTHWEST . . .	xxxxx	xxxxx	xxxxx	xxxxx	xxxxx	xxx											
TOTAL FOR FRANCE .	xxxxx	xxxxx	xxxxx	xxxxx	xxxxx	xxxxx	xxxxx	x									

[123]

TABLE V
THE GEOGRAPHIC INCIDENCE
PERCENTAGE CATEGORIES

Department	Population[a]	Area[b]	Émigrés	Per Cent of Population
LESS THAN 1/5 OF 1 PER CENT				
Corse (Liamone)	163,900	8,747	43	.03
Loire	290,900	4,760	105	.03
Alpes, Hautes-	112,500	5,590	105	.09
Cher	217,700	7,199	239	.10
Rhône	299,400	2,790	332	.11
Loire, Haute-	229,800	4,962	271	.12
Pyrénées, Basses-	355,600	7,623	449	.12
Allier	248,800	7,308	340	.13
Creuse	218,000	5,568	280	.13
Indre	205,600	6,795	277	.13
Isère	435,900	8,289	632	.14
Lot	377,200	5,212	569	.15
Nièvre	232,600	6,817	344	.15
Yonne	320,600	7,428	472	.15
Puy-de-Dôme	507,100	7,950	840	.17
Ardèche	266,600	5,527	451	.17
Loiret	286,100	6,771	520	.18
Loir-et-Cher	209,900	6,351	385	.18
Aveyron	326,300	8,743	597	.18
Vosges	308,900	5,853	567	.18
TOTALS	5,613,400	130,283	7,818	.14
FROM 1/5 TO 2/5 OF 1 PER CENT				
Seine-et-Marne	299,100	5,736	623	.20
Oise	350,900	5,855	732	.20
Indre-et-Loire	268,900	6,114	551	.20
Charente	299,000	5,942	633	.21
Gard	300,100	5,836	638	.21
Ain	297,000	5,799	660	.22
Pyrénées, Hautes-	174,700	4,529	391	.22
Gers	270,600	6,280	611	.23
Gironde	502,700	9,740	1,186	.23
Saône-et-Loire	452,700	8,552	1,052	.23
Ariège	196,400	4,894	480	.24
Hérault	275,400	6,198	659	.24
Aisne	425,900	7,352	1,128	.26
Eure-et-Loir	257,800	5,874	760	.26
Landes	224,300	9,321	586	.26
Drôme	235,300	6,522	632	.27
Eure	408,800	5,958	1,112	.27
Lozère	126,500	5,170	338	.27
Somme	459,500	6,161	1,286	.28
Sarthe	388,100	6,207	1,090	.28
Garonne, Haute-	405,600	6,290	1,157	.29

TABLE V. PERCENTAGE CATEGORIES   125

TABLE V—(*Continued*)

Department	Population[a]	Area[b]	Émigrés	Per Cent of Population
Saône, Haute-	291,600	5,340	889	.30
Aube	231,400	6,001	728	.31
Jura	288,200	4,994	910	.32
Tarn	270,900	5,742	846	.32
Cantal	220,300	5,741	709	.32
Corrèze	243,700	5,866	807	.33
Charente-Inférieure	399,100	6,826	1,335	.33
Marne, Haute-	226,700	6,220	759	.33
Mont-Blanc (Savoie) . . .	542,446	10,075	1,806	.33
Seine (Paris)	631,600	479	2,069	.33
Seine-Inférieure	609,800	6,035	2,038	.33
Aude	225,200	6,313	759	.34
Marne	304,700	8,180	1,040	.34
Morbihan	401,200	6,798	1,353	.34
Nord	765,000	5,681	2,635	.34
Alpes, Basses-	134,000	6,954	510	.38
Manche	530,600	2,928	2,005	.38
Seine-et-Oise	421,500	5,604	1,598	.38
TOTALS	13,249,246	240,107	39,101	.30

FROM 2/5 TO 3/5 OF 1 PER CENT

Department	Population	Area	Émigrés	Per Cent
Ille-et-Vilaine	488,800	6,726	2,072	.42
Maine-et-Loire	375,500	7,121	1,643	.44
Pas-de-Calais	505,600	6,606	2,260	.45
Ardennes	259,900	5,233	1,201	.46
Calvados	451,800	5,521	2,080	.46
Meurthe	338,100	6,090	1,544	.46
Loire-Inférieure	369,300	6,875	1,750	.47
Orne	395,700	6,097	1,870	.47
Vendée	243,400	6,703	1,142	.47
Finistère	439,000	6,722	2,086	.48
Haute-Vienne	245,100	5,517	1,165	.48
Dordogne	409,500	9,183	2,000	.49
Sèvres, Deux-	241,900	6,000	1,200	.50
Lot-et-Garonne	323,900	5,354	1,610	.50
Côtes-du-Nord	504,300	6,886	2,575	.51
Côte-d'Or	340,500	8,761	1,781	.52
TOTALS	5,932,300	105,395	27,979	.47

FROM 3/5 OF 1 PER CENT TO 1 PER CENT

Department	Population	Area	Émigrés	Per Cent
Meuse	269,500	6,228	1,640	.61
Vaucluse	191,400	3,584	1,275	.67
Vienne	241,000	5,970	1,710	.71
Doubs	216,200	5,228	1,930	.89
Rhin, Haut-	303,800	4,108	2,746	.90
TOTALS	1,221,900	25,118	9,301	.76

TABLE V—(*Continued*)

Department	Population[a]	Area[b]	Émigrés	Per Cent of Population
MORE THAN 1 PER CENT				
Mayenne	305,700	5,171	3,253	1.06
Moselle	348,100	5,369	3,827	1.10
Alpes-Maritimes	238,057	3,742	3,000	1.26
Bouches-du-Rhône	285,000	5,105	5,125	1.80
Var	271,700	6,028	5,331	1.96
Pyrénées-Orientales . . .	110,700	4,122	3,854	3.48
Bas-Rhin	450,200	4,553	20,510	4.56
TOTALS	2,009,457	34,090	44,900	2.23

RECAPITULATION

Category	Population	Area	Émigrés	Per Cent of Population
Less than 1/5 of 1 per cent	5,613,400	130,283	7,818	.14
1/5 to 2/5 of 1 per cent . .	13,249,246	240,107	39,101	.30
2/5 to 3/5 of 1 per cent . .	5,932,300	105,395	27,979	.47
3/5 of 1 per cent to 1 per cent	1,221,900	25,118	9,301	.76
More than 1 per cent . . .	2,009,457	34,090	44,900	2.23
TOTALS	28,026,303	534,993	129,099	.46

[a]Based on the census of 1801.
[b]In square kilometers.

TABLE VI. THE SOCIAL INCIDENCE 127

TABLE VI

THE SOCIAL INCIDENCE
VARIATIONS WITH THE EXCLUSION OF THE DEPARTMENTS OF THE
HEAVIEST EMIGRATION

Social Category	All classified émigrés		Without the Bas-Rhin		Without the Bas-Rhin, the Pyrénées-Orientales and the Var		Without the Bas-Rhin, the Bouches-du-Rhône, the Mayenne, the Moselle, the Pyrénées-Orientales and the Var	
	No.	%	No.	%	No.	%	No.	%
Clergy	24,596	25¼	23,660	30¾	22,843	33¾	20,792	37½
Nobility	16,431	16¾	15,932	20¾	15,306	22½	13,955	25
Upper Middle Class	10,792	11	9,799	12¾	8,283	12¼	5,729	10¼
Lower Middle Class	6,012	6¼	3,899	5	2,882	4¼	1,574	2¾
Working Class . .	13,953	14¼	7,902	10¼	6,064	9	4,003	7¼
Peasants	18,910	19½	9,309	12	7,097	10½	4,380	8
No Status Given .	6,851	7	6,534	8½	5,375	7¾	5,212	9¼
TOTALS	97,545	100	77,035	100	67,850	100	55,645	100

Note on the Bas-Rhin: The 20,510 émigrés of the Bas-Rhin represent 21 per cent of all the classified émigrés.
   The 9,601 peasant émigrés of the Bas-Rhin represent 51 per cent of all the classified peasant émigrés.
   The 6,051 working class émigrés of the Bas-Rhin represent 43 per cent of all the classified working class émigrés.
   The 2,113 lower middle class émigrés of the Bas-Rhin represent 35 per cent of all the classified lower middle class émigrés.

TABLE VII
THE SOCIAL INCIDENCE
CIRCUMSTANTIAL CORRELATIONS

REGION I: CIVIL WARS OF THE WEST

Department	*Clergy*		*Nobility*		*Upper Middle Class*		*Lower Middle Class*		*Working Class*		*Peasants*		*No Status Given*		*Totals*
	No.	*%*	*No.*	*%*	*No.*	*%*	*No.*	*%*	*No.*	*%*	*No.*	*%*	*No.*	*%*	
Calvados[a]	114	*38¾*	75	*25½*	10	*3½*	9	*3*	36	*12¼*	42	*14¼*	8	*2¾*	294
Eure[a]	52	*24½*	40	*19*	15	*7*	12	*5¾*	23	*11*	41	*19½*	28	*13¼*	211
Ille-et-Vilaine	758	*36¼*	793	*38½*	43	*2*	30	*1½*	71	*3½*	71	*3½*	306	*14¾*	2072
Maine-et-Loire	609	*37*	483	*29½*	109	*6¾*	34	*2*	152	*9¼*	235	*14¼*	21	*1¼*	1643
Manche	812	*40½*	394	*19½*	83	*4¼*	24	*1¼*	239	*12*	358	*17¾*	95	*4¾*	2005
Mayenne	589	*18¼*	294	*9*	25	*¾*	100	*3*	628	*19¼*	1454	*44¾*	163	*5*	3253
Morbihan	741	*54¾*	136	*10*	97	*7¼*	66	*4¾*	108	*8*	145	*10¾*	60	*4½*	1353
Orne[a]	267	*47¼*	97	*17¼*	101	*18*	19	*3¼*	22	*4*	39	*7*	19	*3¼*	564
Sarthe[a]	95	*20*	115	*24¼*	87	*18¼*	9	*2*	59	*12½*	97	*20½*	12	*2½*	474
Sèvres, Deux-[a]	169	*33*	235	*46*	45	*8¾*	10	*2*	20	*4*	32	*6¼*			511
Vendée	500	*43¾*	409	*35¾*	21	*1¾*	23	*2*	62	*5½*	127	*11¼*			1142
TOTALS	4706	*34¾*	3071	*22¾*	636	*4½*	336	*2½*	1420	*10½*	2641	*19¾*	712	*5¼*	13522

REGION II: CIVIL WARS OF THE SOUTHEAST

Department	*Clergy No.*	*%*	*Nobility No.*	*%*	*Upper Middle Class No.*	*%*	*Lower Middle Class No.*	*%*	*Working Class No.*	*%*	*Peasants No.*	*%*	*No Status Given No.*	*%*	*Totals*
Bouches-du-Rhône	480	*9¼*	360	*7*	2049	*40*	945	*18½*	819	*16*	472	*9¼*			5125
Rhône	98	*29½*	91	*27½*	111	*33½*	13	*4*	10	*3*	1	—	8	*2½*	332
Var	335	*6½*	374	*7*	1131	*21¼*	808	*15¼*	1407	*26¼*	535	*10*	741	*14*	5331
Vaucluse	311	*24½*	223	*17½*	196	*15¼*	107	*8½*	227	*17¾*	33	*2½*	178	*14*	1275
TOTALS	1224	*10*	1048	*8¾*	3487	*29*	1873	*15½*	2463	*20½*	1041	*8½*	927	*7¾*	12063

REGION III: SOUTHERN FEDERALIST CENTERS

Gard	336	*52¾*	68	*10¾*	78	*12½*	14	*2¼*	31	*4¾*	20	*3*	91	*14¼*	638
Garonne, Haute- . .	525	*45½*	300	*26*	92	*8*	21	*1¾*	65	*5½*	6	*½*	148	*12¾*	1157
Gironde	331	*28*	360	*30¼*	196	*16½*	53	*4½*	79	*6¾*	34	*2¾*	133	*11¼*	1186
Hérault	338	*51¼*	81	*12¼*	94	*14¼*	34	*5¼*	37	*5½*	29	*4½*	46	*7*	659
TOTALS	1530	*42*	809	*22¼*	460	*12¾*	122	*3¼*	212	*5¾*	89	*2½*	418	*11½*	3640

REGION IV: OTHER MAJOR INSURRECTIONS

Doubs	521	*27*	216	*11¾*	88	*4½*	39	*2*	294	*15¼*	684	*35½*	88	*4½*	1930
Loire, Haute- . . .	110	*40½*	85	*31½*	17	*6¼*	3	*1*	10	*3¾*	23	*8½*	23	*8½*	271
Lozère	209	*61¾*	59	*17½*	21	*6¼*	4	*1¼*	7	*2*	22	*6½*	16	*4¾*	338
TOTALS	840	*33*	360	*14¼*	126	*5*	46	*1¾*	311	*12¼*	729	*28¾*	127	*5*	2539

REGION V: INVADED TERRITORY

Aisne	368	*32½*	329	*29¼*	105	*9¼*	62	*5½*	141	*12½*	44	*4*	79	*7*	1128
Ardennes	339	*28¼*	251	*21*	128	*10½*	56	*4½*	170	*14¼*	173	*14½*	84	*7*	1201
Corse	4	*9¼*	29	*67¼*	6	*14*			2	*4¾*			2	*4¾*	43
Meurthe	519	*33½*	292	*19*	186	*12*	11	*¾*	150	*9¾*	386	*25*			1544
Meuse	488	*29¾*	594	*36¼*	266	*16¼*	47	*2¾*	151	*9¼*	37	*2¼*	57	*3½*	1640
Moselle	982	*25½*	697	*18¼*	480	*12½*	263	*6¾*	614	*16½*	791	*20½*			3827
Nord	738	*28*	374	*14½*	436	*16½*	188	*7¼*	277	*10½*	600	*22¾*	22	*¾*	2635
Pyrénées, Basses- . .	137	*30½*	66	*14¾*	27	*6*	16	*3½*	45	*10*	25	*5½*	133	*29¾*	449
Pyrénées-Orientales .	482	*12½*	252	*6½*	385	*10*	209	*5½*	431	*11¼*	1677	*43½*	418	*10¾*	3854
Rhin, Bas-	936	*4½*	499	*2½*	993	*5*	2113	*10¼*	6051	*29½*	9601	*46¾*	317	*1½*	20510
TOTALS	4993	*13½*	3383	*9¼*	3012	*8¼*	2965	*8*	8032	*21¾*	13334	*36¼*	1112	*3*	36831

TABLE VII—(*Continued*)

REGION VI: QUIET DEPARTMENTS

Department	*Clergy*		*Nobility*		*Upper Middle Class*		*Lower Middle Class*		*Working Class*		*Peasants*		*No Status Given*		*Totals*
	No.	*%*	*No.*	*%*	*No.*	*%*	*No.*	*%*	*No.*	*%*	*No.*	*%*	*No.*	*%*	
Allier	70	*20½*	128	*37¾*	59	*17¼*	3	*1*	7	2	4	*1¼*	69	*20¼*	340
Alpes, Basses-	205	*40½*	119	*23¼*	57	*11¼*	9	*1¾*	22	*4¼*	2	*½*	96	*18¾*	510
Alpes, Hautes-	39	*37¼*	39	*37¼*	13	*12¼*							14	*13¼*	105
Ardèche	122	*27*	184	*40¾*	49	*10¾*	4	*1*	14	*3¼*	7	*1½*	71	*15¾*	451
Ariège	277	*57¾*	54	*11½*	29	*6*	4	*1*	59	*12½*	35	*7¼*	22	*4½*	480
Aube	157	*21½*	229	*31½*	133	*18¼*	53	*7¼*	36	*5*	80	*11*	40	*5½*	728
Aude	507	*66¾*	125	*16¼*	19	*2½*	4	*½*	14	2	4	*½*	86	*11¼*	759
Aveyron	274	*46*	177	*29½*	19	*3¼*	5	*¾*	12	2	13	*2½*	97	*16¼*	597
Cantal	402	*56¾*	241	*34*	37	*5¾*	4	*½*	11	*1½*	1	*¼*	13	*1¾*	709
Charente	173	*27¼*	191	*30¼*	25	*4*	5	*¾*	5	*¾*			234	*37*	633
Cher	92	*38½*	102	*42¾*	27	*11¼*	1	*½*	3	*1¼*			14	*5¾*	239
Corrèze	316	*39¼*	236	*29¼*	104	*13*	4	*½*	19	*2¼*	43	*5¼*	85	*10¼*	807
Côte d'Or	346	*19½*	449	*21¼*	424	*23¾*	136	*7½*	150	*8½*	46	*2½*	230	*13*	1781
Creuse	135	*48½*	101	*36*	8	*3*			1	*¼*	9	*3¼*	26	*9¼*	280
Gers	262	*43*	197	*32¼*	51	*8¼*	4	*¾*	22	*3½*	14	*2¼*	61	*10*	611
Indre	57	*20½*	117	*42¼*	39	*14*	6	*2¼*	7	*2½*	3	*1*	48	*17½*	277
Indre-et-Loire	285	*51¾*	160	*29*	24	*4½*	6	*1*	4	*¾*	2	*½*	70	*12¾*	551
Isère	320	*50¾*	142	*22½*	50	*8*	4	*½*	2	*¼*			114	*18*	632
Jura[a]	131	*30¼*	138	*32*	87	*20*	2	*½*	20	*4½*	2	*½*	53	*12¼*	433
Landes	383	*65¼*	119	*20¼*	32	*5¼*	3	*½*	4	*¾*	4	*¾*	41	*7*	586
Loir-et-Cher	111	*29*	137	*35½*	47	*12½*	3	*¾*	5	*1¼*			82	*21¼*	385
Lot	130	*22¾*	187	*33*	65	*11½*	12	*2*	19	*3¼*	7	*1¼*	149	*26¼*	569
Marne	350	*33¾*	269	*25¾*	110	*10½*	33	*3¼*	43	*4¼*	65	*6¼*	170	*16¼*	1040
Marne, Haute-	283	*37¼*	189	*25*	97	*12¾*	31	*4*	47	*6¼*	21	*2¾*	91	*12*	759
Mont-Blanc	1033	*57¼*	349	*19¼*	283	*15½*	55	*3*	37	*2*	16	*1*	33	2	1806
Nièvre	123	*35¾*	183	*53¼*	11	*3¼*			5	*1½*	3	*¾*	19	*5½*	344
Oise	238	*32½*	162	22	142	*19½*	7	*1*	25	*3½*	6	*¾*	152	*20¾*	732
Pyrénées, Hautes-	228	*58½*	50	*12¾*	15	*3¾*	5	*1¼*	4	*1*	34	*8¾*	55	*14*	391

Rhin, Haut-	855	*31¼*	323	*11¾*	224	*8¼*	93	*3¼*	686	*25*	407	*14¾*	158	*5¾*	2746
Saône, Haute- . . .	443	*49¾*	219	*24¾*	136	*15¼*	12	*1¼*	41	*4¾*	20	*2¼*	18	*2*	889
Saône-et-Loire . . .	437	*41½*	375	*35¾*	144	*13½*	25	*2½*	27	*2½*	13	*1¼*	31	*3*	1052
Seine-et-Marne . . .	177	*28½*	166	*26¾*	50	*8*	14	*2½*	7	*1*	7	*1*	202	*32½*	623
Seine-Inférieure[a] . .	335	*38¾*	290	*33½*	74	*8¼*	31	*3½*	29	*3¼*	16	*2*	90	*10½*	865
Somme	666	*51¾*	221	*17¼*	142	*11*	54	*4¼*	32	*2½*	71	*5½*	100	*7¾*	1286
Tarn	546	*64½*	131	*15½*	20	*2¼*	6	*¾*	29	*3½*	12	*1½*	102	*12*	846
Vosges	204	*36*	156	*27½*	56	*10*	9	*1½*	23	*4*	99	*17½*	20	*3½*	567
Yonne	129	*27¼*	163	*34½*	76	*16*	14	*3*	28	*6*	10	*2¼*	52	*11*	472
TOTALS	10841	*40¼*	6818	*25½*	2978	*11*	661	*2½*	1499	*5½*	1076	*4*	3008	*11¼*	26881

REGION VII: PARIS

Seine	462	*22¼*	942	*45½*	93	*4½*	9	*½*	16	*¾*			547	*26½*	2069

RECAPITULATION

Department	*Clergy*		*Nobility*		*Upper Middle Class*		*Lower Middle Class*		*Working Class*		*Peasants*		*No Status Given*		*Totals*
	No.	*%*	*No.*	*%*	*No.*	*%*	*No.*	*%*	*No.*	*%*	*No.*	*%*	*No.*	*%*	
Civil Wars of the West	4706	*34¾*	3071	*22¾*	636	*4½*	336	*2½*	1420	*10½*	2641	*19¾*	712	*5¼*	13522
Civil Wars of the Southeast	1224	*10*	1048	*8¾*	3487	*29*	1873	*15½*	2463	*20½*	1041	*8½*	927	*7¾*	12063
Southern Federalist Centers	1530	*42*	809	*22¼*	460	*12¾*	122	*3¼*	212	*5¾*	89	*2½*	418	*11½*	3640
Major Insurrections .	840	*33*	360	*14¼*	126	*5*	46	*1¾*	311	*12¼*	729	*28¾*	127	*5*	2539
Invaded Territory .	4993	*13½*	3383	*9¼*	3012	*8¼*	2965	*8*	8032	*21¾*	13334	*36¼*	1112	*3*	36831
Quiet Departments .	10841	*40¼*	6818	*25½*	2978	*11*	661	*2½*	1499	*5½*	1076	*4*	3008	*11¼*	26881
Paris	462	*22¼*	942	*45½*	93	*4½*	9	*½*	16	*¾*			547	*26½*	2069
TOTALS	24596	*25¼*	15431	*16¾*	10792	*11*	6012	*6¼*	13953	*14¼*	18910	*19½*	6851	*7*	97545

[a]Partial classification. See Table I for totals.

TABLE VIII
THE VOCATIONAL INCIDENCE

1. THE CLERGY

	No.	%		No.	%
Upper	2,298	11	Secular	18,688	90
Lower	18,493	89	Regular	2,103	10
			(Monks . . 1,890)		
TOTAL	20,791	100	(Nuns . . . 213)		
No rank given	3,805				
			TOTAL	20,791	100
TOTAL	24,596		No status given	3,805	
			TOTAL	24,596	

2. THE NOBILITY

	No.	%
Nobles of the gown (*noblesse de robe*)	872	5
Officers (including retired officers)	5,695	35
No profession indicated	7,358	45
Women	2,506	15
TOTAL	16,431	100

3. THE UPPER MIDDLE CLASS

High ranking functionaries of the Monarchy or the Republic

Administrators (*administrateurs*), unqualified	231
Chiefs, directors (*chefs, directeurs*) of the customs, posts, salt farms, munitions, supplies, military hospitals, etc.	60
Captains, lieutenants (*capitaines, lieutenants*) of the customs, police, tax farms, ports, etc.	29
Controllers (*contrôleurs*) of the customs, posts, taxes, etc.	46
Clerks (*greffiers*), administrations of the Monarchy or the Republic	50
Deputies (*députés*) in the revolutionary assemblies (*Constituante, Législative, Convention, Cinq-Cents, Anciens*)	36
Diplomats and consuls (*ambassadeur*, 1; *consuls*, 3)	4
Inspectors (*inspecteurs, verificateurs*) of the customs, taxes, state manufactures, munitions, transports, etc.	54
Intendants and sub-intendants (*intendants, subdélégués*)	35
Mayors (*maires*) of towns of more than 1,000 inhabitants	83
Municipal officers (*officiers municipaux, échevins,* etc.)	38
National agents (*agents nationaux*)	5
Presidents (*présidents*), *Bureaux des Finances, Élection,* etc.	6
Receivers (*receveurs*) of customs, taxes, lotteries, etc.	221
Treasurers (*trésoriers*) of customs, taxes, lotteries, etc.	26
Secretaries (*secrétaires*), departmental, district, municipal, intendance, etc.	55

Total number of high functionaries 979

The professions

Actors (*comédiens*, 7) and musicians (*musiciens*, 40)	47
Architects (*architectes*)	43
Archivists (*archiviste*, 1) and roll keepers (*commissaires à terrier*, 5) .	6
Artists (*artistes*, unqualified, 3), painters (*peintres*, 11), and sculptors (*sculpteurs*, 8)	22

TABLE VIII. THE VOCATIONAL INCIDENCE   133

Authors (*hommes de lettres*, 12) and journalists (*journalistes*, 11) . .   23
Doctors (*médecins*, 294), oculist (*oculiste*, 1), and surgeons
   (*chirurgiens*, 292)   587
Engineers (*ingénieurs*)   30
Lawyers and magistrates ("*hommes de loi*," *avocats*, *avoués*,
   procureurs, *commissaires du roi*, *juges*, *juges de paix*, *baillis*,
   gardes-marteaux, *lieutenants particuliers*, *maîtres particuliers*,
   prévôts, *sénéchaux*, etc.)   1741
Professors, scholars, scientists (*professeurs*, *savants*, etc.)   34
Ships' captains and pilots (*capitaines marchands*, *pilotes*)   150
     Total number of members of the professions   2,683
Business
Bankers (*banquiers*, 30) and brokers (*agents de change*, 17)   47
Brewers (*brasseurs*, 7) and distillers (*distillateurs*, 7)   14
Contractors (*entrepreneurs*)   17
Executives (*directeurs*)   5
Manufacturers (*manufacturiers*, *marchands-fabricants*, 14; *maîtres
   de verrerie*, *manufacturiers de verre*, 16; *maîtres de forges*, *métallur-
   gistes*, 7; *fabricants de drap*, *de soie*, *de laine*, etc., 24)   61
Merchants (*marchands drapiers*, *toiliers*, 40; —*de fer*, 11; *de soie*, 10;
   de blé, 21)   82
Merchants, wholesale (*négociants de draps*, *vins*, *fer*, *blé*, *huile*, etc.) .   645
Printers (*imprimeurs*) and publishers (*imprimeurs-éditeurs*)   18
Refiners (*raffineurs de sucre*, etc.)   2
Shipbuilders (*constructeurs de navires*)   5
     Total number engaged in business   896
Miscellaneous
"Bourgeois" (494), non-noble landed proprietors (269), and
   "rentiers" (171)   934
Managers and overseers of large estates (*agents*, *hommes-d'affaires*,
   intendants, *régisseurs*)   39
Private secretaries (*secrétaires particuliers*)   10
Students (*étudiants*)   296
Tax farmers (*fermiers généraux*)   14
     Total number in the miscellaneous group   1,293

Officers   1,818

Male members of upper middle class families   1,598

Women   1,525

    Total number of upper middle class emigrants   10,792

4. THE LOWER MIDDLE CLASS

Petty functionaries and employees of the Monarchy or the Republic
(*commis*, *préposés*, *secrétaires*, *écrivains*, *employés* in government
bureaux, etc., in the customs, police, lotteries, etc.; *gardiens*, *gardes-
magasins*, *magasiniers*, and *concierges* of public buildings, warehouses,
etc.)   564

Clerks (*greffiers*) in the lower courts and petty legal people (*clercs de
notaires*, etc.)   34

Shopkeepers and tradesmen

Barbers (*coiffeurs*, 34), hairdressers and wig-makers (*perruquiers*, 139) 173
Bathing establishments, owners of (*baigneurs*) 4
Booksellers (*libraires*) 11
Clothing trades
  Button merchants (*marchands de boutons*) 2
  Drygoods merchants (*merciers*, 12; *marchands de toile, de laine*, etc., 24) 36
  Furriers (*pelletiers*) 7
  Tailors (*tailleurs, culottiers*) 661
      Total of persons engaged in the clothing trades 706
Druggists (*droguistes*, 50), apothecaries (*apothicaires*, 68), and pharmacists (*pharmaciens*, 15) 133
Food trades
  Bakers (*boulangers*) 278
  Butchers (*bouchers*) 166
  Caterers (*traiteurs, rotisseurs*) 34
  Confectioners (*confiseurs*) 26
  Delicatessen proprietors (*charcutiers*) 15
  Fruit merchants (*marchands de fruit*) 9
  Grocers (*épiciers*) 34
  Pastry cooks (*patissiers*) 7
  Salt merchants (*marchands de sel*) 2
  Wine and liquor merchants (*marchands de vin, liquoristes*) 18
      Total of persons engaged in the food trades 589
Hardware merchants (*quincaillers*) 6
Hotel, restaurant, café, and cabaret keepers (*hotelliers*, 5; *aubergistes*, 117; *taverniers*, 17; *cabaretiers*, 33; *cafetiers*, 26) . . . 198
Jewelers (*bijoutiers*, 12; *orfèvres*, 67) 79
Leather and hide merchants (*marchands de cuir*, etc.) 3
Livery stable proprietors (*loueurs de voitures*) 2
Milliners (*marchands de mode*) 2
Perfumers (*marchands parfumeurs*, etc.) 6
Stationers (*papetiers*) 6
Stock dealers (*marchands de porcs, chevaux*, etc.) 3
Tobacconists (*marchands de tabac*) 7
Wood merchants (*marchands de bois*) 9
Shopkeepers, unqualified or miscellaneous ("*marchands*") 661
      Total number of shopkeepers and tradesmen 2,598

Miscellaneous vocations

Brewers in villages and the countrysides (*brasseurs*) 27
Dentists (*dentistes*) 3
Draftsmen (*dessinateurs*) 2
Millers (*meuniers*) 165
Nurses (*infirmiers*) 7
Organists (*organistes*) 3
Postmasters (*maîtres de poste*) 26
Sacristan (*sacristain*) 1
Salesmen (*voyageurs de commerce, courtiers*, etc.) 13
Schoolteachers (*maîtres d'école, instituteurs*, etc.) 248
Scribes (*écrivains*) 45
Surveyors (*arpenteurs, arpenteurs-toiseurs, experts*, etc.) 35
Tutors (*précepteurs*), dancing, fencing, drawing, riding, music masters (*maîtres de dance, d'armes*, etc.) 31

TABLE VIII. THE VOCATIONAL INCIDENCE   135

Veterinarians (*vétérinaires*) 6
White-collar help (*commis, teneurs de livres*, etc.) 62
     Total number engaged in miscellaneous vocations 674

Male members of lower middle class families 1,007

Women
  Shopkeepers and tradeswomen
     Bakers (*boulangères*) 27
     Booksellers (*libraires*) 2
     Butchers (*bouchères*) 37
     Confectioners (*confiseuses*) 3
     Drygoods merchants (*mercières*, etc.) 11
     Grocers (*épicières*) 25
     Hairdressers (*coiffeuses*) 16
     Hotel, restaurant, café, and cabaret keepers (*aubergistes*,
      32; *cabaretières*, etc., 22) 54
     Jewelers (*bijoutières*, etc.) 2
     Merchants, unqualified ("marchandes") 97
      Total number of shopkeepers and tradeswomen 274
  Miscellaneous vocations
     Governesses (*gouvernantes*) 11
     Nurses and midwives (*infirmières, sages-femmes*) 17
     Schoolteachers (*institutrices*, etc.) 59
      Total engaged in miscellaneous vocations 87
  Female members of lower middle class families 774
      Total number of women 1,135

      Total number of lower middle class emigrants 6,012

5. THE WORKING CLASS

Apprentices and journeymen (*apprentis, compagnons*, 70); helpers
   (*garçons*, 274) 348
Artisans and workmen, unqualified (*artisans*, 49; *fabricants*, 55; *ouvriers*, 143) 247
Blacksmiths (*maréchaux-ferrants*, 184; *forgerons*, 57; *ferruriers*, 26) and
   wheelwrights (*charrons*, 86) 353
Bookbinders (*relieurs*) 5
Building trades
   Carpenters (*charpentiers*, 340), joiners (*menusiers*, 286), turners
    (*tourneurs*, 37) 657
   Masons (*maçons*, 520) and stone masons (*tailleurs de pierre*, 85) . . 605
   Painters (*peintres*) 19
   Plasterers (*plâtriers*) 4
   Roofers and tilers (*couvreurs*, 23; *tuiliers*, 35) 58
     Total number engaged in the building trades 1,343
Carters and drivers
   Carters (*charretiers, rouliers, voituriers*) 92
   Drivers and outriders (*conducteurs, messagers, piqueurs*) 10
   Muleteers (*muletiers*) 5
   Postilions (*postillons*) 6
     Total number of carters and drivers 113
Chimney sweeps (*ramoneurs*) 4
Concierges (house porters) 5
Coopers (*tonneliers*, 149) and hoop-makers (*cercliers*, 12) 161

Cork-cutters (*bouchonniers*) 2
Drummers (*tambours*) 3
Earthenware and glass trades
   Crockery-makers (*faïenciers*) 8
   Finishers of demijohns (*garnisseurs de dames-jeannes*) 2
   Glass blowers (*verriers*) 23
   Glaziers (*vitriers*) 53
   Potters (*potiers*) 50
      Total engaged in earthenware and glass trades 136
Engravers (*graveurs*) 6
Executioners (*bourreaux*) 4
Fishermen (*pêcheurs*) 133
Fountain-makers (*fonteniers*) 3
Furniture and fixture trades
   Cabinetmakers and turners (*ébénistes, tabletiers, tourneurs de chaises, mouleurs de bois*, etc.) 20
   Clock-makers (*horlogers*) 27
   Gilders (*doreurs*) 2
   Mattress-makers (*matelassiers*) 2
   Mirror-makers (*miroitiers*) 2
      Total engaged in the furniture and fixture trades 53
Gelders (*chatreurs*) 2
Grave-diggers (*fossoyeurs*) 3
Household supply trades
   Basin and tub-makers (*baquetiers*, 5; *cuvettiers*, 8) 13
   Basket-makers (*vanniers*) 25
   Candle-makers (*chandeliers, mangonniers*, 19; *ciriers*, 10) 29
   Coal-dealers (*charbonniers*) 27
   Soap-makers (*savonniers, fabricants de savon*) 32
   Starch-makers (*amidonniers*) 7
   Sieve-makers (*cribliers, tamisiers*) 2
      Total engaged in the household supply trades 135
Garment trades
   Button-makers (*boutonniers*) 16
   Dressmakers (*couturiers*) 2
   Embroiderers (*brodeurs*) 2
   Glovers (*gantiers*) 13
   Hatters (*chapeliers*) 56
   Lace-makers (*passementiers*) 12
   Ribbon-makers (*rubaniers*) 4
   Stocking-makers (*bonnetiers*, 17; *fabricants de bas*, 40) 57
      Total engaged in the garment trades 162
Knife-grinders (*rémouleurs*) 3
Leather, hide, and harness trades
   Harness-makers (*bourreliers*) 17
   Leather-curriers (*corroyeurs*, 5; *mégissiers*, 10) 15
   Moleskin-curriers (*taupiers*) 10
   Saddlers (*selliers*, 27; *bâtiers*, 6) 33
   Shammy-dressers (*chamoiseurs*) 4
   Tanners (*tanneurs*) 75
      Total number engaged in the leather trades 154
Metal, arms, and tool trades
   Armorers (*armuriers*) 14
   Coppersmiths (*chaudronniers*) 24
   Cutlers (*couteliers*) 15

TABLE VIII. THE VOCATIONAL INCIDENCE   137

Founders (*fondeurs*, 9; *fondeurs de cloches*, 4)   13
Furbishers (*fourbisseurs*)   6
Goldsmiths (*tireurs d'or*)   2
Pewtersmiths and tinsmiths (*ferblantiers*, 30; *étameurs*, 6; *potiers*
    d'étain, 5)   41
Locksmiths (*serruriers*)   96
Machinists (*machinistes*)   16
Nail-makers (*cloutiers*)   43
Tool-makers (*taillandiers*)   15
     Total engaged in the metal, arms, and tool trades   285
Miners (*mineurs*)   4
Pavers (*paveurs*)   4
Peddlers and hawkers (*colporteurs*, 18; *marchands-forrains*, 5)   23
Police, gendarmes (*gardiens*, 15; *gardes villages*, 2; *gendarmes*, 25; *sergents de*
    ville, 3)   45
Porters and carriers (*portes-chaises*, 2; *portefaix*, 17; *portiers*, 4; *facteurs*, 2) .   25
Rope-makers (*cordiers*)   53
Saltpeter-makers (*salpêtriers*)   6
Seamen, boatmen, longshoremen
   Seamen (*marins*, 81; *navigateurs*, 5; *timoniers*, 17)   103
   Boatmen (*bateliers*, 15; *flotteurs*, 2)   17
   Stevedores (*chargeurs*)   25
     Total of seamen, boatmen, and longshoremen   145
Scales-makers (*balanciers*)   8
Servants
   Bodyguards (*gardes du corps*, etc.)   4
   Coachmen (*cochers*, 34; *palefreniers*, 7)   41
   Cooks (*cuisiniers*)   91
   Footmen (*chasseurs*)   9
   Gamekeepers, foresters (*gardes-chasse*, 34; *forestiers*, 22)   56
   Gardeners (*jardiniers*)   71
   Maîtres d'hotel   3
   Servants, unqualified ("*domestiques*")   1020
     Total number of servants   1,295
Shearers, fleecers (*tondeurs*, 5; *écorcheurs*, 4)   9
Shoemakers and cobblers (*condonniers*, 579; *sabotiers*, 96; *savetiers*, 2)   677
Shipbuilding and ship chandler trades
   Cable-makers (*aussiers*, at Toulon)   8
   Calkers (*calfats*, 26) and borers (*perceurs*, 4)   30
   Mast-makers (*mâteurs*)   13
   Pulley or block-makers (*poulierus*)   10
   Sail-makers (*voiliers*)   14
     Total engaged in the shipbuilding and chandler trades   75
Street merchants and secondhand dealers
   Fish vendors (*poissonniers*, *marchands de carpes*, etc.)   5
   Lemonade vendors (*limonadiers*)   2
   Old clothes dealers (*fripiers*, *hardiers*)   10
   Ragpickers (*chiffonniers*, *marchands de chiffon*)   3
   Secondhand dealers (*regrattiers*, *brocanteurs*)   20
   Vinegar-makers (*vinaigriers*)   2
     Total number of street merchants and secondhand dealers   42
Textile trades
   Dyers (*teinturiers*)   46
   Finishers (*apprêteurs* (at Lyon), 3; *pareurs*, 4)   7
   Flax-dressers (*filassiers*, 24; *peigneurs de chanvre*, 4)   28

Serge-weavers (*sergiers*)   3
Silk-throwers (*mouliniers*, 2) and curriers (*degraisseurs*, 2)   4
Spinners (*fileurs, filatiers*)   34
Taffeta-weavers (*taffetiers*)   2
Tapestry-weavers (*tapissiers*)   12
Trimmers (*garnisseurs*)   3
Weavers, unqualified (*tisserands*)   935
Wool-combers (*cardeurs, peigneurs de laine, lainiers*, etc.)   30
    Total number of textile workers **1,104**
Tobacco-graters (*râpeurs de tabac*)   3
Washermen (*blanchisseurs*)   5
Warders, gaolers, prison guards (*argousins*, 2; *guichetiers*, 2; *pertuisaniers*, 2)   6
Woodcutters, sawyers (*bûcherons, coupeurs de bois, scieurs*)   16
Day laborers (*brassiers, journaliers, terrassiers, manoeuvriers* and *gagnes-deniers*)   203
Bandits, convicts, poachers (*miquelets*, in Roussillon, 2; *forçats*, 8; *braconniers*, 2)   12
Beggars, vagabonds, and imbeciles (*mendiants*, 3; *vagabonds*, 3; *imbéciles*, 2) .   8
Miscellaneous vocations represented by not more than one person.
    Examples: stove-maker (*poêlier*), maker of playing cards (*cartier*), maker
    of plaster of Paris (*gypseur*), etc.   77
Soldiers and sailors (*soldats, matelots*), including deserters and fugitives
    from conscription   2,237
Male members of working class families   1,322
Women
Basket-makers (*vannières*)   4
Button-makers (*boutonnières*)   12
Fish vendor (*marchande de poisson*)   1
Lace-makers (*dentellières*)   3
Laundresses (*blanchisseuses*, 7; *lingères*, 5; *repasseuses*, 2)   14
Milliners (*faiseuses de modes, modistes*)   4
Ribbon-maker (*rubanière*)   1
Seamstresses (*couturières*, 48; *tricoteuses*, 2)   50
Secondhand dealer (*regrattière*)   1
Servants (*domestiques*, 373; *cuisinières*, 20)   393
Stocking-makers (*bonnetières*, 2; *fabricants de bas*, 12)   14
Textile workers (*filassières*, 3; *fileuses*, 22; *tisserands*, 160;
    tapissières, 4)   189
Wool-combers (*cardeuses de laine*)   5
Day laborers (*journalières*, 37; *ouvrières*, 70)   107
Beggars (*mendiantes*, 3), prostitutes (*filles publiques*, 6), and camp
    followers ("*vivandière de mauvaise vie*," 1)   10
Female members of working class families   2078
    Total number of women **2,886**

    Total number of working class emigrants **13,953**

6. PEASANTS

Men   14,223
Women   4,687

    Total number of peasant emigrants **18,910**

BIBLIOGRAPHY OF MATERIAL USED IN COMPILING TABLES

I. General

"Liste générale par ordre alphabétique des émigrés de toute la république," 4 vols.; Paris, an II. Bibliothèque nationale (BN), La[34] 5; also in the Archives nationales (AN) and in many of the Archives départementales (AD).

"Premier [deuxième, troisième, etc. . . . . septième] supplément à la liste générale . . . des émigrés de toute la République," 7 vols.; Paris, an II–an IX (1793–1801). BN, La[34] 5; also AN and various AD.

"Liste des émigrés ayant obtenu la radiation des listes des émigrés," 5 vols.; Paris, an III–an VII (1794–1799). BN La[34] 6; also AN and various AD.

"Liste des émigrés maintenus ou rétablis sur les listes des émigrés," 3 vols.; Paris, an V–an VII (1797–1799). BN, La[34] 7; also AN and various AD.

"Liste officielle des individus rayés définitivement de la list des émigrés . . . en exécution . . . de la loi du 25 brumaire an III . . .," Paris, s.d. BN, La[35] 3.

"Liste des propriétaires aux colonies qui ont fourni leurs certificats de résidence," s.d. [1793?]. AD Yonne, Q 611.

"État des officiers de tous grades déserteurs ou émigrés classés par régiment," Paris, 1793. BN, LF[195] 5.

II. Clergy

Armel, l'ère, "Les martyrs de l'ordre franciscain pendant la Révolution," *Annales franciscaines*, 1925–1928 (series of articles).

Guillon, Aimé, *Les martyrs de la foi pendant la Révolution française* (4 vols.; Paris, 1821).

Lemonnier, Pierre, *Martyrologe de la déportation ecclésiastique à Rochefort-sur-Mer, 1794–1795* (Paris, 1917).

Manseau, Abbé, *Les prêtres et religieux déportés sur les côtes et dans les îles de la Charente-Inférieure* (2 vols.; Lille, 1886).

139

Pierre, Victor, *La déportation ecclésiastique sous le Directoire* (Paris, 1896).

Pisani, Paul, *Répertoire biographique de l'épiscopat constitutionnel, 1791–1802* (Paris, 1907). (See especially for bibliographies.)

Rousseau, François, *Moines bénédictins martyrs et confesseurs de la foi pendant la Révolution* (Paris, 1926).

Sabatié, A. C., *La justice pendant la Révolution. La déportation du clergé français* (2 vols.; Paris, s.d. [1917]).

Sevestre, E., Eude, E., et Le Corbeiller, E., *La déportation du clergé orthodoxe pendant la Révolution. Registres des ecclésiastiques insermentés embarqués dans les principaux ports de France* (Paris, 1913).

III. Local

AIN

Based on André Gain's indemnity hypothesis (see above, pp. 19–20). Indemnities: 132; émigrés: 660.

Cf. Dubois, Eugène, *Histoire de la Révolution dans l'Ain* (3 vols.; Bourg, 1931–1933), II, 435–437 (list of émigrés issued in March, 1792); and Rochet, S. (Abbé), "Le clergé de l'Ain pendant la Révolution," *Bulletin de la Société Gorini* (1910), VII, 193–211, 249–271, 387–407; (1911) VIII, 142–152, 253–269; (1912) IX, 337–344 (fragmentary data on the deported clergy).

AISNE

"Relevé général des émigrés portés sur les listes arrêtées par le département de l'Aisne," ms., s.d. AD Aisne, Q 291.

"Première [deuxième, troisième, etc. . . . huitième] liste supplétive des émigrés du département de l'Aisne," an II–an III. *Ibid.*, Q 294–314; also AD Gironde, Q 1475.

"Liste des prêtres du diocèse [de Soissons] émigrés, déportés ou arrêtés," 1795. Bibliothèque de Soissons, Collection Perrin, no. 4909.

Divers lists of *radiations*, an V–an VII. AD Aisne, Q 315–316.

Cf. Fleury, E., *Le clergé du département de l'Aisne pendant la Révolution* (2 vols.; Paris et Laon, 1853), II, 49–58 (lists).

ALLIER

Cornillon, J., *Le Bourbonnais sous la Révolution française* (5 vols.; Riom, 1888–1895), II, 319–334 (list; apparently complete for the émigrés but does not include the deported clergy).

Divers lists and dossiers. Especially *Dossiers individuels des déportés.* AD Allier, Q unclassified.

ALPES, BASSES-

"Liste des émigrés du département des Basses-Alpes," 10 mars 1793. AD Basses-Alpes, Q unclassified.

"Liste supplétive des émigrés . . . des Basses-Alpes," 19 août 1793; "Seconde liste supplétive . . .," 1 floréal an II; "Troisième liste supplétive . . .," 5 thermidor an II. *Ibid., idem.*

Cf. Maurel, M. J. (Abbé), *Histoire religieuse du département des Basses-Alpes pendant la Révolution* (Marseille et Digne, 1902), 299–505, 508–511 (lists and brief biographies of the deported clergy).

ALPES, HAUTES-

Uncaptioned, undated list of the émigrés of the department (the most comprehensive of the several lists in the departmental archives). AD Hautes-Alpes, Q 103.

"État des émigrés du département [des Hautes-Alpes]," ms., s.d. *Ibid., idem.*

"Département des Hautes-Alpes. District d'Embrun. État des noms des émigrés et leurs biens," ms., s.d. *Ibid., idem.*

"Département des Hautes-Alpes. District de Gap. États par communes des citoyens absents dont les biens sont dans ces communes," ms., s.d. *Ibid.,* Q 112.

"Département des Hautes-Alpes. État des ecclésiastiques émigrés avant le 18 septembre 1792, époque de la publication de la loi du 26 août," ms., s.d.; "État des ecclésiastiques émigrés sans passports depuis la publication de la loi du 26 août," ms., s.d. *Ibid,* Q 103.

"Département des Hautes-Alpes. Procès verbaux de main mise sur les biens des prêtres émigrés, condamnés ou déportés," ms., an II–an III. *Ibid.,* Q 112.

"Registre servant à constater la délivrance des certificats de non-inscription sur la liste des émigrés [des Hautes-Alpes]," ms., s.d. [an VI]. *Ibid.,* Q 102.

"État des émigrés [des Hautes-Alpes] rentrés et rayés de la liste," 6 floréal an IV. *Ibid.,* Q 112.

"État des émigrés [des Hautes-Alpes] rayés ou amnistiés," 10 fructidor an X. *Ibid., idem.*

Dossiers individuels des émigrés et des déportés des Hautes-Alpes (about one hundred). *Ibid.,* Q 108–111.

ALPES-MARITIMES

"Liste générale des émigrés . . . des Alpes-Maritimes," 26 juin 1793; supplements and district lists, an II–an VII. AD Alpes-Maritimes, Q unclassified.

Combet, Joseph, *La Révolution dans le comté de Nice et la principauté de Monaco, 1792–1800* (Paris, 1925), 239 (totals of various lists and estimate of 3,000 émigrés for the department); Tisserand, E., *Histoire de la Révolution française dans les Alpes-Maritimes* (Nice, 1878), 467–469 (list of émigrés for the district of Grasse, which was attached to the Var during the Revolution, and an estimate of from "4,000 to 5,000 émigrés" for the Alpes-Maritimes).

ARDÈCHE

Répertoire des émigrés du département de l'Ardèche (typed manuscript, 62 pp., dated February 28, 1939), prepared by Jean Régné, archivist of the Ardèche. AD Ardéche, unclassified; AN, Bureaux de l'administration, no. 2753.

ARDENNES

"Département des Ardennes. Liste des personnes émigrées," 8 octobre 1792. AD Ardennes, Q 625.

"Liste des émigrés dont le dernier domicile est fixé dans le département des Ardennes . . .," ms., s.d. (late, probably an VI). *Ibid., idem.*

"Seconde liste des biens immobiliers . . . séquestrés dans le département des Ardennes," 1793; "Troisième liste des biens immobiliers . . .," 2 brumaire an II. *Ibid.*, Q 616.

Four lists captioned "Liste des personnes absentes dont le dernier domicile était dans le département des Ardennes," dated respectively 7 germinal an IV, 26 ventôse an V, 8 nivôse an VI, 1 pluviôse an VI. *Ibid., idem.*

District lists: Couvin ("Liste générale des prévenus d'émigration . . .," 4 ventôse an III), Sedan ("Première liste des citoyens . . . prévenus d'émigration . . .," 1 germinal an III), Grandpré ("Première liste des citoyens prévenus d'émigration . . .," 9 prairial an III), and Rethel ("Liste des citoyens . . . prévenus d'émigration . . ., 1 nivôse an IV). *Ibid., idem.*

"Tableau contenant les noms des personnes [des Ardennes] qui ont obtenu du Directoire exécutif les arrêtés de radiation de la liste des émigrés," ms., s.d. *Ibid.*, Q 625.

Petitions for cancellation; lists of cancellations. *Ibid.*, Q 656*–660*.

Dossiers individuels des émigrés des Ardennes. Ibid., Q 661–760.

ARIÈGE

"Liste générale des émigrés et des déportés . . . de l'Ariège arrêtée par l'administration du département . . .," 1 ventôse an II. AD Ariège, Q 49.

"Troisième supplément à la liste des émigrés . . . de l'Ariège," 27 nivôse an VI. *Ibid.*, *idem.*

Dossiers individuels des émigrés et des prêtres déportés de l'Ariège. Ibid., Q unclassified.

AUBE

"État général des émigrés et de leurs propriétés situées dans le département de l'Aube," s.d. BN, Lb⁴¹ 3034.

Dossiers des émigrés, condamnés et déportés de l'Aube. AD Aube, Q 4 (*138 cartons*).

Prévost, Abbé, *Histoire du diocèse de Troyes pendant la Révolution* (3 vols.; Troyes, 1909), II, 694–699 (list of deportees). Cf. Ecalle, P. F. (Mgr.), *Le schisme constitutionnel à Troyes, 1790–1801* (Troyes, 1905), 217.

AUDE

"Répertoire général des émigrés, déportés ou reclus du département de l'Aude," ms., s.d. (late, perhaps 1795, and comprehensive). AD Aude, Q 139.

"État général des émigrés propriétaires dans le département de l'Aude . . . fait en exécution de l'adresse de M. Roland . . . aux corps administratifs," ms., s.d. *Ibid.*, *idem.*

"Liste générale des émigrés du département de l'Aude," 25 juin 1793. *Ibid.*, *idem.*

"État des émigrés [de l'Aude]," ms., s.d. [1794] (fragment). *Ibid.*, *idem.*

"Liste supplétive des émigrés du département de l'Aude dressée en exécution . . . de la loi du 25 brumaire an III," ms., s.d. [an VI]. *Ibid.*, *idem.*

"Renseignements sur les émigrés, déportés . . . [de l'Aude] fournis par les administrations de canton en an 6," ms., s.d. *Ibid.*, *idem.*

Lists for the districts of Carcassonne, Castelnaudary, Limoux, Narbonne, and Quillan, an II–an X. *Ibid.*, Q 140.

Divers lists of fathers and mothers of émigrés (". . . astreints au paiement de la solde de l'habillement de deux volontaires pour chaque enfant émigré."—". . . qui ont offert ou refusé le partage des biens . . .", etc.), an II–an VII. *Ibid.*, Q 142–143.

Cancellations. *Ibid.*, Q 140. Certificates of residence. *Ibid.*, Q 144. *Dossiers individuels . . . Ibid.*, Q 72–101.

AVEYRON

"Département de l'Aveyron. Liste des émigrés," s.d. AD Aveyron, Q unclassified.

"Premier supplément à la liste des émigrés [de l'Aveyron]," s.d. *Ibid.*
"Liste des citoyens absens (*sic*) . . . du district de Saint-Afrique . . .,"
   1 prairial an III; "Liste des citoyens absens (*sic*) . . . du district
   d'Aubin," 20 messidor an III; "District de Millau. Liste des émigrés
   formée en exécution . . . de la loi du 25 brumaire an III," 16 germinal
   an III. *Ibid.*
Cf. Verlaguet, A., *La vente des biens nationaux du département de
   l'Aveyron* (3 vols.; Rodez, 1931–1932), *passim.*
For the clergy, Fabre, Augustin, *Les 500 prêtres de l'Aveyron déportés
   pendant la Révolution* (2 vols.; s.l., s.d. [1912]), II, 303–400 (lists);
   and Verlaguet, A., *Notices sur les prêtres du Rouergue déportés
   pendant la période révolutionnaire* (4 vols.; Rodez, 1927–1932),
   passim.

BOUCHES-DU-RHÔNE

"Liste des biens des français émigrés situés dans le département des
   Bouches-du-Rhône," an II–an VI (?). (Comprehensive, but fragile,
   faded, and in part illegible.) AD Bouches-du-Rhône, Q 37–38.
"Relevé général des émigrés et prévenus d'émigration du département
   des Bouches-du-Rhône," 15 nivôse an II. AD Gironde, Q 1475.
Cf. on the clergy, Valence, Apollinaire de, *Études franciscaines sur la
   Révolution dans le département des Bouches-du-Rhône* (Nîmes, 1898),
   passim.
(*Note*: The total number of émigrés and deportees inscribed in the above
   cited comprehensive "Liste des biens des français émigrés . . .,"
   in the departmental archives at Marseille is about 5,370. But since
   this list is in part unreadable and replete with duplications, I have
   accepted the total of 5,124 exiles given by Paul Moulins, *Documents
   relatifs à la vente des biens nationaux. Département des Bouches-du-
   Rhône* (4 vols.; Marseille, 1908–1911), I, p. xii).

CALVADOS

The figure for the total number of émigrés (Tables I–V) is based on
   Gain's indemnity hypothesis. Indemnities: 416; émigrés: 2,080.
   Before the Second World War the Archives départementales de
   Calvados, at Caen, contained a considerable amount of material on
   the émigrés, including numerous *dossiers individuels*, but it was
   unclassified and unavailable.
The partial social classification (Tables I and VII) is based on the follow-
   ing sources:
"Liste des prévenus d'émigration . . . de Calvados," 15 ventôse an II.
   AD Gironde, Q 1475.

"Premier supplément à la liste des émigrés . . . de Calvados," 15 ventôse an VI; "Deuxième liste supplémentaire des émigrés . . . de Calvados," 23 ventôse an VI. *Ibid.*, *idem.* "Troisième liste supplémentaire des émigrés . . . de Calvados," 7 fructidor an VI. AD Yonne, Q 612.

"Liste des prévenus d'émigration . . . du ci-devant district de Falaise," 25 brumaire an III. AD Gironde, Q 1475.

For the clergy, Sevestre, E., *Problèmes religieux de la Révolution et de l'Empire en Normandie* (2 vols.; Paris, 1924), II, 793–808 (statistics on the deported clergy; esp. p. 803 for 545 clergy of Calvados deported from Norman ports alone).

CANTAL

"Liste générale des émigrés . . . du Cantal," 5 octobre 1793. AD Gironde, Q 1475.

Dossiers individuels des émigrés et des prêtres déportés du Cantal. AD Cantal, Q unclassified (but alphabetically filed).

Cf. Serres, Jean Baptiste, *Histoire de la Révolution en Auvergne* (6 vols.; Paris, 1895–1896), V, 109–110, 163–179 (lists); and Delmas, J., "Les prêtres du Cantal déportés pendant la Révolution," *Revue de la Haute-Auvergne*, année 1911, pp. 257–275.

CHARENTE

"Relevé général des émigrés portés sur les listes arrêtées par le Directoire du département de la Charente jusqu'au 27 septembre 1793," ms., s.d. [1793]. AD Charente, Q 10^4.

"Liste des émigrés dont les biens ont été vendus dans le département de la Charente," ms., s.d. *Ibid.*, *idem.*

"Liste supplétive des émigrés possessionés dans le départment de la Charente . . .," 27 septembre 1793. *Ibid.*, Q 10^2.

"Table générale des émigrés [de la Charente]: liste par ordre alphabétique des émigrés rayés ou amnistiés," *registre*, ms., s.d. *Ibid.*, Q 20^1.

Certificates of non-inscription, 28 thermidor an VI–3 germinal an VIII. *Ibid.*, Q 10^6. Certificates of residence, 18 février 1793–8 prairial an VII. *Ibid.*, Q 10^5. *Dossiers individuels . . . Ibid.*, Q 12$^{1-55}$.

Cf. Saint-Marc, C. de, "Les émigrés du Poitou (Deux-Sèvres, Vendée, Vienne) et des anciens grands gouvernements d'Angoumois, Aunis et Saintonge (Charente et Charente-Inférieure), 1792–1793 . . .," *Mémoires de la Société historique et scientifique des Deux-Sèvres*, année 1905, pp. 165–375; and Blanchet, J. P. G. (Abbé), *Le clergé charentais pendant la Révolution* (Angoulême, 1898), 218ff., 518–528 (lists of deported clergy).

CHARENTE-INFÉRIEURE

Based on Gain's indemnity hypothesis. Indemnities: 267; émigrés: 1335. Cf. Saint-Marc, C. de, *loc. cit.*, *passim*; and, on the émigré and deported clergy, Lemonnier, Pierre (Abbé), *Le clergé de la Charente-Inférieure pendant la Révolution* (La Rochelle, 1905), 116–117 (list of 197 clergy; probably incomplete).

CHER

"Liste générale des émigrés du département du Cher," 3 août 1793. AD Cher, Q 399; also AD Gironde, Q 1475, and AD Pyrénées-Orientales, Q 730.

"Première liste supplétive des émigrés, déportés, reclus et condamnés du Cher," 12 vendémiaire an III. AD Cher, Q 399, and AD Gironde, Q 1475. "Seconde liste supplétive . . . du Cher," 1 floréal an VII. AD Cher, Q 399.

"Liste des émigrés . . . du Cher," 24 août 1792. *Ibid.*, *idem.*

"Liste des prêtres du département du Cher déportés en exécution des lois du 26 août 1792, 21 avril 1793 et 30 vendémiaire an II," ms., 29 messidor an II (?); "Liste des prêtres [du Cher] qui se sont déportés volontairement et avec passports," ms., 29 messidor an II; "Liste des prêtres exceptés de la déportation à cause de leur âge ou de leurs infirmités," 29 messidor an II. AD Cher, Q 399.

"Liste des personnes du Cher notoirement connues pour avoir émigré et qui ne sont pas rentrés," s.d. *Ibid.*, *idem.*

Dossiers individuels des émigrés, des prêtres déportés . . . etc. du Cher. *Ibid.*, Q 352–391.

Cf. Brimont, Vicomte de, *M. de Puységur et l'église de Bourges pendant la Révolution* (Bourges, 1896), 169–170 (incomplete list of deported clergy).

CORRÈZE

Audubert, A., "Liste des émigrés de la Corrèze," *Bulletin de la Société du Musée départemental d'éthnographie et d'art populaire du Bas-Limousin* (1901), II, 46–48, 103–107 (incomplete list).

Forot, Victor, *Les émigrés corrèziens avec la nomenclature et la valeur de leurs biens séquestrés* (Paris, 1922), *passim*. (A satisfactory critical reconstruction of the local lists.)

CORSE (GOLO AND LIAMONE)

"Liste des individus qui ont émigré en suivant les anglais lors de leur évacuation de la Corse . . .," 10 messidor an V. AD Gironde, Q 1477.

"Premier supplément à la liste des émigrés du département du Liamone," 20 vendémiaire an VI. *Ibid.*, *idem.*

(*Note*: There seems to be no record of any emigration from the department of Golo, the northeastern section of the island. Probably, however, there were a few émigrés from this region; if so, our data for Corsica are incomplete.)

CÔTE-D'OR

"Relevé général des émigrés [de la Côte-d'Or] portés sur les listes arrêtées par le Directoire du département ... depuis le 2 juillet 1792 jusqu'au 3 octobre 1793," octobre, 1793. AD Côte-d'Or, Q 514 (printed copy) and Q 516 (ms. copy). Also under Q 514 another list bearing the same caption as the foregoing but only partially duplicating it.

"Relevé général des émigrés portés sur les listes arrêtées par le Directoire ... de la Côte-d'Or le 10e jour du 2e mois de l'an II ...," [31 octobre 1793]. *Ibid.*, Q 514 (printed copy) and Q 516 (ms. copy).

"Relevé général des émigrés ... de la Côte-d'Or ...," 29 brumaire an II. *Ibid.*, *idem.*

Partially duplicating the above: "Liste des biens des émigrés ... [de la Côte-d'Or]," 5 juillet 1792–28 novembre 1792; "Liste supplétive des biens des émigrés ... Septième liste," 3 octobre 1793; "Liste des biens des émigrés ... Huitième liste," le 2e jour du 2e mois de l'an II; "Liste des biens des émigrés ... Neuvième liste," 29 brumaire an II. *Ibid.*, *idem.*

"Département de la Côte-d'Or. Liste des noms et des biens des émigrés. Dixième liste," 29 frimaire an II; and in sequence, identically captioned, "Onzième ... vingtième liste," 29 nivôse, 29 pluviôse, 29 ventôse, 29 germinal, 29 floréal, 29 prairial, 29 messidor, 29 thermidor, 29 fructidor an II, 17 brumaire an III, respectively. *Ibid.*, Q 514 (printed copies) and Q 515 (ms. copies).

CÔTES-DU-NORD

Based on Gain's indemnity hypothesis. Indemnities: 515; émigrés: 2575. Among other documents pertaining to the emigration the Archives départementales des Côtes-du-Nord, at Saint-Brieuc, contain a répertoire in five volumes of the émigrés of the department (Q unclassified).

Cf. on the deported clergy the works of Auguste Lemasson, *Manuel pour l'étude de la persécution religieuse dans les Côtes-du-Nord pendant la Révolution française* (Rennes, 1926), and *Les actes des prêtres insermentés du diocèse de Saint-Brieuc ... déportés à Rochefort et à l'Île de Ré* (2 vols.; Saint-Brieuc, 1914–1920).

CREUSE

"Arrêté du Directoire du département de la Creuse contenant la liste générale des émigrés du département," 22 juillet 1793. AD Gironde, Q 1475.

"Arrêté du Directoire du département de la Creuse contenant la première liste supplétive des émigrés de ce département," 2 prairial an II. *Ibid.*, *idem.*

"Extrait des registres des délibérations du Directoire du département de la Creuse," 20 octobre 1792 (ms. draft of first list issued in the Creuse). AD Creuse, L 139.

"Liste alphabétique des prévenus d'émigration amnistiés ou radiés depuis l'arrêté des consuls du 28 vendémiaire an IX en surveillance dans la Creuse," ms., s.d.; "État des prévenus d'émigration [de la Creuse] dans le cas d'amnistie ou qui ont obtenu leur radiation depuis l'arrêté consulaire du 28 vendémiaire an IX qui restent en surveillance dans le département . . .," ms., s.d. AD Creuse, L 138.

Certificates of residence, etc. *Ibid.*, L 136. Émigré suspects imprisoned in the Creuse. *Ibid.*, L 137.

DORDOGNE

"Liste des biens des émigrés du département de la Dordogne," s.d. AD Dordogne, Q 43. Cf. other lists of émigré property under the same *côte* partially duplicating the "Liste des biens . . ."

"Liste des émigrés [de la Dordogne]," ms., s.d. *Ibid.*, Q 40.

"Liste des individus inscrits sur la liste des émigrés [de la Dordogne] qui n'ont pas fourni leurs actes de naissance," ms., s.d. *Ibid.*, Q 41.

"Liste supplétive des émigrés de la Dordogne," 30 fructidor an II; "Quatrième supplément à la liste des émigrés de la Dordogne," 5 vendémiaire an VII. AD Gironde, Q 1475.

"Arrondissement de Périgueux. Liste des émigrés," ms., s.d. AD Dordogne, Q 42.

DOUBS

"Liste générale des émigrés . . . du Doubs," s.d. AD Gironde, Q 1475.

"Première liste supplétive des émigrés . . . du Doubs," s.d. *Ibid.*, *idem.*

"Cinquième liste supplétive . . ." s.d. AD Pyrénées-Orientales, Q 730; "Sixième liste supplétive . . .," s.d. AD Gironde, Q 1475.

Pigallet, M., *Rapport annuel au Conseil général [du Doubs]* (Besançon, 1910), appendix (list of the émigrés of the Doubs).

Sauzay, Jules, *Histoire de la persécution révolutionnaire dans le département du Doubs de 1789 à 1801* (10 vols.; Besançon, 1867-1873), III, 786-805; V, 199-247, 655-682 (lists of émigrés and deportees).

DRÔME

"Liste des émigrés du département du Drôme, 1792–an V (?)." AD
Drôme, Q 278.

"Tableau général des émigrés [du Drôme] et de leurs biens, 1792–an II."
AD Drôme, Q 332.

Divers lists of émigrés and deportees in part duplicating the above items.
Ibid., Q 334–335.

Dossiers individuels des émigrés et des déportés du Drôme. Ibid., Q 282–321,
323–325.

EURE

"Émigrés du département de l'Eure," ms., s.d. (an VI?). AD Eure,
Q 10.

"Émigrés du département de l'Eure. Première liste des biens des français émigrés . . .," 30 juillet 1792. *Ibid.*, Q 11.

"Premier [deuxième, troisième, quatrième, cinquième] supplément à
la liste des biens des français présumés émigrés [de l'Eure]," 26
novembre 1792, 30 septembre 1793, 1 nivôse an II, 8 germinal
an II, and 11 frimaire an VII, respectively. *Ibid.*, Q 11 and Q 12;
also for the "Cinquième supplément . . .," AD Gironde, Q 1475.

"Département de l'Eure. District de Bernay. Liste des émigrés formée
en exécution de la loi du 25 brumaire an III," an III. AD Eure, Q 12.

Sevestre, E., *Les problèmes religieux de la Révolution et de l'Empire en
Normandie* (2 vols., Paris, 1924), II, 794–795, 803; and, by the
same author, *Liste critique des ecclésiastiques fonctionnaires insermentés et assermentés en Normandie, janvier–mai 1791* (Paris, 1922),
297–301, and *passim.*

EURE-ET-LOIR

Based on Gain's indemnity hypothesis. Indemnities: 152; émigrés: 760.
The Archives départementales de l'Eure-et-Loir, at Chartres, are
virtually devoid of material on the émigrés.

FINISTÈRE

"Liste générale des émigrés ci-devant domiciliés ou ayant des biens dans
le département du Finistère," 28 fructidor an II. AD Finistère,
Q unclassified; also AD Gironde, Q 1475.

Dossiers individuels des émigrés du Finistère. AD Finistère, Q unclassified.

Cf. on the clergy, Peyron, Abbé, *Documents pour servir à l'histoire du
clergé et des communautés religieuses dans le Finistère pendant la
Révolution* (Quimper, 1892), *passim*; Téphany, Joseph Marie,
*Histoire de la persécution religieuse dans les diocèses de Quimper et
de Léon de 1789 à 1801* (Quimper, 1879), 649–654 (list of *déportés*);

and Uzureau, François, "Les prêtres insermentés du Finistère," *Annales de Bretagne* (1920), XXXIV, 261–272; (1921), XXXV, 89–91.

GARD

"Liste générale des émigrés . . . du Gard," s.d. AD Gard, Q unclassified.

"Troisième [quatrième, septième, huitième . . . douzième] liste supplétive des émigrés du Gard," an II–an VII. AD Gironde, Q 1475.

Rouvière, François, *L'aliénation des biens nationaux dans le Gard* (Nîmes, 1900), 655–744 (for a "Table par ordre alphabétique de noms d'émigrés"); and, by the same author, *Histoire de la Révolution française dans le Gard* (4 vols.; Nîmes, 1887–1889), II, 504–523 (list of deportees); III, 445–464 (list of émigrés).

GARONNE, HAUTE-

"Relevé général des émigrés portés sur les listes arrêtées par le Directoire du département de la Haute-Garonne jusqu'au (*sic*) loi du 25 juillet 1793," ms., s.d. AD Haute-Garonne, Q 110.

"Liste des émigrés du département de Haute-Garonne," ms., s.d. *Ibid., idem.*

"Liste des émigrés . . . de la Haute-Garonne," 24 juin 1793. *Ibid.,* Q 109.

"Répertoire des noms des émigrés des districts de Toulouse, Castelsarrasin, Grenade et Muret," ms., s.d. *Ibid., idem.*

"Premier supplément à la liste des émigrés et des prêtres déportés ou reclus [de la Haute-Garonne]," juin 1794–juillet 1795; "Deuxième [troisième, quatrième, cinquième] liste des citoyens absens (*sic*) [de la Haute-Garonne]," 13 thermidor an V, 6 nivôse an VI, 21 germinal an VI, and 1 germinal an VII, respectively. *Ibid.,* Q 609; also, except for the "Cinquième liste . . .," AD Gironde, Q 1476.

Dossiers individuels des émigrés et des prêtres déportés de la Haute-Garonne (1792–an VIII). AD Haute-Garonne, Q 40–107.

Cf. Martin, Henri, *Documents relatifs à la vente des biens nationaux. Département de la Haute-Garonne* (2 vols.; Toulouse, 1912–1924), I, 148–247, 541–557; II, 137–178, 187–254.

(*Note*: The total number of clergy comprised in the lists of the Haute-Garonne is 1,025. Almost half of them, however, were *reclus,* many of whom were sent to Toulouse from other departments—62 from the Aveyron alone. See Augustin Fabre, *op. cit.,* II, 350–353.)

GERS

"Liste des émigrés du département du Gers," 1 octobre 1793. AD Gers, Q 336.

"Liste supplétive des émigrés . . . du Gers," 25 floréal an II; "Troisième [quatrième] supplément à la liste des émigrés du Gers," 14 nivôse an VI, and 19 brumaire an VII, respectively. AD Gers, Q 336. Cf. Lamazouade, P. (Abbé), *La persécution contre le clergé du département du Gers sous la Révolution française* (Paris et Auch, 1879), 111–121 (list of deportees).

GIRONDE

"Département du Bec-d'Ambès (Gironde). Relevé général des émigrés portés sur les listes arrêtées par le Directoire du département du 6 juin 1792 jusqu'au 29 floréal an II," 17 fructidor an II. AD Gironde, Q 1473; also AD Haute-Saône, 1 Q 12.

"Répertoire des émigrés du département de la Gironde," ms., s.d. AD Gironde, Q 1479.

"Supplément au relevé général des émigrés [de la Gironde] portés sur les listes . . . du 6 juin 1793 jusqu'au 29 floréal an II," 14 frimaire an III. *Ibid., idem.*

Dossiers individuels des émigrés et des prêtres déportés de la Gironde. Ibid., Q 1494–1520.

Cf. Marion, M., Benzacar, J., and Caudrillier, G., *Documents relatifs à la vente des biens nationaux. Département de la Gironde* (2 vols.; Bordeaux, 1911–1912), I, 123–150 (list of émigrés); II, p. xiv, 161–170 (list of deportees).

HÉRAULT

"Liste générale des émigrés du département de l'Hérault . . .," an II. AD Hérault, Q unclassified.

"Supplément aux listes des émigrés . . . de l'Hérault," an II; "Second supplément aux listes des émigrés . . . de l'Hérault," 7 floréal an II. AD Hérault, Q unclassified; also AD Gironde, Q 1476. "Troisième [quatrième, cinquième, sixième, septième, dixième, douzième] supplément aux listes des émigrés . . . de l'Hérault," 3 thermidor an II, 12 fructidor an II, 29 fructidor an II, 19 vendémiaire an III, 13 frimaire an III, 11 pluviôse an V, and 8 messidor an VI, respectively. AD Gironde, Q 1476.

Cf. Saurel, F., *Histoire religieuse du département de l'Hérault pendant la Révolution* (4 vols.; Montpellier et Paris, 1894–1896), II, pp. lix–lxviii; III, pp. i–xii (lists of deportees).

ILLE-ET-VILAINE

Tanguy, E., "L'émigration dans l'Ille-et-Vilaine et la vente des biens nationaux de 2e origine," *Annales de Bretagne* (1906), XXI, 160–165. Cf. Guillou, Adolphe, "La vente des biens du clergé et des émigrés à Rennes pendant la Révolution," *Annales de Bretagne* (1910), XXVI, 1–99.

Corson, Guillotin de (Abbé), *Les confesseurs de la foi pendant la grande Révolution sur le territoire de l'archdiocèse de Rennes* (Rennes, 1900), *passim*.

INDRE

"Liste des absens (*sic*) de leurs propriétés [dans l'Indre]." s.d. [1792]. AD Indre, Q 547.

"Première [seconde, troisième, quatrième, cinquième] addition à la liste des absens (*sic*) de leurs propriétés [dans l'Indre]," 10 août 1792, 17 août 1792, 4 septembre 1792, 12 novembre 1792, and s.d. [1792], respectively. *Ibid.*, *idem*.

"Liste des émigrés [de l'Indre] par ordre alphabétique . . .," ms., s.d. (an V ?). *Ibid.*, *idem*.

"Liste des citoyens absens (*sic*) [de l'Indre] prévenus d'émigration," an III. *Ibid.*, Q 550.

"Liste supplétive des émigrés . . . de l'Indre," 2 floréal an II; "Liste supplétive . . .," 3 frimaire an VII. *Ibid.*, Q 553.

Lists of fathers and mothers of émigrés. *Ibid.*, Q 551.

Dossiers individuels des émigrés et des prêtres déportés de l'Indre. Ibid., Q 573–790.

INDRE-ET-LOIRE

"Relevé général des émigrés . . . de l'Indre-et-Loire," 8 février 1793. AD Indre-et-Loire, Q unclassified.

"Seconde liste supplétive des émigrés . . . de l'Indre-et-Loire," 23 floréal an II. *Ibid.*

"État nominatif des noms . . . des individus portés sur la liste générale des émigrés . . . qui en ont été rayés définitivement," ms., s.d. *Ibid.*

Dossiers individuels des émigrés et des prêtres déportés de l'Indre-et-Loire. Ibid.

Cf. Carré de Busserolle, J. X., *Souvenirs de la Révolution dans le département de l'Indre-et-Loire de 1790 à 1798* (Tours, 1864), 168ff. (list of deportees).

ISÈRE

Dossiers individuels des émigrés et des prêtres déportés de l'Isère. AD Isère, L 245–251.

Franclieu, M. de, *La persécution religieuse dans le département de l'Isère de 1790 à 1802* (3 vols.; Tournai, 1904–1905), II, 681–693 (list of émigré clergy).

(*Note*: The author was unable to locate any lists of émigrés in the Archives départementales de l'Isère, at Grenoble. The file of dossiers, however, seems to be complete.)

JURA

"Liste des émigrés du département du Jura dressée par la commission administrative séante à Dole," 29 pluviôse an II. AD Jura, Q unclassified; also AD Gironde, Q 1476.

Dossiers individuels des émigrés et des prêtres déportés du Jura. AD Jura, Q unclassified.

LANDES

"Département des Landes. Émigrés. Liste générale formée par le procureur-général-syndic du département . . . des particuliers qui possédaient des biens dans l'arrondissement de ce département et qui ont été declarés émigrés par le Directoire du département . . .," 13 juillet 1793. AD Landes, 1 Q 133.

"Relevé général des émigrés portés sur les listes arrêtées par le Directoire du département des Landes jusqu'au 15 septembre 1793 . . .," ms., 18 septembre 1793. *Ibid., idem.*

"Relevé général des émigrés et des prévenus d'émigration . . . des Landes provisoirement arrêté le 6 ventôse an VI . . .," an VI. *Ibid., idem.* Cf. divers supplements, 1793–an V, partially duplicating the "Relevé . . ." of 6 ventôse an VI. *Ibid.,* 1 Q 134.

"Liste des émigrés formée en exécution de la loi du 25 brumaire an III. Département des Landes. District de Mont-de-Marsan," 27 ventôse an III. *Ibid.,* 1 Q 133.

"Observations sur les personnes et les biens des émigrés . . . des Landes . . .," ms., s.d. *Ibid., idem.*

"Registre des prévenus d'émigration . . . des Landes à qui a été delivré un certificat d'amnistie conformément au senatus-consulte du 6 floréal an X," ms., s.d. *Ibid., idem.*

Légé, Abbé, *Les diocèses d'Aire et de Dax pendant la Révolution française* (2 vols.; Aire, 1875), I, 181–186 (lists of deportees, *reclus,* etc.).

LOIR-ET-CHER

"Tableau des émigrés ou absens (*sic*) qui ont des propriétés dans le département de Loir-et-Cher," 1793. AD Loir-et-Cher, Q 48.

"État contenant les noms des émigrés du département de Loir-et-Cher . . .," ms., s.d. *Ibid., idem.*

"Relevé général des émigrés portés sur les listes arrêtées par le Directoire du département de Loir-et-Cher jusqu'au 12 septembre 1793," 12 septembre 1793. *Ibid., idem.*

"Liste supplétive des émigrés . . . de Loir-et-Cher," 13 brumaire an II; "Liste provisoire des personnes émigrées du Loir-et-Cher," 8 floréal an II; "Liste supplétive . . .," 1 brumaire an VII; "Liste supplétive . . .," 27 pluviôse an VII. *Ibid., idem.*

District lists: Blois, 2 frimaire an III; Clarismont, 26 fructidor an II, and 1 pluviôse an III; Vendôme, 7 germinal an III. *Ibid.*, Q 47.

Inscriptions, cancellations, sequestrations. *Ibid.*, Q 1756–1767. See also Q 901–904, 1045–1049, 1152–1154, 1217–1231, 1294–1307, and 1360–1364 for a vast quantity of material on the émigrés filed by districts.

Dossiers individuels des émigrés et des déportés de Loir-et-Cher. Ibid., Q 314–736.

Cf. Vallière, H. de la, "Notes sur les émigrés de Loir-et-Cher et liste des émigrés," *Revue de Loir-et-Cher* (1899), XII, 100–110 (uncritical and incomplete); and, for the clergy, Gallerand, J. (Abbé), *Les cultes sous la Terreur en Loir-et-Cher* (Blois, 1928), 753–757; 761–768; 771–773 (excellent lists of deportees and *réfractaires*).

LOIRE

Based on Gain's indemnity hypothesis. Indemnities: 21; émigrés: 105. Cf. "Liste générale des émigrés du département de Rhône-et-Loire . . .," s.d. [1793]. AD Rhône, Q unclassified; also BN, 4^0 Lb^{40} 3035. Note that the Loire was detached from the Rhône-et-Loire on August 10, 1793, by decree of the representatives on mission in the region, confirmed in November by the Convention.

LOIRE, HAUTE-

"État général des biens des émigrés situés dans l'étendue du département de la Haute-Loire . . .," 15 octobre 1793. AD Gironde, Q 1476.

"Relevé général des émigrés ou prévenus d'émigration portés sur la première liste arrêtée par le département de la Haute-Loire le 15 octobre 1793," 9 thermidor an II. AD Gironde, Q 1476. For an exact reproduction of this list see *Annales de la Société d'agriculture, sciences, arts et commerce du Puy* (1889-1897), XXXV, 239–258.

For the clergy, not included in the above sources, Gonnet, Ernest, *Essai sur l'histoire du diocèse du Puy-en-Velay, 1789–1802* (Paris, 1907), 209–210; and for a complete reconstruction of the emigration from the Haute-Loire, Rioufol, Maxime, *La Révolution de 1789 dans le Velay* (Le Puy, 1904) 282ff. and 293ff.

LOIRE-INFÉRIEURE

Based on Gain's indemnity hypothesis. Indemnities: 350; émigrés: 1750. The Archives départementales de la Loire-Inférieure, at Nantes, contain no local lists of émigrés. But in the Archives départementales de la Creuse, at Guéret, are the following: "Département de la Loire-Inférieure. Troisième supplément aux listes d'émigrés formées en exécution de la loi du 25 brumaire an III," 14 prairial an VII; and "... Quatrième supplément ...," 28 messidor an VII. L 139.

Cf. on the clergy, Lallié, Alfred, *Le diocèse de Nantes pendant la Révolution* (2 vols.; Nantes, 1893), II, *passim*; and Briand, P. M. (Abbé), *Notices sur les confesseurs de la foi dans le diocèse de Nantes pendant la Révolution* (2 vols.; Nantes, 1903), *passim*.

LOIRET

Based on Gain's indemnity hypothesis. Indemnities: 104; émigrés: 520.

LOT

"Relevé général des émigrés portés sur les listes arrêtées par le Directoire du département du Lot jusqu'au 1er octobre 1793," ms., 4 octobre 1793. AD Lot, Q 1.

"Liste supplétive des émigrés ... du Lot arrêtée par le Directoire du département le 16 février 1793," ms. *Ibid., idem.*

"Département du Lot. Liste supplétive des émigrés pour le mois de brumaire an II," ms., 29 brumaire an II. *Ibid., idem.*

"Quatrième supplément à la liste des émigrés du Lot," 27 vendémiaire an VII. *Ibid., idem.*; also AD Gironde, Q 1477.

District lists: Cahors, ms., 14 septembre 1793, and (a supplement containing the names of the deported clergy) 1 ventôse an II; Gourdon, ms., 6 septembre 1793; Lauzerte, ms., 28 septembre 1793; Montauban, ms. s.d. [2 juin 1793]. Also "Tableau des citoyens de la ville de Mountauban ... présumés émigrés ...," ms., 22 decembre 1792. AD Lot, Q 1 and Q 2.

Cf. on the clergy, Gary, Justin (Abbé), *Notice sur le clergé de Cahors pendant la Révolution* (Cahors, 1897), 285–295 (lists of deportees); and Sol., E., *Le clergé du Lot et le serment exigé des fonctionnaires publics ecclésiastiques* (Paris, 1926), *passim*.

LOT-ET-GARONNE

Based on Gain's indemnity hypothesis. Indemnities: 322; émigrés: 1610.

The following material on the émigrés, unavailable when the author sought to use it, is contained in the Archives départementales de Lot-et-Garonne, at Agen: "Liste des émigrés ou présumés tels ... de Lot-et-Garonne," s.d. Q 280. "Liste des émigrés ... de Lot-et-Garonne," 7 juillet 1793; and three supplements, 1793–an VII. Q 279. "Registre contenant les noms des émigrés ... de Lot-et-Garonne," ms., s.d. Q 278. "Répertoire alphabétique des noms des émigrés . . . de Lot-et-Garonne," 1825. Q 311. "État nominatif des prêtres déportés . . . [de Lot-et-Garonne]" (about 420 priests), an VIII. L 521.

LOZÈRE

"Liste générale des français émigrés de la Lozère," 22 avril 1793. AD Lozère, L unclassified.

District lists: Florac, 24 floréal an II; Langogne, 22 avril 1793; Marvéjols, 5 janvier 1793; Meyrueis, 20 juillet 1793 (?); Saint-Chély, an III; Villefort, an III. *Ibid.*, Q 22, 44, 52, 112–114, 135–136, respectively.

Pourcher, P. (Abbé), *L'épiscopat français et constitutionnel et le clergé de la Lozère durant la Révolution de 1789* (3 vols.; Saint-Martin-de-Boubaux, 1895–1900), II, 215–216; III, 449–464, 487–490 (lists of émigrés, deportees and *reclus*); André, Louis, *La Révolution en Lozère* (Marvéjols, 1894), 34; and Delon, J. B., *La Révolution en Lozère* (Mende, 1922), 68–69 (on the *réfractaires*).

MAINE-ET-LOIRE

"Relevé général des émigrés portés sur les listes arrêtées par le Directoire du département du Maine-et-Loire . . .," 15 vendémiaire an VI. AD Maine-et-Loire, Q unclassified.

"Table des émigrés dépossédés . . . du Maine-et-Loire," s.d. *Ibid.*

Dossiers individuels des émigrés et des prêtres déportés du Maine-et-Loire (files in confusion and apparently very incomplete). *Ibid.*

Queruau-Lamerie, Émile, *Le clergé du département du Maine-et-Loire pendant la Révolution* (Angers, 1899), *passim*; and "Les victimes de la Terreur en Anjou. Les religieuses condamnées à la déportation," *L'Anjou historique* (1903–1904), IV, 21–44.

MANCHE

"Relevé . . . des émigrés compris sur la première liste arrêtée par le Directoire du département de la Manche," 28 juillet 1792. AD Manche, Q unclassified.

"Liste générale des noms des prévenus d'émigration qui ont des biens dans ce département [La Manche]," 15 decembre 1793. AD Gironde, Q 1477; also AD Manche, Q unclassified.

Dossiers individuels des émigrés et des prêtres déportés de la Manche (apparently incomplete). AD Manche, Q unclassified.

Tesson, A. de, "Les biens des émigrés dans l'Avrachin (districts d'Avranches et de Mortain) en 1792," *Mémoires de la Société d'archéologie, littérature, sciences et arts des arrondissements d'Avranches et de Mortain* (1900–1902), XV, 201–232 (lists of émigrés and deportees).

Sevestre, E., *Problèmes religieux de la Révolution et de l'Empire en Normandie* (2 vols.; Paris, 1924), II, 795–797, 803 (statistics on the deportees); and, by the same author, *Liste critique des ecclésiastiques fonctionnaires publics insermentés et assermentés en Normandie* (Paris, 1922), 297–301 (statistics on the *réfractaires*).

MARNE

"Liste générale des émigrés et prévenus d'émigration, déportés, reclus et condamnés du département de la Marne," 27 prairial an II. AD Marne, L unclassified; also AD Gironde, Q 1477.

"Liste des citoyens étrangers qui, possessionnés dans . . . la Marne, ont discontinué ou n'ont pas produit leurs certificats de résidence . . .," 30 ventôse an II. AD Gironde, Q 1477.

"Liste supplétive des émigrés du district de Chalons . . .," ms., 25 brumaire an III. AD Marne, L unclassified.

Dossiers individuels des émigrés et des prêtres déportés de la Marne. AD Marne, L unclassified (but alphabetically filed and apparently complete).

MARNE, HAUTE-

"Département de la Haute-Marne. Liste générale . . . des émigrés dont le dernier domicile était dans le département de la Haute-Marne et de ceux qui y possédaient des biens," 20 brumaire an VI. AD Haute-Marne, Q unclassified; also BN, 8⁰ Lb⁴¹ 5347.

Cf. Bresson, A. (Abbé), *Les prêtres de la Haute-Marne déportés sous la Convention et le Directoire* (Langres, 1913), 131–227 (fragmentary data on the deportees).

MAYENNE

"Liste générale . . . des émigrés, prêtres et autres ecclésiastiques déportés, reclus et condamnés à mort du département de la Mayenne," 18 floréal an II. AD Mayenne, Q 103; also AD Gironde, Q 1477.

"Liste supplétive des émigrés . . . de la Mayenne," ms., 12 ventôse an IV. AD. Mayenne, Q 106; also, for a printed copy, AD Gironde, Q 1477. "Liste supplétive . . .," ms., 18 fructidor an IV; "Liste supplétive des émigrés . . . de la Mayenne dans laquelle sont compris tous les individus . . . omis sur les listes anciennes, tous les prêtres réfractaires rentrés sur le territoire de la République ou qui n'en ont jamais sortis, et enfin tous les hommes notoirement signalés pour faire partie des bandes d'assassins et de brigands armés contre le gouvernement," ms., 5 pluviôse an VII. AD Mayenne, Q 106.

Cf. among the several works treating the clergy of the Mayenne, Piolin, Paul, "L'Église du Maine pendant la Révolution (4 vols.; Le Mans, 1868–1871), II, 555–631; III, 514–575; Le Coq, Frédéric, *Documents pour servir à l'histoire de la constitution civile du clergé dans le département de la Mayenne* . . . (7 vols.; Laval, 1890–1893), *passim*; and *Mémoires ecclésiastiques concernant la ville de Laval et ses environs* . . . *pendant la Révolution*, par un prêtre de Laval (Laval, 1842), 114, 124, 417.

MEURTHE

Troux, Albert, *La vie politique dans le département de la Meurthe d'août 1792 à octobre 1795* (2 vols.; Nancy, 1936), II, 900–901 (statistics on the émigrés of the Meurthe).

Mangenot, Eugène (Abbé), *Les ecclésiastiques de la Meurthe martyrs et confesseurs de la foi pendant la Révolution française* (Nancy, 1895), 137ff., 299ff., 445ff. (lists and statistics concerning the deportees).

MEUSE

Dubois, Jean, *Liste des émigrés, des prêtres déportés et des condamnés pour cause révolutionnaire du département de la Meuse* (Bar-le-Duc, 1911), *passim*. (A critical edition of the lists; the model for many of the later works of the sort.)

MONT-BLANC (SAVOIE AND HAUTE-SAVOIE)

Descostes, François, *Les émigrés en Savoie, à Aoste et dans le pays de Vaud, 1790–1800* (Chambéry, 1903), *passim*.

Mottard, Antoine, "Extrait du relevé général des émigrés du département du Mont-Blanc," *Travaux de la Société d'histoire et archéologie de Maurienne* (1871), III, 17ff.

MORBIHAN

"Département du Morbihan. Liste des biens des émigrés . . .," four lists identically captioned, 23 mai, 16 juin, 2 juillet, 22 décembre, 1792. AD Morbihan, Q 568.

"Relevé général des émigrés qui ont des biens dans le département du Morbihan," 27 septembre 1793. *Ibid.*, Q 569; also AD Gironde, Q 1477, and BN, Lb⁴¹ 3337.

"Liste supplétive des émigrés . . . du Morbihan," 7 germinal an II; "Liste supplétive . . .," 7 prairial an II; "Liste supplétive . . .," 30 brumaire an III. AD Morbihan, Q 570; also, except for the "Liste supplétive . . .," of 30 brumaire an III, AD Gironde, Q 1477.

"Liste des individus . . . du district de Vannes absens (*sic*) de leurs communes depuis le premier floréal dernier pour se réunir aux

chouans et pour cette raison regardés comme émigrés . . .," 7
nivôse an IV. AD Morbihan, Q 570.

Cf. Le Fahler, J., *Acta martyrum*. *Les prêtres du Morbihan victimes
de la Révolution, 1792–1800* (Vannes, 1921), *passim* (incomplete
data on the deportees).

MOSELLE

Gain, André, *Liste des émigrés, déportés et condamnés pour cause révolutionnaire du département de la Moselle* (2 vols.; Metz, 1925-1932),
passim. (One of the best of the critical works on the émigrés.)

NIÈVRE

Meunier, Paul, *La Nièvre pendant la Convention* (2 vols.; Nevers, 1895),
I, 49–64 (list of émigrés, apparently complete for laymen).

Charrier, J., *Histoire religieuse du département de la Nièvre pendant la
Révolution* (2 vols.; Paris, 1926), I, 92, 185–204 (lists of deportees).

Five registers, dated an II, containing the names of the émigrés of the
Nièvre. Also 400 *dossiers individuels*. AD Nièvre, Q unclassified.

NORD

"Liste générale des émigrés . . . du Nord," 20 août 1793. AD Nord,
L 1080.

"Premier supplément à la liste générale des émigrés . . . du Nord,"
28 ventôse an VII. *Ibid.*, L 1079.

District lists: Avesnes, Bergues, Cambrai, Hazebrouck, Le Quesnoy,
Lille, Valenciennes, ms., s.d. *Ibid.*, L 1093–1102.

Cf. Denis du Péage, P., "Inventaire des dossiers concernant les émigrés
du Nord aux Archives nationales," *Annales du Comité flamand de
France* (1921), XXXII, 109–170 (serves as a list of the émigrés
of the Nord); and Peter, J., et Poulet, C., *Histoire religieuse du
département du Nord pendant la Révolution, 1789–1802* (2 vols.;
Lille, 1930–1933), *passim* (an excellent scientific monograph).

OISE

"Département de l'Oise. Émigrés. Liste générale formée par le procureur-général-syndic du département . . . des particuliers qui
possédaient des biens dans . . . ce département et qui ont été declarés
émigrés . . .," 19 avril 1793. AD Oise, Q unclassified.

"Département de l'Oise . . . Liste des personnes declarées émigrées
depuis le mois de mai 1793 jusqu'au 29 pluviôse an II pour servir
de premier supplément à la Liste générale arrêtée le 19 avril 1793,"
s.d.; "Second [troisième, quatrième, cinquième, sixième, septième]
supplément à la Liste générale des émigrés [de l'Oise] . . .," 3

fructidor an II, 9 frimaire an III, s.d., 17 frimaire an VII, 5 pluviôse an VII, and 24 floréal an VII, respectively. AD Oise, Q unclassified; also, for the "Premier supplément," BN, 4^0 Lb^{41} 3713; and for the "Second supplément . . ." and the "Sixième supplément . . .," AD Gironde, Q 1477.

Dossiers individuels des émigrés et des prêtres déportés de l'Oise. AD Oise, Q unclassified (but alphabetically filed and complete).

ORNE

"Table des personnes portées sur la liste des émigrés du département de l'Orne," ms., s.d. AD Orne, Q 472.

"Tableau des noms des prévenus d'émigration [de l'Orne]," ms., s.d. [an VII]. *Ibid.*, Q 492.

"Liste des personnes [de l'Orne] declarées emigrées le 9 octobre 1793," ms., s.d. *Ibid.*, *idem.*

"Table générale des émigrés dont les biens sont séquestrés [dans l'Orne]," ms. s.d. *Ibid.*, Q 643.

District lists of émigrés: Argentan, an II. *Ibid.*, Q 130. Argentan, an III. *Ibid.*, Q 128. Argentan, an III. *Ibid.*, Q 129. Laigle, 3 ventôse an II. *Ibid.*, Q 243.

District lists of deportees: Argentan, an III. *Ibid.*, L 1648. Argentan, an IV. *Ibid.*, L 2519. Bellême, an IV. *Ibid.*, L 2811. Domfort, an III. *Ibid.*, L 3013. Domfort, an IV. *Ibid.*, L 3014, 3015.

"Table alphabétique des individus compris sur les listes des émigrés [de l'Orne] qui ont obtenu main-levée des saisies exercées sur leurs biens," 1812. *Ibid.*, Q 585.

Divers lists and materials ("Sommier de biens d'émigrés et déportés," an II. *Ibid.*, Q 620; "Sommier . . . par bureaux." *Ibid.*, 621–642; "Sommier des biens des prêtres déportês . . ." *Ibid.*, Q 649; "État des émigrés . . .," [a fragment]. *Ibid.*, Q 473; "Registre des émigrés . . ." *Ibid.*, Q 494; and "Table des émigrés . . ." *Ibid.*, Q 498).

Cf. on the clergy, the works of E. Sevestre, as cited above under Calvados, Eure, and Manche.

PAS-DE-CALAIS

Based on Gain's indemnity hypothesis. Indemnities: 452; émigrés: 2260. The Archives départementales du Pas-de-Calais, at Arras, contain a number of district lists and extensive material on émigré property (Q unclassified) which might serve for a reconstruction of the pattern of the emigration from the department.

Cf. Sangier, Georges, *La terreur dans le district de Saint-Pol, 10 août 1792–9 thermidor an II* (2 vols.; Blanquermont, 1938), 255–260

("Prêtres et religieux déportés ou émigrés,"—a total of 250 from the single district of Saint-Pol).

PUY-DE-DÔME

Based on Gain's indemnity hypothesis. Indemnities: 168; émigrés: 840. The Archives départementales du Puy-de-Dôme, at Clermont-Ferrand, contain incomplete departmental and district lists (Q unclassified). A copy of one of the latter ("Liste des biens des émigrés situés dans le district de Clermont," 26 juin 1792) is in the Bibliothèque nationale (Lb⁴¹ 3674).

Cf. Champfour, Commandant de, *La coalition d'Auvergne, avril 1791. Carnet du comte d'Espinchal* (Rion, 1899), 49–119, 125–138, 141–158.

PYRÉNÉES, BASSES-

Dubarat, V., "État des émigrés du département [des Basses-Pyrénées] inscrits sur les listes générales et supplémentaires . . .," *Revue historique et archéologique du Béarn et pays basque* (1912), III, 496–507 (reproducing the local lists); and, by the same author, "Les prêtres déportés du diocèse de Bayonne sous la Terreur," *ibid.* (1911), II, 433–434 (fragmentary data on the deportees).

PYRÉNÉES, HAUTES-

"Relevé général des émigrés portés sur les listes arrêtées par le Directoire du département des Hautes-Pyrénées jusqu'au 16 brumaire an II," 16 brumaire an II. AD Gironde, Q 1476.

"Premier supplément à la liste générale des émigrés des Hautes-Pyrénées," 13 vendémiaire an III. AD Pyrénées-Orientales, Q 730.

(*Note:* The Archives Départementales des Hautes-Pyrénées, at Tarbes, contain no local lists. They do contain some dossiers, and other material on the émigrés. Q unclassified.)

PYRÉNÉES-ORIENTALES

"Tableau des émigrés du département des Pyrénées-Orientales jusqu'au 3 brumaire an II," 23 brumaire an II. AD Pyrénées-Orientales, Q 734.

"Supplément au tableau des émigrés . . . des Pyrénées-Orientales jusqu'au 30 nivôse an II," 30 nivôse an II; "Deuxième supplément a la liste des émigrés . . . des Pyrénées-Orientales," ms., 9 prairial an II; "Troisième supplément . . .," ms., 23 thermidor an II; "Quatrième supplément . . .," ms., 4 fructidor an II; "Cinquième liste supplétive des émigrés ou prévenus d'émigration . . . des Pyrénées-Orientales connus pendant le mois de fructidor [an II] . . .," 9 vendémiaire an III; "Liste des émigrés . . . connus pendant le mois de vendémiaire an III," 23 brumaire an III; "Liste des émigrés . . . connus pendant le mois de brumaire an III," ms., 15 frimaire an III; "Liste supplémentaire des émigrés . . . des Pyrénées-Orientales," 3 frimaire an IV; "Liste des individus émigrés ou prévenus d'émigration . . . des Pyrénées-Orientales . . .," 1 floréal an IV; "Liste des individus émigrés . . .," ms., 23 floréal an V. *Ibid.*, *idem.* Also for printed copies of the lists of 9 prairial, 23 thermidor, 4 fructidor an II, 23 brumaire, 15 frimaire an III, and 1 floréal an IV, AD Gironde, Q 1477.

Cancellations: "Liste des émigrés . . . des Pyrénées-Orientales qui ont obtenu des arrêtés favorables de l'administration du département . . .," 11 prairial an III; "Liste des individus inscrits sur la liste des émigrés qui ont été admis par les administrations de district ou de département à jouir de la faveur des lois des 22 nivôse et 4e jour complémentaire an III," ms., s.d. *Ibid.*, Q 746. "Liste des individus . . . qui ont obtenu des arrêtés de radiation provisoires du préfet du département des Pyrénées-Orientales jusqu'au 29 germinal an IX," s.d. *Ibid.*, Q 749. "État nominatif des individus . . . qui ont été éliminés . . . en exécution de l'arrêté . . . du 26 vendémiaire an IX," s.d. *Ibid.*, Q 750. "État nominatif des individus qui ont été amnistiés conformément au senatus-consulte du 6 floréal an X," s.d. *Ibid.*, Q 757.

Dossiers individuels des émigrés et des prêtres déportés des Pyrénées-Orientales. Ibid., Q 532-729; and, divers material, *ibid.*, Q 730-733, 735-745.

Cf. Torreilles, Philippe (Abbé), *Perpignan pendant la Révolution, 1789–1800* (2 vols.; Perpignan, 1896–1897), II, 168ff. (statistics on the émigrés); and, by the same author, *Histoire du clergé dans le département des Pyrénées-Orientales pendant la Révolution française* (Perpignan, 1890), *passim.* (Torreilles estimated [p. 580] about 1,000 local clergy in exile—twice as many as the sources indicate.)

RHIN, BAS-

The department of the Bas-Rhin never issued a general recapitulative list of émigrés. Each district issued general and supplementary lists, and beginning in the Year IV the department issued supplementary lists.

"État général des émigrés du district de Barr," s.d.; "Liste supplétive des émigrés du district de Barr," 19 vendémiaire an II; "Liste supplétive . . .," 25 ventôse an II. AD Bas-Rhin, Q unclassified; also, for the two supplements, AD Gironde, Q 1475, and AD Pyrénées-Orientales, Q 730.

"État général des émigrés du district de Benfeld," 19 février 1793. AD Bas-Rhin, Q unclassified.

"État général des émigrés du district de Haguenau," 7 février 1793; "Liste supplétive des émigrés du district de Haguenau," 19 vendémiaire an II; "Liste supplétive . . .," 4 messidor an II. *Ibid.*; also, for the two supplements, AD Gironde, Q 1475, and AD Pyrénées-Orientales, Q 730.

"Liste des émigrés du district de Neu-Sarwerden [Saarwerden], 26 ventôse an II; "District de Saar-Union [Saarwerden]. Liste des citoyens absens (*sic*) . . .," 1 brumaire an IV. AD Bas-Rhin, Q unclassified; also, for the list of 26 ventôse, AD Gironde, Q 1475, and AD Pyrénées-Orientales, Q 730.

"Liste supplétive des émigrés du district de Schlestat [Sélestat]," 26 prairial an III. AD Bas-Rhin, Q unclassified.

"État général des émigrés du district de Strasbourg," 15 janvier 1793 (reproduced in *Revue catholique d'Alsace*, année 1867, pp. 71ff.); "Liste supplétive des émigrés du district de Strasbourg," 19 vendémiaire an II; "Liste supplétive . . .," 13 germinal an II; "Liste supplétive . . .," 5 thermidor an II; "Liste supplétive . . .," 7 thermidor an III. AD Bas-Rhin, Q unclassified; also, for the supplements of 19 vendémiaire and 5 thermidor an II, AD Gironde, Q 1475, and AD Pyrénées-Orientales, Q 730.

"État général des émigrés du district de Wissembourg," 19 février 1793; "Liste supplétive des émigrés du district de Wissembourg," 19 vendémiaire an II; "Liste supplétive . . .," 4 fructidor an II; "Liste supplétive . . .," 12 fructidor an II; "Liste supplétive . . .," 16 messidor an III; "Liste supplétive . . .," 7 brumaire an IV. AD Bas-Rhin, Q unclassified; also, for the supplement of 19 vendémiaire an II, AD Gironde, Q 1475, and AD Pyrénées-Orientales, Q 730.

"Liste supplétive des émigrés des districts de Strasbourg, Selestatt [Sélestat], Haguenau et Wissembourg," 10 brumaire an III; "Liste supplétive des émigrés des districts de Strasbourg, Selestatt [Sélestat], et Saar-Union," 19 frimaire an III. AD Bas-Rhin, Q unclassified.

"Liste supplétive des émigrés du département du Bas-Rhin," 6 messidor an IV; "Liste supplétive . . . du Bas-Rhin," 29 frimaire an V; "Liste supplétive . . .," 13 ventôse an V; "Liste supplétive . . .," 30 germinal an V; "Liste supplétive . . .," 21 prairial an V; "Liste supplétive . . .," 2 prairial an VI. AD Bas-Rhin, Q unclassified;

also, for the supplements of 13 ventôse an V, 2 prairial an VI, and an undated fragment, BN, Lb^{42} 2623, 2624.

Dossiers individuels des émigrés et des prêtres déportés du Bas-Rhin. AD Bas-Rhin, Q unclassified (but alphabetically filed and complete).

RHIN, HAUT-

"Liste générale des émigrés . . . du Haut-Rhin . . .," 27 août 1793. AD Gironde, Q 1476; also probably AD Haut-Rhin, Q unclassified.

"Deuxième [troisième] supplément à la liste générale des émigrés du Haut-Rhin," 29 prairial an II, 24 germinal au V, respectively. AD Gironde, Q 1476; also AD Haut-Rhin, Q unclassified.

Schaedelin, Félix, *L'émigration révolutionnaire du Haut-Rhin, première partie* (Colmar, 1937), *passim*, especially pp. 72–91, for statistics and social classification of the émigrés.

Cf. Bardy, H., "Les émigrés du district de Belfort en 1793," *Revue d'Alsace* (1905), LVI, 13–34.

RHÔNE

"Liste générale des émigrés du département de Rhône-et-Loire," 1793. AD Rhône, Q unclassified; also BN, 4^0 Lb^{40} 3035.

"Liste supplémentaire des émigrés . . . du Rhône," 29 pluviôse an VI. AD Rhône, Q unclassified.

Charléty, Sébestien, *Documents relatifs à la vente des biens nationaux. Département du Rhône* (Lyon, 1906), 89–99, 116–173 (lists of émigrés).

Cf. Descostes, François, *Les émigrés en Savoie . . . 1790–1800* (Chambéry, 1903), 270–331 (list of French émigrés at Lausanne; among them were 234 Lyonnais).

SAÔNE, HAUTE-

"Liste générale des émigrés qui ont des propriétés dans le département de la Haute-Saône . . .," 29 vendémiaire an II. AD Gironde, Q 1476, and AD Pyrénées-Orientales, Q 730.

"Premier supplément à la liste générale des émigrés . . . de la Haute-Saône," 15 floréal an II; "Seconde liste supplémentaire des émigrés . . . de la Haute-Saône," 25 messidor an II; "Troisième supplément . . .," 15 brumaire an III; "Quatrième supplément . . .," 18 messidor an VI. AD Gironde, Q 1476, and, except for the "Quatrième supplément . . .," AD Pyrénées-Orientales, Q 730.

Cf. Gauthier, L., *Les émigrés de la Haute-Saône* (Gray, 1913), *passim*. (A list of the émigrés who applied for cancellation, based on the dossiers in AN, F^7 5579–5587^3); and Maréchal, P., *La Révolution dans la Haute-Saône* (Paris, 1903), 466ff. (list of *réfractaires*).

SAÔNE-ET-LOIRE
"Liste générale des émigrés . . . de Saône-et-Loire," 9 frimaire an II.
AD Gironde, Q 1477, and AD Pyrénées-Orientales, Q 730.
"Première [seconde, quatrième, cinquième] liste supplétive des émigrés
. . . de Saône-et-Loire," 6 pluviôse, 27 pluviôse, 22 prairial, 4
fructidor an II, respectively. AD Gironde, Q 1477.
Montarlot, Paul, "Les émigrés de Saône-et-Loire," *Mémoires de la
Société éduenne* (1913), XLI, 75–139; (1914), XLII, 149–242;
(1919), XLIII, 17–132; (1920–1923), XLIV, 9–100, 129–198, 314–
327, 343–370; (1924–1927), XLV, 5–64, 113–158, 231–296, 347–
398; (1928–1931), XLVI, 7–46, 105–158, 217–268. (Based on the
dossiers in AN, F^7 5012–6327. Detailed and complete for the
émigrés, but does not include the deported clergy.)
Bauzon, L. (Abbé), Muguet, Paul (Abbé), et Chaumont, Louis (Abbé),
*Recherches historiques sur la persécution religieuse dans le département
de Saône-et-Loire pendant la Révolution, 1789–1803* (4 vols.; Chalon-
sur-Saône, 1889–1903), *passim* (complete data on the deported
clergy).

SARTHE
The figure for the total number of émigrés (Tables I–V) is based on
Gain's indemnity hypothesis. Indemnities: 218; émigrés: 1090.
The partial social classification (Tables I and VII) is based on the follow-
ing sources:
"Liste générale . . . des émigrés [de la Sarthe] avec indication des
districts, du dernier domicile connu, et . . . de la situation des
biens de chaque émigré," 28 ventôse an II. AD Sarthe, Q 21bis/15;
also AD Gironde, Q 1478.
"Cinquième liste supplétive des émigrés . . . de la Sarthe," 19 floréal
an VII. AD Yonne, Q 612.
Cf. on the clergy, Giraud, M. (Abbé), *Essai sur l'histoire religieuse de la
Sarthe de 1789 à l'an IV* (Paris, 1920), 547; and Piolin, Paul,
L'Église du Maine pendant la Révolution (4 vols.; Le Mans, 1868–
1871), II, 555–563; III, 514–573 (lists of deportees).

SEINE (PARIS)
"Noms, qualités et derniers domiciles des personnes dont les biens
ont été portés sur les listes d'émigrés arrêtées par le Directoire du
département de Paris . . .," 23 octobre 1792. AD Seine, D^4/AZ
1024.
"Liste par ordre alphabétique des émigrés du département de Paris,"

an II. BN, Lb⁴¹ 3338; also AD Pyrénées-Orientales, Q 730 (two copies).

"Supplément . . . à la liste des émigrés de la Seine," s.d. AD Gironde, Q 1478.

"Noms des individus du département de la Seine qui ont été rayés définitivement de la liste des émigrés," s.d. BN, 8⁰ La³⁴ 28.

Dossiers individuels des émigrés et des prêtres déportés de Paris. AD Seine, Q unclassified.

Cf. for fragmentary data on the *déportés*, Pisani, P., *L'Église de Paris pendant la Révolution* (4 vols.; Paris, 1908–1911), *passim.*

SEINE-ET-MARNE

"État contenant les noms . . . et ci-devant qualités des émigrés des cinq districts . . . du département de Seine-et-Marne," 1793. AD Seine-et-Marne, 1 Q 2310.

"Relevé général des émigrés portés sur les listes arrêtées par le Directoire du département [de Seine-et-Marne]," s.d. [an V]. *Ibid., idem.*

"Deuxième [troisième, quatrième] liste supplétive des émigrés . . . de Seine-et-Marne," 22 germinal an II, 11 frimaire an III, and 23 floréal an V, respectively. *Ibid., idem.*

District lists: Meaux, Melun, Nemours, Provins, Rozoy, 1793–an V. *Ibid.,* Q 2302–2306.

Dossiers individuels des émigrés et des prêtres déportés de Seine-et-Marne. Ibid., Q 2312–2679.

Cf. on the clergy, Néret, L. (Abbé), *Martyrs et confesseurs de la foi du diocèse de Meaux, 1792–1799* (Meaux, 1905), 118–123 (incomplete list of deportees).

SEINE-ET-OISE

"Émigrés: affiches généraux. Collection de listes. États des personnes comprises aux listes 1–9 [de Seine-et-Oise]," (lists dated respectively July 26, August 23, September 24 [two lists], November 19, 1792, February 5, 1793; 7th, 8th, and 9th lists undated but appeared in 1793). AD Seine-et-Oise, Q 373.

"Supplément à la sixième liste des émigrés de Seine-et-Oise," 16 février 1793. *Ibid., idem.*

"Dixième liste des émigrés du département de Seine-et-Oise," s.d. [decembre 1793]. *Ibid., idem.*

"Département de Seine-et-Oise. Liste des citoyens absens (*sic*) qui ont leur domicile dans . . . le district de Saint-Germain-en-Laye et qui sont prévenus d'émigration," 5 prairial an III. BN, Lb⁴¹ 4730.

"Département de Seine-et-Oise. Inventaire des biens d'émigrés," 1793. Bibliothèque de Versailles, t. IX, no. 616. (A *registre* of 192 pages.) Cf. Alliot, J. M., *Le clergé de Versailles pendant la Révolution française* (Versailles, 1913), *passim* (fragmentary data on the deportees).

SEINE-INFÉRIEURE

"Liste générale des émigrés . . . de la Seine-Inférieure," juin 1793; and divers supplements, 1793–an V (?). AD Seine-Inférieure, Q unclassified.

Bouloiseau, Marc, *Liste des émigrés, déportés et condamnés pour cause révolutionnaire dans le district de Rouen, 1792–an X* (Paris, 1937), *passim*. (The most meticulous of the critical editions of the lists of émigrés).

For the deported clergy see the works of E. Sevestre as cited above under Calvados, Eure, and Manche. For other works on the émigrés and deportees of the Seine-Inférieure see Marc Bouloiseau, 27–28, 92–93. Among those *not* cited by Bouloiseau, Langlois, P. (Abbé), *Essai historique sur le chapitre de Rouen pendant la Révolution, 1789–1792* (Rouen, 1856), 117–124 (list of 81 priests deported to Rochefort).

SÈVRES, DEUX-

"Liste générale des émigrés . . . des Deux-Sèvres," 8 ventôse an II. AD Gironde, Q 1475.

"Tableau alphabétique . . . [des émigrés des Deux-Sèvres]," *registre*, 2 v., ms., s.d. (Replete with duplications and difficult to use, but apparently the only comprehensive list of local émigrés). AD Deux-Sèvres, Q 38–39.

Lastie-Saint-Jal, Vicomte de, *L'Église et la Révolution à Niort et dans les Deux-Sèvres* (Poitiers, 1870), 294–318 (incomplete list of deportees); and Saint-Marc, C. de, *loc. cit.* (under Charente), pp. 165–375.

SOMME

"Liste générale des émigrés . . . de la Somme," 8 juin 1793. AD Somme. Q 231.

"État général des émigrés ou présumés d'être qui ont des propriétés dans l'étendue des cinq districts du département de la Somme," ms., s.d. *Ibid.*, Q 232.

"Liste supplétive des émigrés . . . de la Somme," 10 brumaire an II; and, with the same caption, five other supplements dated in sequence 3 frimaire an II, 10 frimaire an II, 30 pluviôse an II, 30 floréal an II, and 5 fructidor an VII. *Ibid.*, Q 231.

"District de Péronne. Liste supplétive . . .," s.d. *Ibid.*, *idem.*

Petitions for cancellation. *Ibid.*, L 1399–2720. Draft lists of émigrés and deportees. *Ibid.*, L 1399–2720.

Cf. Le Sueur, Abbé, *Le clergé picard pendant la Révolution* (2 vols.; Amiens, 1904), *passim.*

TARN

"Département du Tarn. État général des émigrés formé d'après les états particuliers fournis par les commissaires du département en exécution de la loi du 8 avril 1792," 15 février 1793, ms. and printed copies. AD Tarn, Q 451.

"Département du Tarn. Deuxième [troisième] liste des individus absens (*sic*) prévenus d'émigration," 26 pluviôse an VI, and 28 fructidor an VII, respectively; "Supplément à la quatrième liste arrêtée le 2 prairial an VII . . .," 13 ventôse an VII. *Ibid.*, Q 451–452.

District lists: "Liste supplétive des émigrés et déportés du district d'Albi," ms. and printed copies, 6 germinal an III; "État des émigrés du district de Castres . . .," ms., s.d.; "District de Castres. Liste générale supplétive des émigrés . . . ou déportés déclarés aussi émigrés par la loi des 29 et 30 du premier mois de l'an II," ms., 16 ventôse an II; "Liste supplétive des émigrés et déportés du district de Gaillac," ms. and printed copies, 25 floréal an III; "District de Lacaune. Liste des citoyens absens (*sic*) . . . qui sont prévenus d'émigration . . .," ms. and printed copies 29 pluviôse an III; "État des émigrés [du district] de Lavaur," ms., s.d. [an III]. *Ibid.*, *idem.*

Dossiers individuels des émigrés du Tarn. Ibid., Q 479–560.

Rossignol, Élie, *Les prêtres du Tarn persécutés pendant la Révolution* (Albi, 1895), 8–21, 98–202 (list of deportees).

VAR

Honoré, Louis, "L'émigration dans le Var, 1789–1825," *Bulletin de la Société d'études scientifiques et archéologiques de Draguignan* (1923), XXXIV, 5–781. (One of the most thorough and complete of the critical editions of the lists of émigrés.)

Cf. Coulet, E., "Les fugitifs de Toulon et les anglais dans la Mediterranée," *Bulletin de la Société d'études . . . de Draguignan* (1929), XXXVII, 1–87.

VAUCLUSE

"Liste générale des émigrés du département de Vaucluse," 4 prairial an II. AD Gironde, Q 1478; also AD Pyrénées-Orientales, Q 730, and Bibliothèque de Carpentras, 1933, fol. 46.

Joannis, J. de, *Le fédéralisme et la Terreur à L'Isle* . . . (Avignon, 1884), 166–168 (incomplete list of the émigrés of L'Isle).
(*Note*: Apparently the Archives départementales de Vaucluse, at Avignon, contain no material of any consequence on the émigrés.)

VENDÉE

"Liste générale . . . des émigrés qui possédent des biens dans l'étendue du département de la Vendée dressée en exécution des lois des 5 avril et 25 juillet 1793," 1 fructidor an II. AD Gironde, Q 1478; also Bibliothèque de Nantes, no. 2518.
Dossiers individuels des émigrés de la Vendée. AD Vendée, Q unclassified (probably very incomplete).
Saint-Marc, C. de, *loc. cit.* (under Charente), pp. 165–375; Beauchet-Filleau, H., *Tableau des émigrés du Poitou aux armées des princes* . . . (Poitiers, 1845), *passim*; Baraud, A. (Abbé), *Le clergé vendéen victime de la Révolution française, 1790–1801* (2 vols.; Luçon, 1904–1905), I, 43–53; and Bourloton, Edgar, "Le clergé de la Vendée pendant la Révolution," *Revue du Bas-Poitou* (1898–1906), XII–XIX, *passim* (a series of articles on the deportees, etc.).

VIENNE

Based on Gain's indemnity hypothesis. Indemnities: 342; émigrés: 1710. The Archives départementales de la Vienne, at Poitiers, contain the "Relevé général des émigrés de la Vienne," an II, and probably other material as well.
Cf. De Roux, M., *La Révolution à Poitiers et dans la Vienne* (Paris, s.d.), 411–420, 441ff.; Saint-Marc, C. de, *loc. cit.* (under Charente), pp. 165–376; and Beauchet-Filleau, H., *op. cit., passim*.

VIENNE, HAUTE-

Based on Gain's indemnity hypothesis. Indemnities: 233; émigrés: 1165. The Archives départementales de la Haute-Vienne, at Limoges, contain extensive material on the emigration—departmental and district lists (Q 289–293), and *dossiers individuels* of the émigrés and deportees (Q 155–242, 245–251).
Cf. Lecler, A. (Abbé), *Martyrs et confesseurs de la foi du diocèse de Limoges pendant la Révolution française* (3 vols.; Limoges, 1892–1903), *passim* (lists of deportees).

VOSGES

"Liste générale des émigrés . . . des Vosges formée suivant les dispositions de l'article X de la loi du 28 mars 1793, de toutes les personnes émigrées ou présumées telles . . .," s.d. (Comprises three lists:

the "Liste générale . . .," and two undated supplements.) AD Vosges, Q unclassified.

Dossiers individuels des émigrés des Vosges. Ibid., II Q 1–71.

Cf. Schwab, Léon, *Département des Vosges. Documents relatifs à la vente des biens nationaux. District d'Épinal* (Épinal, 1911), 273–335 (list of *indemnified* émigrés).

YONNE

"Liste alphabétique des émigrés du département [de l'Yonne]," ms., s.d. AD Yonne, Q 607.

"Liste des noms et derniers domiciles des particuliers déclarés suspects d'émigration . . . [de l'Yonne]," s.d. *Ibid.,* Q 608.

"Liste générale des émigrés . . . de l'Yonne," ms., s.d. *Ibid., idem.*

"Premier [deuxième, troisième . . . sixième] supplément à la liste des émigrés . . . de l'Yonne (first five ms., s.d.; the sixth printed, 19 pluviôse an VII). *Ibid., idem.*

"Première [deuxième] liste supplétive des noms et derniers domiciles des particuliers déclarés suspects d'émigration . . . [de l'Yonne]," ms., s.d. *Ibid.,* Q 609–610.

Ms. lists for 1792, duplicated in the above. *Ibid.,* Q 607.

"Liste des personnes qui ont obtenu mainlevée de leur séquestre jusqu'au 1er nivôse an IV," ms., s.d. *Ibid.,* Q 611.

Dossiers individuels des émigrés et des prêtres déportés de l'Yonne. Ibid. Q 412–565 (émigrés), Q 567–583 (deportees).

Cf. Bonneau, Abbé, *Notes pour servir à l'histoire du clergé de l'Yonne pendant la Révolution, 1790–1800* (Sens, 1900), *passim.*

INDEX

HARVARD HISTORICAL MONOGRAPHS